positively gay

POSITIVELY GAY

New Approaches to Gay and Lesbian Life

Edited by Betty Berzon, Ph.D.

Foreword by Barney Frank
U.S. House of Representatives

Updated and Expanded

CELESTIALARTS

Berkeley, California

Text and cover design by David Charlsen
Typesetting by Jeff Brandenburg/ImageComp
Logo design by Robert Hu

FIRST CELESTIAL ARTS PRINTING 1992

Library of Congress Cataloging in Publication Data

Positively gay : new approaches to gay and lesbian life / edited by Betty Berzon.
    p.   cm.
    ISBN 0-89087-676-2 : $9.95
    1. Homosexuality—United States. 2. Gays—United States. 3. Lesbians—United States. I. Berzon, Betty.
HQ76.3.U5P683 1992
305.9'0664—dc20   92-28419
                                                       CIP

1   2   3   4   5   6   7   8   9   10   /   96   95   94   93   92

*This book is lovingly dedicated to
Teresa DeCrescenzo
for continuing to make my life so positively gay.*

ACKNOWLEDGMENTS

To Paul Reed for approaching me and initiating this updated revision of *POSITIVELY GAY*.

To David Hinds and David Charlsen for making it happen.

To my partner, Terry DeCrescenzo, for being my best sounding board, for freeing me to chase a rainbow, and for loving me so resolutely.

To Barney Frank for his courage, his eloquence, and his presence among us.

To Mark Thompson for his knowledge and helpfulness as my major guide to the world of gay and lesbian writers.

To all the early pioneers of gay liberation, particularly Morris Kight, not often enough acknowledged for being out there always, raising my consciousness very early on, working tirelessly to make it possible for *all* of us to be more positively gay.

TABLE OF CONTENTS

FOREWORD

We live in a very skeptical time marked by a fierce debunking of the usual reasons for doing things. But not even those most cynical about the appearance of updated versions of old books can question the relevance of this volume. Few aspects of American life have changed as radically as the position of lesbians and gay men in our society since the first time Betty Berzon brought out a set of essays on the subject in 1979.

Overshadowing everything is the terrible tragedy of AIDS with the inexpressible personal sorrow it has brought to so many. But paradoxically, there have simultaneously been significant improvements in the social, legal and political place of gays and lesbians in America. The fact that the fight against homophobia has made its most important advances while America was confronting the AIDS epidemic is evidence of what I believe to be central in understanding the struggle of lesbians and gay men for equal rights in our society: Americans are not only less homophobic than they used to be, they are less homophobic than they think they are supposed to be.

I realize that both these points are bitterly contested, not just by the right wingers determined to clothe their prejudice in the armor of majority sentiment, but by many gays and lesbians who have been too battered by their experiences with prejudice to accept any such description of our society. While I consider it one of the great advantages of my job that I get to debate the right wing on this and other issues, in various forums, my focus here, given the likely readership of this book, is on the latter — the men and women whose fight I share.

As I said above, Exhibit A for my argument is the fact that gay men and lesbians have made our greatest gains in combating anti-gay prejudice during the very period in which our society has learned about AIDS. Those who most disagree with what they consider my excessively optimistic view had exactly the opposite expectation. In the early and mid-80s, many activists warned passionately and articulately of the repression that would come in the wake of the AIDS crisis. To some it seemed likely that anti-gay Americans who resented the small gains we had made would use the AIDS epidemic as a screen for their prejudice, whipping up anti-gay feelings and instituting repressive measures in the guise of containing the epidemic. To others, the repression would be less malignantly motivated, being instead, to some extent, an honestly mistaken reaction to the terrible nature of AIDS; but the results would be no less bitter.

Society's reaction to AIDS has been badly lacking in many respects, most grievously in its consistent refusal to provide the funds needed for maximum efforts both to combat its spread and seek its cure. But the predictions of quarantine, widespread public exposure of people with HIV, massive firings, systematic denial of medical treatment, etc., have fortunately been proven wrong. We have not seen officially sanctioned mistreatment either of gay men in general or of people with AIDS in particular.

Quite the contrary has happened — at the federal level we have passed a law which bans discrimination against people with the HIV virus, and threats of quarantine, publicly maintained lists, etc., have remained largely threats. At the same time, the number of states with laws protecting people against discrimination based on their sexual orientation has gone from one — Wisconsin — when the first version of this book appeared, to six, with a large number of cities also joining the list; the federal law banning homosexuals from immigrating to the U.S. has been completely repealed, openly gay and lesbian employees are becoming a fact of life in the federal and many state civil services, etc. . . . My experience as a Member of Congress participating in the national battles involving gay and lesbian rights, and AIDS, convinces me that not only has AIDS not hindered us in our fight against prejudice, but that it has in fact been one of the major reasons why we have made many of the gains.

At this point two disclaimers are necessary. First, no matter what political benefits may have accrued to gay men and lesbians out of the fight against AIDS, it is not a cloud with a silver lining, or a mixed blessing. It is a tragic, unmitigated plague. Second, while the advances we have made in combating prejudice are important as a mark of whether or not we are moving in the proper direction, they are not a cause for rejoicing. Having succeeded in diminishing the corrosive effects of a bigotry that should never have existed in the first place does not require the victims of the bigotry to appear grateful. In the years since the first edition of this book appeared, gay men and lesbians, with our allies, have done a great deal to reduce the scope and impact of homophobia, but it remains a serious problem.

When I came to the U.S. House of Representatives in 1981, gay-related issues rarely came up. The two matters debated in my first term were both assaults on our rights — an amendment to ban gay men and lesbians from receiving help from the Legal Services Program, and a resolution overruling the Washington, D.C. law repealing the sodomy statutes. Our efforts to block these measures failed badly in both cases. What I found when I lobbied my colleagues to vote against these bills was that a large number of Representatives were sympathetic but that they were unwilling to vote their sympathies for two connected reasons.

First, they did not see that there was a real need for protecting the rights of gay men and lesbians — they saw the issues as largely symbolic. Second, because of this perception, they were unwilling to take what they saw as the significant political risk that would accrue to them if they voted in a way opponents could construe as "pro-homosexual."

There are some Members of legislative bodies who are strongly ideological, and almost always vote their convictions no matter what public opinion is at the moment. Others have few strongly held views, and are generally on what they understand to be the popular side. But most legislators, in my experience, fall well between these poles. For them, voting is a constant ongoing effort to balance two sets of factors — their own sense of correct public policy, and what they think the public wants of them.

Consequently, the less a legislator believes an issue has intrinsic importance, the more likely he or she is to vote with what is considered to be public opinion. It is not that Representatives will not risk voting on the unpopular side; it is rather that they are generally disinclined to do so, for what they think are insignificant reasons.

This was the problem in the matter of gay and lesbian rights in 1981. We had collectively and individually succeeded so well in hiding our pain from the majority in society that many honest, well-intentioned Representatives and Senators had little idea how serious a problem homophobia was. And again, because so many of us had so ably concealed ourselves, few of these legislators knew openly gay people, or knew how others in society reacted to those they knew to be gays or lesbians. As Adam DeBaugh pointed out in the first edition of this book, in 1979 very few legislators at the state or federal level had ever been lobbied by someone who had identified himself or herself as gay. Thus they tended to share the prevailing view that the attitude of most straight people towards homosexuality was a mixture of active dislike, contempt, and fear.

Politically, we had then the worst of both worlds. Politicians thought of us as people asking them to take significantly unpopular steps for insignificant reasons. "Why should I stir up all of that angry controversy," one colleague asked me when I lobbied him on the D.C. sodomy repeal, "when they never enforce the law anyway? I'm not going to get into a political jam over something that is purely symbolic."

Fortunately, for lesbians and gay men, and the many others who think America is a better place when prejudice recedes in any area of our life, both aspects of this viewpoint were in the process of changing even as they were expressed in 1981.

The first, most important aspect of this occurring is the movement energized by the self-defense action at Stonewall. The earlier version of this book was a part of the determination of lesbians and gay men to end our invisibility, to document the nature of that oppression faced by lesbian and gay Americans, and to assert our right to lives unmarred by other people's prejudices.

Most of that effort took the form of organized activity — political, cultural, economic. But a prerequisite for such organization was a series of individual acts by men and women who acknowledged their homosexuality to more than the small circle of friends and relatives who had previously known of it. Not every member of every group needs to be public, but organizations that are largely anonymous cannot expect to have maximum social impact

By the mid-80s, the number of Americans who were acquainted with people they knew to be gay and lesbian, and unashamed, had increased enormously from ten years previously. And, as part of that process, the majority of Americans discovered two things. First, that gay men and lesbians were among their friends, coworkers, relatives, bosses, teammates, favorite authors, etc., and were very much like most other people. Second, that it was okay not to be prejudiced against them. Before this, people in America who did have lesbian and gay friends generally considered themselves to be exceptional in their lack of bigotry. "It's fine with me," we heard from so many of those closest to us, "but you had better not tell (mother, father, grandma, the boss, Joe, Mary, etc.) they wouldn't understand."

My recognition that this was a general phenomenon and not just the individualized reaction that many of us were encountering came in 1987 when I polled in my congressional district after publicly acknowledging my homosexuality. When asked if they thought I would be damaged politically by this statement, 43% of the voters said yes. When asked if they personally would be less inclined to vote for me because of it, only 21% said yes — most of them probably voters who already had more reasons why they wished to vote against me than this occasion provided. That is, fully 20% of the voters who did not think my sexual orientation politically relevant, believed that many other voters did — the equivalent of "it's okay with me but don't tell Uncle Charlie."

One of the greatest benefits of the increased visibility of gay people in the 80s was that this attitude was severely undermined. Straight people found that it was not un-American to be unprejudiced. As more and more lesbians and gay men let people know who we really were, more and more straight Americans learned that they had friends, relatives, and people they liked and admired who were suffering because of anti-gay prejudice.

This sets the stage for the political changes that came about as Congress grappled with AIDS. While people in the society at large were responding more favorably than most of us expected, my congressional colleagues were still affected by one of the most potent forces in the political process: cultural lag.

Many Members of Congress were supportive of the right of gay men and lesbians to fair treatment; others opposed this ideologically. But, the swing vote still belonged to those who believed prejudice to be both wrong *and* politically potent, and declined still to risk losing votes for what they saw as symbolic gains. And then came AIDS.

By the mid-80s, when Congress took votes on gay-related issues, they were almost always on AIDS-related matters. Two linked factors led to a turnaround from a situation where the anti-gay position almost always won, to the current situation where it loses more often than not. First AIDS, and its treatment, could hardly be dealt with as if it was of little real importance. Everyone knew we were dealing here literally with matters of life and death, and with a disease that struck gay men disproportionately but not exclusively. Second, the conservatives did us the reverse favor of being obviously demonstrably wrong on most aspects of this set of issues.

While they argued that ideology should not displace science in fighting a terrible disease, the right wing in fact found itself caught doing precisely that. In virtually every vote that has been taken in Congress on AIDS-related matters, the overwhelming majority of public health and medical professionals have been on the same side as the gay community. The American Public Health Association, the AMA, the American Nurses Association and, most significantly from the political standpoint, Surgeon General Koop and the other health professionals in the Reagan administration honored themselves by their opposition to the right wing's efforts to obstruct the fight against AIDS.

This combination of factors finally produced congressional majorities against the homophobes and in favor of positions that could be identified in some ways as "pro-gay." That is, of course, the way the right wing did in fact identify these positions beginning with the elections of 1984 and thereafter. In every congressional election since that time, Representatives and Senators who have voted against the anti-gay amendments that have been offered by right wingers to various appropriations bills — especially those involving AIDS — have been criticized by some groups for giving in to the "homosexual lobby." That much was expected. Many of the members who voted to oppose demagogic amendments were convinced to do so by the support of public health groups and by their conviction that it was necessary to take the appropriate steps to combat a terrible plague, but they also expected to pay some price at the polls.

In fact, the price paid has been far less than almost anyone anticipated. We have no record of anybody losing his or her seat in the House or Senate because he or she voted to oppose efforts to divert the fight against AIDS into a crusade against gay people. And this has become a reinforcing trend. Many Members originally voted in what they feared would be interpreted as a "pro-homosexual" manner in '84, '85, and '86 because they thought that the life and death nature of the AIDS issue gave them no choice but to do what they knew to be the right thing, despite possible adverse consequences. When they found that there were either no adverse consequences or far fewer than they had anticipated, many of these people then felt confident in voting against homophobia even when AIDS was not the issue.

The culmination of all this came in 1990, when as part of a generally controversial immigration bill both Houses accepted without a formal vote an amendment that completely repealed one of the most explicitly anti-gay provisions in American law: the amendment adopted in 1952, and strengthened in 1965, which prohibited any gay men or lesbians from coming to America as either permanent residents, or even as tourists.

In fact, the history of the gay and lesbian immigration exclusion is a good example both of how far we have come in the fight against prejudice and how far we have yet to go. An anti-gay provision was put into the immigration law in 1952, but, unwilling to use indecorous language, the authors of that provision used the phrase "psychopathic personality" to designate homosexuals for exclusionary purposes. In 1965, fearful that the liberal Warren Court might find that language constitutionally inaccurate as a basis for excluding lesbians and gay men, the Johnson administration and the very liberal Congress, elected in 1964, collaborated to tighten the language, lest any lesbians or gay people slipped through the net. They added the phrase "sexual deviation."

The 1965 immigration law was generally regarded as a liberal one, and it was supported by all of the liberal organizations in America. The fact that this liberalization of immigration law included a tightening of the anti-gay and lesbian provision did not appear to make much difference to its supporters. A search of the appropriate records shows that at no point in the process was there any articulated opposition to including that effort to further strengthen the homophobic content of the immigration law.

Twenty-five years later, when Congress next revised the illegal immigration law, an amendment which I offered at the House Judiciary Committee — to strike this anti-gay and lesbian language entirely from the law — was accepted with equally little controversy, and was included in the House/Senate compromise version enacted at the end of that session. Obviously there were people in Congress at the time who vigorously opposed this repeal, but just as in 1965 those who supported gay and lesbian rights felt that they lacked the political context in which to raise the issue, it was the bigots in 1990 who apparently felt there would be no point in trying to start a fight. Consequently, the section of the 1990 law repealing this enactment of prejudice passed as easily as the original enactment had twenty-five years earlier.

At the same time, the 1990 bill repealed the provision of the law that had been successfully inserted by Senator Jesse Helms in 1986 which required that all people with HIV infections be excluded from immigrating to this country. The effect of replacing this provision was to give the President the authority to make regulations regarding people with HIV in exactly the same manner as with any other disease. In 1991, when this had taken effect, the public health officials in the Bush administration recommended to the President that he use his authority to drop the restriction from the law. But, he refused to do so. The recommendation of his public health officials was not enough to counter the political pressure from the right wing, which proved itself to be the greater power in setting public health policy within this administration.

And so, the fight goes on. The book Betty Berzon brought forward in 1979 was one salvo in what was to become a very significant assault on anti-gay and lesbian prejudice. A large part of our problem before 1980 was our very invisibility. By helping to increase not only the visibility, but an understanding of who gay men and lesbians really are, the original version of this volume became a significant resource in the movement which has led to many of the gains that we have won in the 1980s. I hope this updated version will play an equally significant part in helping us to win the important battles against prejudice that remain.

Barney Frank
U.S. House of Representatives
Washington, D.C.

INTRODUCTION TO
THE UPDATED EDITION

Twelve Years Later:
 • In the hospital I hold the hand of my psychotherapy client who is dying at the age of thirty-five. We cry, and laugh a little, and sit in silence. I go to his memorial service. I do the same with another client, and another, and another, and another.
 • A quilt memorializing people who have died of AIDS is so large that it covers more than six football fields..
 • The New York Times which previously had not allowed use of the word "gay" in their pages, headlines an editorial condemning the armed forces ban on gays: "GAY SOLDIERS, GOOD SOLDIERS."
 • The Democratic candidate for President of the United States says publicly, "We can't afford to waste the capacities, the contributions, the hearts, the souls, the minds of the gay and lesbian Americans."
 • The Gay and Lesbian Alliance Against Defamation (GLAAD) sits down with the heads of movie studios, with television producers and newspaper editors to advise as to how gay and lesbian people should be depicted by them. *They listen.*
 We are a long way from 1979.
 In the gay and lesbian world of 1992 there is a new generation of activists. They show us how good it feels to get the anger out, and up in the faces of the people who have turned a deaf ear to us before. But this makes many of the older activists nervous. Don't be so outrageous. Tone it down. Keep it cool. Play it safe. There is a tension between the activist generations. Imagine how far we've come. *Two generations* of gay and lesbian activists now working on distinctly different fronts to push our agenda. The family grows. So do the problems, as in every family.

Playing the Edge
It has been an illuminating experience to edit this book twelve years after I did it the first time. I had to deal with things that never came up in 1979. Gay and lesbian people have given themselves permission to be justifiably angry these days, a development I believe is healthy and strengthening. However, I felt the need to soft-pedal the anger of some contributors in order not to distract from the main mission of this book: to focus on those aspects of gay and lesbian life that can most directly enhance positive identity.
 I had to fight some of the younger contributors who insisted on using the word "queer" to describe who/what we are. I lost this battle, but at least I got them to acknowledge that this term is both new and controversial. What was I so worried

about? I thought of the older gays and lesbians for whom "queer" has for years been the pejorative used against them. I thought of the mother who just learned her young son was gay and now might go around calling himself *that word* which meant he was radically into some kind of homosexual guerrilla defiance of everything his life was formerly about. I thought of the nongay reader trying to educate him/herself about the *positive* lives of gay and lesbian people and finding all this talk about "queer" so seemingly self-deprecating as to be confusing.

And then, I decided to stop worrying. So now we're queer where before we were gay and lesbian, and before that just gay, and before that just plain old homosexual. The name is part of the game. I suppose it's about seizing the moment and many younger activists (and those more aggressive players of any age) are seizing the moment with a vengeance. This is, after all, a social movement and it has to move along according to the people who are out there on the front lines leading the action. If everybody just behaved nicely, knew their place and accepted the *status quo*, there would have been no reason for any book advocating strategies for growth to be written and published in the first place. If there is one thing that characterizes a successful social movement it is its ability to play the edge, to keep changing. It is essential to understand that.

In 1979 we were all thrilled to have our organizations and our banquets and our "acceptance" by many mainstream politicians. We've built on that to establish a stable and diverse world in which gay and lesbian people can live as openly as they are ready to, and have a myriad of opportunities to be productive and creative, to find love and form families and enjoy a peaceful life.

The activist agenda has changed, however; it is more militant and aggressive. We should all be mindful of what is happening out there in the streets because it affects us, it's happening *for* us, like it or not. But this book is not about that agenda, it's about another side of gay and lesbian life. It's about building relationships and dealing with family and being parents and aging and reconciling religious beliefs. It's about managing money and job security and using our voting power. It's about the special experiences of gay and lesbian people of color, minorities within a minority. It's about the explosion of creativity on the gay and lesbian cultural scene, and the brave new world of gay and lesbian youth. And, it's about how we are coping with AIDS.

A Community of Heroes
How the landscape has changed since 1979. Many of our giants have been run to earth. We are bathed in tears time and time again. We shake our fists at the sky and demand an explanation, "Why? Why?"

There is no explanation beyond the cold clinical facts. A virus flourishes among us. Indiscriminately this virus attacks a life, and moves on to attack another. We are trying to stop it but it is elusive. Just as we think we've got it pinned, it changes its composition, and steals away, out of reach. Someday, we will defeat this plague, but we will never forget two things: the people it has taken from our daily lives, and the absolutely extraordinary competency with which we have dealt with this nightmare.

Never before have we been tested collectively, and individually, as we are being tested now. If anyone ever doubted that being gay meant survival in the face of adversity, surely they can have no doubts now. We are a community of heroes. And if that isn't a reason for pride, I don't know what is.

The care-giving miracle that we have seen emerge in the gay and lesbian community is something that we can all identify with and feel triumphant about. While we do indeed need the world around us, we also have demonstrated that in the clutch we are sufficient unto ourselves. There is a core of courage, a wellspring of spirit that erupted at Stonewall, and now fuels our efforts in the fight against AIDS. We will come out of this crisis sadder, stronger, and more resistant than ever to the miscreants who would crusade us into oblivion. We know our strength now. We've met the *real* demon and we are, as a community, clearly holding our own.

Using This Book

Michelangelo Signorile is the controversial young journalist who gained fame by introducing "outing" as a strategy for uncovering the hypocrisy of certain closeted gay and lesbian public figures. The idea was to bring attention to these people who either actively work against gay rights, or by their failure to disclose themselves, withhold the opportunity to make a significant contribution to the public's understanding of who gay people are. However one might feel about it, these outings have awakened interest in gay and lesbian issues on the part of a great many nongay people who otherwise would have no reason to ever discuss *our* lives around *their* dinner tables. It made one more inroad into the conspiracy of silence that has kept our issues so effectively out of the consciousness of our fellow human beings.

If you can adopt a perspective that is not about any one individual being outed, but is about the larger picture of breaking into the silence and generating debate about our lives, opening the minds of nongay Americans to our issues, perhaps you will believe, as I do, that Mike Signorile did something quite constructive. Because I think that, I was delighted when he told me recently that as a teen-ager he found a copy of the original edition of *POSITIVELY GAY*. It was the first gay book he'd ever seen. He said he tore the cover off to sneak it into the house past his mother, and after he read some he thought, "This woman is crazy. She thinks gay people should *come out*." But, he read on and soon he began to feel less scared and more positive about himself. He says it "outed" him.

With less spectacular results, I know *POSITIVELY GAY* has had that same effect on many people over the past twelve years which is, no doubt, why people kept buying it even though it was becoming increasingly out of date. Now, in this expanded edition, I believe those of you who are gay or lesbian will find much to inform, to guide, and I hope to make you feel more positive about *yourself*. If you are a nongay reader, I hope this window into the universe of gay and lesbian life answers whatever questions you have, or perhaps raises a few you hadn't thought of before.

The contributors here are as different from one another in their approaches, as we gay and lesbian people are different from one another in who we are ethnically, socio-economically, age-wise, educationally, and in our values and interests across the board. Some of these chapters are intensely personal, some are strictly report-age, some are academic and precise in their attention to the information needed to tell the family you're gay, make the best use of your money, understand the process of identity integration, or deal with your sexuality in the age of AIDS. You'll read what it means to be a gay father with an infant, how it feels to be an African-American lesbian, and what is happening in the lives of gay and lesbian youth.

At the end of some of the chapters there is a suggested reading list. Of course as time goes on there will be many additional books. Two bookstores to keep in touch with about new books, because they put out catalogues through the mail, are Lambda Rising in Washington, D.C. (1-800-621-6969) and A Different Light in New York (1-800-343-4002). Lambda also has a store in Baltimore, and A Different Light has stores in San Francisco and West Hollywood.

Finally, even if a given chapter does not address your specific concerns about being gay or lesbian, I hope you will read them all. It's time we understood one another better, looked into each others' lives with more curiosity, expanded our knowledge of who this person is who stands beside us in a community that binds all our lives together, because we have something very precious to us in common. Man, woman, young, old, child-of-the-parent, or parent-of-the-child, coupled or single, Jew, Protestant, Catholic or atheist, white, black, Latino or native, HIV-infected or not, out-and-open or stuck-in-the-closet, activist or onlooker, this book is for and about all of you.

Betty Berzon

BEING GAY: PERSONAL ISSUES, SOCIAL OPTIONS

Developing a Positive Gay and Lesbian Identity

Betty Berzon

Who am I? Am I okay?

Two questions that plague all of us eternally. The answers are elusive and ever-changing, clearer and more dependable at some times, less trustworthy at others. We grow older and find new layers of definition in ourselves. Our values change. Society's values change, or at least shift in emphasis. Our own reference point moves, and moves again. We are greatly affected by external events. We, in turn, affect those events by the way we relate to them. Our lives involve a constant interplay of feelings and behavior, past and present, fantasy and reality. We are the sum of all our parts, but only for a moment. Identity is a moving, changing process, not a fixed, established point. But, this is an intolerable truth. Our sanity requires a compromise. We select components of ourselves to relate to in awareness. We arrange them into a semblance of order and think of ourselves as this configuration as long as it makes sense to us and to those around us.

This is what personal identity is about. It is not immutable. It is not totally fluid. It is somewhere in between. It is amenable to change by design. It is ours to reorder if we have the courage to accept the challenge.

It does take courage.

It takes courage to consult one's self for the direction to take in life rather than consulting tradition. It is often easier to be defined by what other people expect of you, to emerge into a stereotype, to yield individuality, to abdicate responsibility for being who you are and becoming what you want to be. But the price for giving up the prerogative to grow is devastating in spirit, in energy and in integrity. Forever, it seems, gay people have been giving their power away to others: define me, explain me, structure my behavior, decide for me what I can and cannot hope to achieve in my life, make rules for my participation in society, let me know the limits of tolerability if I happen to go beyond the boundaries set for me.

It takes uncommon courage to reclaim power once it has been given away. It is uncommon courage that is called for in developing a positive gay identity in an antigay society.

Such courage has been aroused for many by the accomplishments of the new gay rights movement. Many gay and lesbian people have been inspired to seek a better life through increasing self-definition and self-determination. Many of us are now rejecting tolerance, rewriting the rules, defying the boundaries, embracing the challenge of change by design and implementing that challenge with personal and political action.

It has not always been so for me.

Reinventing Myself

I lived my young adult life in the 1950s and 1960s. I learned to deny my homosexuality almost totally with more than a little help from a series of well-meaning, kind, smart, skillful, miserably misguided psychotherapists. But I had a fantasy. I decided that if I should ever be told that I had a terminal disease and only had a short time to live I would go to another city and become gay. It would no longer matter what others thought of me or what I thought of myself. The fantasy was a pleasant one. Having given myself permission to think homosexually, in the fantasy, I could yearn for the closeness and the passionate connection with women I was deprived of in real life.

I thought I had to die to live.

I found out I was wrong. I'm not sure how that happened exactly. Perhaps I had enough of the kind of loneliness that goes beyond experiencing the absence of other people, that begins at one's core and permeates the entire field of one's being. It is the loneliness of alienation from the true self, as if deep in one's center there is a truth pleading for acknowledgment but lost in denial and dread of exposure to the unknown. Risking the acknowledgment of my gay feelings, the expression, the being known for what is true and so long denied, had been terrifying for me.

I was helped, I think, in moving toward the discovery of my true self by the profession I happened to be in. I was accustomed to asking difficult questions of other people. I finally got around to myself.

I will never forget the anguish of the day when I actually made the final decision to leave my comfortable, secure, conventional existence and move to another city, other work, a new life. Luck provided an unexpected visitor that day, an old friend, the late psychologist Sidney Jourard. I had not yet told my employers of my decision to leave. I told Sid, and all the anxiety I was feeling came out with the disclosure. I broke down. I cried. "Am I crazy? Look what I'm giving up. What am I going to? Am I making a terrible mistake? What am I doing?"

Sid smiled and said in his quiet way, "You are re-inventing yourself."

He was right. I didn't know how wonderfully right until the day I arrived in my new city. That day I met the woman I was to be involved with for the next year and a half. I began to live the truth so long defended against, the fulfillment so long denied. With the living out of that truth came a sense of new strength and optimism, came new prerogatives I had only dared dream of before. I could open my life to lesbian women, the one category of persons I had consistently shut out of my experience, almost out of my awareness. I could (and did) make myself available to deeply involving emotional and sexual experience in which I could give up control for the first time and allow another human being access to the inner reaches of my sensuality. When that happened, and it was really different than it had ever been before, I knew I had made the right decision, that my re-invented self was one I would want to spend the rest of my life with, hold up to others as evidence of the rewards of struggling for truth in self-definition.

The struggle was not over, however. In my fantasies I had longed for intimate connections with women, but when I began to meet many lesbian women I found to my surprise that the old program was still operating. I was often afraid of them. Or, more correctly, I was afraid of the feelings they aroused in me even though there was no longer any reason to deny those feelings. The interplay of past and present, fantasy and reality. Making friends with these women was like making my way back through a mine field that I had myself set. I had to be very cautious for fear I might be destroyed. The old program was strong in me, but from the outside it looked very different. My cautiousness was seen as aloofness, my manner was interpreted as condescending and rejecting. Insight did not often catch up with experience and I felt alienated from the very people I wanted so much to accept me. It was an exceedingly painful part of the coming out process.

I was lucky though to have had some women friends who were able to decode my signals, or ignore them, who reached out to me and encouraged me to continue to move among women. Gradually, I learned to let them in, to let them know me, to let myself be touched by them, sometimes very deeply. I am thankful for these women. Theirs is the kind of understanding and support that all of us need as we learn to identify and replace our old antigay programs.

Deprogramming
Deprogramming ourselves is a long and arduous process. In our formative years we were all exposed to the same antigay jokes as our nongay counterparts, the same stereotypes of lesbians and gay men, the same misinformation from our peers. For we gay and lesbian people who have swallowed all this toxic material, it works against us from the inside while society's homophobes (persons who fear homosexuality and

have an antagonistic and punitive attitude toward gay people) work against us from the outside. In the long run, I am convinced, we will be able to do something collectively about societal oppression. In the short run we each owe it to ourselves to do something now about our self-oppression. We must work to rid our thinking of destructive stereotypes and depersonalizing myths: "Gay people are superficial/immature/disloyal/flighty/narcissistic." "Gay men think only of sex." "Lesbians are angry and over-aggressive." "Gay men can't form lasting relationships."

How often have you heard a gay person stereotype another gay person? Every time we unthinkingly use one of those clichés we tarnish our image. We pay tribute to bigotry and ignorance. Just as we must stop reinforcing the straight world's homophobia by laughing at their fag and dyke jokes, we must stop reinforcing our own homophobia by perpetuating these harmful generalizations about ourselves.

Demythologizing

In addition to deprogramming our homophobia, we must also begin to reprogram our thinking about ourselves as gay people. One of the most effective ways we can do this is to substitute accurate for inaccurate information regarding homosexuality and the lives of lesbians and gay men. For instance:

(1) *Homosexuality has existed in every society since the beginning of recorded history, and in many it has been more accepted than it is in our society.* Ford and Beach's classic cross-cultural investigation of sexual behavior found that in 64% of the human cultures studied, homosexuality was considered to be normal variant of sexual behavior.[1]

(2) *There are over 20 million adults in the United States who are predominantly homosexual in their sexual and affectional orientation.* This widely accepted estimate is supported by statistics provided in 1977 by the (Kinsey) Institute for Sex Research: 13.95% of males and 4.25% of females, or a combined average of 9.13% of the total population, had either extensive or more than incidental homosexual experience.

(3) *It is not known exactly why one person is heterosexual and one is homosexual.* However, there is a growing body of evidence to indicate that sexual orientation is determined prenatally by some interplay of genetic predisposition and in-utero events. In other words, the strong likelihood is that one is born gay or lesbian and therefore that orientation is as immutable as eye and skin color, or the texture of one's hair, some of which can be cosmetically disguised but will remain essentially unchangeable.

(4) *Homosexuality is not immoral or unnatural.* To quote Dr. William Johnson, minister and religious scholar, on the origins of antigay attitudes in Judeo-Christian tradition:

> *Before we look at the evolution of the antigay bias of the Tradition, we need to acknowledge that the Gospel writers and the missionary Paul did not possess*

---

[1]Ford, C.S., and Beach, F.A. Patterns of Sexual Behavior. *New York, Harper & Brothers, 1951.*

the psychological, sociological, and sexological knowledge which now inform our theological reflections about human sexuality. They knew nothing of sexual orientation or of the natural heterosexual-bisexual-homosexual continuum that exists in human life. They did not postulate that persons engaging in same-gender sex acts could have been expressing their natural sexuality. We now know that homosexuality is part of the created order, same-gender sex acts having been observed in a multitude of species from sea gulls to porcupines.

(5) *Homosexuality is not illegal.* There is no state where homosexuality per se is against the law. While these are laws in many states against sexual acts associated with homosexuality, these laws pertain just as much to heterosexuals. However, these laws are enforced in such a way as to discriminate against gay men in particular. Repeal of these laws, which too often provide the rationale for other forms of discrimination, has been urged by the American Law Institute, the International Congress of Criminal Law, the American Law Committee, the National Commission on Reform of the Federal Criminal Laws, the American Civil Liberties Union, the National Institute of Mental Health and the American Mental Health Foundation.

(6) *Homosexuality is not a mental illness.* During the nineteenth century many social issues previously regarded as moral problems were recast in medical terms. For instance, Benjamin Rush, the father of American psychiatry, proclaimed in print that the color of Negroes' skin was due to a mild form of congenital leprosy from which they all suffered.[2] Therefore, according to Rush, whites should not intermarry with Negroes in order to protect posterity from this disorder. Obviously, his diagnosis served as a way to control social conduct. Similarly, homosexuality became a psychiatric diagnosis, and medical stigma replaced religious stigma as a means of social control of a feared and misunderstood group of people. Though homosexuality was erroneously institutionalized over a period of time as a psychiatric problem, it was not until the last few decades that actual research was conducted that demonstrated no greater incidence of mental illness among homosexual persons that among nonhomosexual persons. The most famous of these studies was conducted by Dr. Evelyn Hooker, Chairperson of the National Institute of Mental Health Task Force on Homosexuality.[3] In 1973 the American Psychiatric Association ruled that homosexuality be removed as a mental disorder from its official diagnostic manual. In 1975 the American Psychological Association voted to support the American Psychiatric Association action and passed the following

---

[2]*Rush, Benjamin. "Observations intended to favour a supposition that the black Color (as it is called) of the Negroes is derived from the LEPROSY."* Transactions of the American Philosophical Society, *289–297, 1799.*

[3]*Hooker, Evelyn. "The adjustment of the male homosexual."* Journal of Projective Techniques, *Vol. 21, 18–31, 1957. Also published in Ruitenbeek, Hendrik M. (ed).* The Problem of Homosexuality in Modern Society. *Dutton, 1963.*

resolution: "Homosexuality per se implies no impairment in judgment, stability, reliability or general social or vocational capabilities."

(7) *Since homosexuality is not an illness it has no cure.* Over the years various mental health practitioners have claimed that they have successfully re-oriented the sexuality of their patients. There is, however, no scientific evidence to back up these claims, nor have objective studies been conducted to test them. To quote Dr. John Money, Professor of Medical Psychology, Department of Psychiatry and Behavioral Sciences, Johns Hopkins University School of Medicine, author or editor of many books and papers in the field of sex research:

> *Until the determinants of the complete sequence of human psychosexual differentiation have been discovered, any claim to be able to intervene and influence the outcome will be based not on theoretical logic, but on trial-and-error probability. This means that any claim to be able to change homosexuality into heterosexuality will be only as valid as the validity of its counterparts, namely the claim to be able to change heterosexuality into homosexuality.*[4]

Of interest here is the following statement by Dr. George Weinberg, author of *Society and the Healthy Homosexual:*

> *From what I have seen the harm to the homosexual man or woman done by the person's trying to convert is multifold. Homosexuals should be warned. First of all, the venture is almost certain to fail, and you will lose time and money. But this is the least of it. In trying to convert, you will deepen your belief that you are one of nature's misfortunes. You will intensify your clinging to conventionality, enlarge your fear and guilt and regret. You will be voting in your own mind for the premise that people should all act and feel the same ways. . . Your attempt to convert is an assault on your right to do what you want so long as it harms no one, your right to give and receive love, or sensual pleasure without love, in the manner you wish to.*[5]

(8) *Gay men are not oversexed and have as much control over their sexual impulses as nongay men.* Until recently the penalties for male homosexual behavior were so severe that gay men generally had no place to meet each other except the most clandestine of environments. Such environments put drastic limits on the ways in which people could relate. This, added to the fact that men have been socialized to sexually objectify others, created a tradition of clandestine sexual activity as the main social mechanism through which gay men made contact with one another. The increased opportunities for social interaction now available in the more open gay and lesbian community have supplemented these secret sexual settings as

---

[4]*Money, John. "Bisexual, homosexual, and heterosexual: society, law, and medicine."* Journal of Homosexuality, *Vol. 2, No. 3, Spring 1977.*

[5]*Weinberg, George.* Society and the Healthy Homosexual, *New York, St. Martin's Press, 1972. Re-issue, 1983.*

meeting places for gay men, much to the relief of the many individuals who had always felt uncomfortable pressure in situations that were strictly sexual.

(9) *Gay people are no more prone to molest children than are nongay people.* The facts, according to the National Center on Child Abuse and Neglect, Department of Health, Education and Welfare, are that 90% of all child abuse is committed by heterosexual men on minor females.[6] This myth about gay people is one of the most destructive. It has no basis whatsoever in fact.

(10) *Gay people are not limited in the kinds of careers they can pursue.* I offer a simple device to illustrate this point. The following is a partial listing of gay and lesbian organizations and caucuses within professional organizations. I use it to indicate the fields in which lesbians and gay men have established careers and are actively working to protect those careers:

American Association of Physicians for Human Rights

Gay Nurses Alliance

National Lesbian and Gay Law Associates

Association of Gay and Lesbian Psychologists

Association of Gay and Lesbian Psychiatrists

National Association of Social Workers, Committee on Lesbian and Gay Issues

Gay Public Health Workers, American Public Health Association

National Association for Lesbian and Gay Gerontology

Society of Lesbian and Gay Anthropologists

Lesbian and Gay Academic Union

Association for Gay Seminarians and Clergy

Lesbian and Gay Caucus, American Federation of Teachers

Gay Caucus, American Association of Geographers

National Organization of Gay and Lesbian Scientists and Technical Professionals

Gay and Lesbian Task Force, American Library Association

---

[6] Child Abuse and Neglect: The Problem and Its Management. *Washington, D.C.: U.S. Dept. of Health, Education and Welfare, National Center on Child Abuse and Neglect, DHEW Publication No. (OHD) 75-30073.*

Gay Historians and Political Scientists Association

Publishing Triangle (editors, authors, agents, etc.)

National Conference of Gay and Lesbian Elected and Appointed Officials

Gay Pilots Association

Pride Behind the Badge/Gay Officers Action League

In addition, there are gay and lesbian business and professional organizations in most American cities. The gay dentists have their guilds. Many major corporations now have gay and lesbian employee associations, and there are gay and lesbian student groups on nearly every major college and university campus in the U.S. Increasingly, gay people in a broad range of occupations and professions are organizing.

Obviously, as we have come to say: We are everywhere! And we have been everywhere for a long time. Gay people have been among the world's most renowned and accomplished citizens. Following is a list of prominent individuals who have announced or publicly discussed their homosexuality, compiled for Wallechinsky, Wallace and Wallace's *The Book of Lists*.[7]

Women

Sappho (flourished c. 600 B.C.), Greek poet

Christine (1626-1689), Swedish queen

Madame de Stael (1766-1817), French author

Charlotte Cushman (1816-1876), U.S. actress

Gertrude Stein (1874-1946), U.S. author

Alice B. Toklas (1877-1967), U.S. author-cook

Virginia Woolf (1882-1941), British author

Victoria Sackville-West (1892-1962), British author

Bessie Smith (1894-1937), U.S. singer

Kate Millett (b. 1934), U.S. author

Janis Joplin (1943-1970), U.S. singer

Men

Zeno of Elea (fifth century B.C.), Greek philosopher

Sophocles (496-406 B.C.), Greek playwright

Euripides (480-406 B.C.), Greek dramatist

Socrates (470?-399 B.C.), Greek philosopher

Aristotle (384-322 B.C.), Greek philosopher

Alexander the Great (356-323 B.C.), Macedonian ruler

Julius Caesar (100-44 B.C.), Roman emperor

Hadrian (76-138 A.D.), Roman emperor

Richard the Lion Hearted (1157-1199), British king

---

[7] *Wallechinsky, David; Wallace, Irving; and Wallace, Amy.* The Book of Lists. *New York, Bantam Books, 1978.*

Richard II (1367-1400), British king

Sandro Botticelli (1444?-1510), Italian painter

Leonardo da Vinci (1452-1519), Italian painter-scientist

Julius III (1487-1555), Italian pope

Benvenuto Cellini (1500-1571), Italian goldsmith

Francis Bacon (1561-1626), British philosopher

Christopher Marlowe (1564-1593), British playwright

James I (1566-1625), British king

John Milton (1608-1674), British author

Jean-Baptiste Lully (1637-1687), French composer

Peter the Great (1672-1725), Russian czar

Frederick the Great (1712-1786), Prussian king

Gustavus III (1746-1792), Swedish king

Alexander von Humboldt (1769-1859), German naturalist

George Gordon, Lord Byron (1788-1824), British poet

Hans Christian Andersen (1805-1875), Danish author

Walt Whitman (1819-1892), U.S. poet

Horatio Alger (1832-1899), U.S. author

Samuel Butler (1835-1902), British author

Algernon Swinburne (1837-1909), British poet

Peter Ilyich Tchaikovsky (1840-1893), Russian composer

Paul Verlaine (1844-1896), French poet

Arthur Rimbaud (1854-1900), French poet

Oscar Wilde (1854-1900), British playwright

Frederick Rolfe (Baron Corvo) (1860-1913), British author

Andre Gide (1869-1951), French author

Marcel Proust (1871-1922), French author

E.M. Forster (1879-1970), British author

John Maynard Keynes (1883-1946), British economist

Harold Nicholson (1886-1968), British author-diplomat

Ernst Rohm (1887-1935), German Nazi leader

T.E. Lawrence (1888-1935), British soldier-author

Jean Cocteau (1889-1963), French author

Waslaw Nijinsky (1890-1950), Russian ballet dancer

Bill Tilden (1893-1953), U.S. tennis player

Christopher Isherwood (b. 1904), British author

Dag Hammarskjold (1905-1961), Swedish U.N. secretary-general

W.H. Auden (1907-1973), British-U.S. poet

Jean Genet (b. 1910), French playwright

Tennessee Williams (b. 1911), U.S. playwright

Merle Miller (b. 1919), U.S. author

Pier Paolo Pasolini (1922-1975), Italian film director

Brendan Behan (1923-1964), Irish author

Malcolm Boyd (b. 1923), U.S. theologian

Allan Ginsberg (b. 1926), U.S. poet

David Bowie (b. 1947), British singer

Elton John (b. 1947), British singer

The author has added the names of some of the people who have come out subsequently:

Martina Navratilova (b. 1956), U.S. tennis champion

John Cheever (1912-1982), U.S. author

Andy Warhol (1927-1987), U.S. artist

Edward Albee (b. 1928), U.S. playwright

Charles Reich (b. 1928), Yale professor and author

Benjamin Britten (1913-1976), British composer

Rita Mae Brown (b. 1944), U.S. author

Sir Ian McKellen (b. 1935), English actor

Gore Vidal (b. 1925), U.S. author

James Baldwin (1924-1987), U.S. author

Barney Frank (b. 1940), U.S. Congressman

Gerry Studds (b. 1937), U.S. Congressman

How affirming it would be for young gay and lesbian people to learn of such things early in the development of their gay identity. What a difference it would have made for me to know in my formative years that the thoughts and feelings I was having were not sick and unnatural, that they need not condemn me to a shadow existence outside the mainstream of life. How supportive it would have been to know that so many had gone before me, that so many shared my experience. But to be open to that kind of information I would have first had to label myself as gay, and that I was unwilling to do.

Labeling Oneself

The labeling issue is an important one with regard to the formation of a positive gay identity. Attaching a label to yourself tends to bring that which you are labeling into your consciousness. It becomes a part of your sense of self at a given time. If you are trying to *deny* some aspect of yourself you are unlikely to label yourself in terms of that aspect. Refusing to adopt a particular label will not make that aspect of self less true. It serves only to prolong the process of denial. For years I labeled myself heterosexual. That did not make me one bit less homosexual. It simply delayed resolution of my identity dilemma. And, not incidentally, it also wasted years of my life in an energy-consuming battle between my true sexual nature and the fictional one I devised with the help of my psychoanalytic therapists. I wanted so to please them and all the others who claimed to care about my welfare. But I am convinced that I am diminished as a person because I missed out on those early adult experiences of connectedness in love that expression of my true sexual nature would have brought me. I am very much saddened by the loss of opportunities for natural love in those precious young years.

Many gay people are reticent to apply the labels *lesbian* or *gay* to themselves because they feel they are not ready to integrate that concept into their sense of identity. Or if there is readiness at the private level, they are resisting the label at the interpersonal level. "Why do I have to tell anybody I'm gay? Why do I have to call myself that? What does it matter?" It matters for two reasons. The first involves personal growth; the second is political.

First, personal growth. I believe the ability to be self-disclosing is especially important to the mental health of gay people who have been subjected to long-standing societal directives that say: be silent, be invisible. The repressive effect on one's ability to communicate about self has to be a strong one. In general, the ability to make one's self known to others is critical to the successful establishment of relationships with other people. It is not only critical to one's social development, it is essential to the growth of intimacy in close, loving relationships.

Self-disclosure tends to reduce the mystery that people have for one another. In so doing it facilitates honest communication and builds trust between people. It brings people out of isolation and makes possible understanding of that which was previously perplexing or even frightening. For gay people, this is particularly important — the demystification of gayness through personalized disclosure: The simple words, "I am gay." The affirming act that says, "I will no longer be silent. I will no longer be invisible. I am understandable. I am natural. I have the right to live my truth rather than living a lie to preserve someone else's fantasy of how the world should be." It is the acceptance of reality that is the hallmark of the healthy personality.

There is a subtle variation of the labeling dilemma that also deserves attention. It is the situation in which a person says, "Why do I have to call myself gay (lesbian)? The people I work with know. My family knows. My straight friends know. We just don't *talk* about it." Let's think of this arrangement as an unspoken contract that might read something like this:

> *Party of the first part agrees not to identify reality: "I'm gay. _____ is my lover."*

> *Parties of the second part agree not to withhold social invitations/job advancements/respect/admiration/acceptance/love/etc.*

> *Parties of the second part are allowed the luxury of never having to deal directly with the awful reality of homosexuality in their midst.*

> *Party of the first part is allowed to remain in their midst.*

What is wrong with this? I believe what is wrong shows up in the small print, this unspoken contract where party-of-the-first-part's conduct is even further restricted. It's the statements that are censored before they are spoken because they're too revealing of intimacy. It's the second thoughts about who else to invite. ("He's a little too obvious for Dad to take.") It's the pictures put away, the books slipped to the bottom of the pile, the word *gay* carefully left out of the conversation. It's the caress cut short, the kiss never given, the thousand little compromises that mean nothing individually but add up to the blunting of experience, the demeaning of love, the spoiling of identity that are too much a part of our gay and lesbian lives already. I think it is time to break this deadly contract, to negotiate a new one that enables love and trust rather than fear and embarrassment to determine the limits of relationships with those we care about.

The second reason why it matters for gay people to identify themselves as gay is political. As an individual you may or may not be ready to make this your business, but you should at least be aware of it. The changes that are needed in social policies and in laws in order to improve the quality of life for gay people will come only when there is a political and economic gay and lesbian constituency that is visible and identifiable. We have the numbers of people but as long as we remain a "phantom population" the numbers are useless. The politician will continue to say, "I don't think I have enough gay constituents to warrant my support of your proposed legislation." The regulatory agency will say, "Gay people are not a significantly large enough segment of the community to justify a change in the regulations." The corporate decision makers will say, "There is not enough of a gay buying public to pay attention to your demands or your protests." The social agencies will say, "There is not a demonstrated need for special programs for gay people."

Voting power counts only when the constituency is a visible and identifiable one. Buying power counts only when the consumer group is a visible and identifiable one.

Only when we begin to come out of the shadows in large numbers will we be seen. Only when we begin to speak up and identify ourselves in large numbers will we be heard. Only when we tell them who we are, what we are, and where we are in large numbers will they pay attention to our needs and concerns. Not before. That is the political and economic reality.

Finally, I would like to look at the development of personal identity in the context of what life is about for most gay and lesbian people, and what it might be about in the future.

In heterosexual society there is a tendency to measure the progress of one's life according to a predetermined pattern revolving around the development of the nuclear family: mother, father, children. Much that happens for an individual from about puberty on, takes on meaning in relation to eventually becoming a marriage partner and a parent. This is one of the major "tracks" of modern life. Progress along this nuclear family track is marked by certain events that signify how far one has come and how far there is yet to travel. Because of their symbolic importance I shall call them ritual events: first dates, courtships, engagements, weddings, childbirth, etc. There is comfort in the knowledge that someone has passed this way before, that there is precedence for one's experience, that something is known about the passage ahead. These ritual events give form to one's life and the notion that it is all about something quite understandable.

For gay and lesbian people it is different. What does give form and continuity to our lives?

First of all, gay people have the same needs that nongay people have. We too need to feel worthwhile, to feel safe, to feel free of pain and suffering. We too need to achieve and acquire. We too need to love and be loved. We too need to do for others and to generate projects that will endure beyond our own lifetime. These are the internally generated needs that motivate most of human endeavor, including involvement in the nuclear family drama.

Where we *are* different is in some of the mechanisms we are developing to meet our needs for affiliation, security, altruism and immortality. For instance, we have replaced the straight marriage with the same-sex lover partnership. Many of us have replaced or supplemented our straight family of origin with a gay and lesbian friendship/support group with whom we can more easily share the joys and struggles of our gay lives. The gay movement itself is a resource for support and positive identification, offering opportunities for involvement in a collective effort to change the quality of life for gay and lesbian people in our lifetime and beyond.

What we have been lacking is a way of formally calibrating our progress through life. To remedy this we should begin to think in terms of our own special, life-affirming, gay growth track. The end point of the track is the validation of our gay existence just as the nuclear family track validates the heterosexual existence of those who follow it. As with the nuclear family track, ritual events would be the symbolic markers of forward movement along the gay growth track. Such ritual events have the purpose of signaling the end of one period in a person's life and the beginning of another. They give us permission to leave behind many of the thoughts, feelings and behaviors that belong to the period that is ending and to adopt new ones for the period being entered into. Some of these ritual events by which we might calibrate our gay lives are:

(1) The first acknowledgment of gayness to one's self.
(2) The first sexual experience with a person of the same gender.
(3) The first disclosure of gayness to a nongay person.
(4) Beginning the first lover relationship.
(5) Moving into the first domicile shared with a lover.
(6) First involvement in the organized gay and lesbian community.
(7) Other important disclosures to family, friends, co-workers.

Nongay people tend to center their lives around courtship, marriage, and the arrival and ongoing care of children. More and more gay and lesbian people also have children, but the organizing principle of any gay life should always involve movement toward an open and integrated gay identity. That includes the ability to be who one truly is not only at home, but on the job, with family and friends, and in the world generally. The process by which we achieve this, both personally and collectively, is what will give form and purpose and continuity to our lives. It is, and will continue to be, the crisis of courage out of which our gay future will be born.

Coming Out Inside

Mark Thompson

At some point or another, you've been there too: It's the dead of night, that special hour when the silence seems spooky, and suddenly you are awakened. On the surface, it could be for any reason; a fragment of a disturbing dream, some stressful remnant from the day before. But as you lie there sinking back into sleep, something else rises up to grasp your conscious mind. It's more than just an anxious feeling cresting on a cloudy surface, it's a whisper from way down deep, past the layers of worry, anxiety, and need. It's a small voice buried in the very center of who you are. And the voice asks, "Am I okay? Am I really satisfied with the way I am? Maybe there is something wrong about being gay, after all."

We've all experienced this kind of self-doubt, whether fleetingly at four in the morning or, at some time, as an all-consuming reality. This is the judging voice of the oppressor within, a voice more hurtful than the taunts and jeers of a homophobe could ever be.

From the moment one begins to suspect that they might be "different" from others the seed of doubt is sown, sending out its corrosive roots to obstruct and inhibit the process by which self-esteem naturally grows. The source of this insidious programming is society's punishing attitudes and actions toward anyone who deviates from its rigid norms. When these destructive attitudes are internalized, the punishment comes from within the person who is cast in the role of outsider. Thus begins the heterosexual majority's effort to control the homosexual minority.

This enemy within is invisible, elusive, and difficult to fight against, until one is able to achieve the understanding that the problem originates with society and is *not* a function of one's own flawed being. The journey to selfhood is particularly difficult when society's damning views about differentness are channeled through a person crucial to your feelings about yourself, such as a parent.

I perceived that something was not right with me the very first time I was told that I threw a ball like a girl. The remark hit me like a missile, launched right there in my grammar school playground. I don't think I had ever thought about the *correct* way to loft a ball before — I just threw it in the manner that seemed most natural to me. If the truth were to be known, I would have much preferred not to throw the ball at all. The cozy solitude of the school library seemed an innately more comfortable place to be. Learning to throw the ball as it was deemed necessary felt odd. Somehow, I could not learn to do it the way others wanted.

Late one afternoon, my father took the matter into his own hands. He marched me into the backyard, positioned himself on the opposite end of a grassy patch, and proceeded to hurl a baseball at me until it became too dark to see. It was obvious that his concern over my manhood grew as the hours went by; the ball was returned to my mitt with increasing force until I had tears in my eyes and a blistered palm. For the life of me, I could still not throw the ball "like a boy" — or so I was sharply told.

Rather than a lesson in sportsmanship, my frustrating session with my father turned out to be a lesson in everything I was *not*: neither someone adept in sport nor, by anyone's standard measure, a man. This was a lesson in failure that would stay with me for a long, long time. On that day, I was suspect for evermore; suspectful of not being normal in other people's eyes, self-doubtful in my own. An acid rain had fallen where I lived, seeping through my innocence. Like cracks in the pavement that erode into dangerous fissures, my soul was rutted by secret misery and shame. No quick patch job would ever cover what had been taken away.

Most gay people learn — as I did — to adapt to their conditional acceptance. It's one reason why we're masterful survivors. But the price we have to pay in order to endure such damage to a young spirit is high. We can see the stressful signs of having to cope in this way throughout our lives and community. Alcoholism and substance abuse, self-destructive behavior and failed relationships — these are the ill effects of a compromised self-image that many of us have had to privately struggle with, usually to a higher degree than our nongay peers. All of these things are the product of that poisonous seed within once it matures.

Restoring our esteem of self is the most essential task at hand when we do admit to ourselves that yes, indeed, we are gay and proud of it. But coming out of the closet can be a paper-thin declaration if it's not part of a bigger, ongoing commitment to personal and social change. The gay and lesbian community provides a kind of safe harbor for us when we do come out, a supportive environment in which to anchor our feelings and mend old wounds.

However, stepping into a prescribed gay lifestyle — as tolerant as it may be — is not enough. The excitement of bonding with similar others can obfuscate the often difficult and lonely work of putting one's demons to rest. Becoming a productive member of gay society is an important first step, but coming out does not end there. Coming out is the initial wake-up call for the real process of personal liberation: A trail-blazing inner journey where we keep on "coming out" over and over again.

Outer lives are easily enough decorated with signs of pride and activist slogans, but what are the markers of coming out inside? How many of us have sought after our rights, while subtly retaining the mistaken notion that we might not be worthy of them? One youthful rallying cry of the early gay movement put forth the idea that we are the people our parents warned us about. But, in truth, we become more like our parents every day. A product of the same genealogy and system of values, we may visibly reject our forebears while still carrying around fears and prejudices similar to theirs. That's why the real spade work of excavating ourselves — of finding out who we truly are — lies in digging through our personal and familial history for clues as to why we are the way we are.

The spiritual cost of not doing this important inner work can be tragically high. We can all look at the people in our lives and find examples of what I am talking about. One friend of mine, Gary, was such a person. On the surface, Gary seemed to have everything a gay man could want; bright and attractive, he was admired by others for his charm and masculine good looks. He set his own pace by working as a well-paid gardener at expensive Los Angeles homes, taking time off when he wanted to travel the world. Gary prided himself on his adventures and active sex-life, yet despite all the outward signs of fulfillment he was continually haunted by a nagging sense of personal lack. His moods could change quickly; under a sunny veneer lay a treacherous interior landscape pocked with despondency and self-doubt.

Gary's feelings about himself were in many ways colored by his history with his father. A deep silence existed between them, a void never addressed by either man. Their absence of communication was first created by early childhood abuse and later widened by Gary's coming out. That rift could have been bridged by Gary and his father talking together about the burdens they carried with regard to one another. Instead, the wounds went unattended. For Gary, this was a lifelong source of pain that could — and did — affect him in unpredictable ways. My friend's bouts of despair were only intensified when he discovered he had AIDS. And while he did seek out some therapy near the end of his life in order to better deal with his hurt, Gary nevertheless died feeling incomplete and flawed.

Gary's story is, unfortunately, not unique. Many of us, including myself, wage a daily struggle for equilibrium. We're on a high wire, trying to keep balance above the spongy soil where our worst fears about ourselves thrive. So how does one begin to take steps away from this predicament? Where does one turn for help? A good way to start recovering self-worth is to learn how to properly frame the past.

While such complex issues as the loss of a father's love can perhaps never be resolved, the ability to put family history in perspective can be helpful, especially when it comes to one's own intimate relationships. The trick is to know what feelings belong to the unfinished business of parental dramas and which ones belong to your own contemporary relationships. Early childhood traumas can grow to defeat us if not properly examined. Such ruptures have a tendency to breed secrets, and with secrets come shame.

Unlike my late friend, Gary, I was able to complete some unfinished business with my father. Twenty years had gone by since that fateful game of catch. But having learned to put my anger and feelings of abandonment in some perspective, I sought my father out. A few summers ago, I drove over 700 miles to the place where he lived, a sprawling cattle ranch in southeastern Oregon. At first, we greeted each other awkwardly. But as we sat talking about our lives on the veranda of his old ranch house, we began to sense how much we really had to share. The day grew late, until finally it was time to make a final round of the land. As we drove from one pasture to another, I jumped out of the truck to open each gate separating the herds. I stood there as my dad steered the truck through, and then latched the metal divider behind us before clambering back into the high weathered cab. It was a ritual done in silence, but it spoke volumes about our willingness to work together, the new bond we had initiated that afternoon.

Within a year, my father was dead from cancer. But the opportunity to say, "I love you, Dad," and to hear, in turn, "I'm proud of you, son," had not been lost.

Establishing a workable relationship with your parents, through dialogue, is an essential point of coming out inside. Staking an autonomous place of your own from which to build that dialogue allows self-respect to grow. You probably cannot do this successfully, however, until you are able to let go of the anger toward your parents that the child within you holds tight. And that requires courage, conviction, and a major sorting of feelings before you can be forgiving enough to find a common ground. That is what happened with my own father. Being able to open the gates for him to drive through symbolically facilitated the easing of two decades of mutual grief.

Many times, parents or other authority figures are not as ready as my father was to come out of their emotional closets. But, whether they're prepared or not, the real liberation comes in the trying, in the commitment you have made to yourself to engender change in a relationship that has been burdened by unresolved conflict. That is the real point of coming out: to dare to confront that buried voice that says you are not okay. By meeting this challenge, with eyes wide open, we enhance our ability to speak directly to the oppressor within.

Coming out inside means connecting with your inner "warrior." It is a powerful archetype that will serve you well, if properly acknowledged. Think of this symbolic figure as a kind of guide, an ally, a secret presence known only to you, that can help make a way through the difficult choices we sometimes face in being gay or lesbian. If possible, try to locate the hero within yourself. When you are through reading this chapter, set the book aside for a few minutes and imagine what such a figure would look like, how he or she would be dressed and might act. Establish contact, say "hello" if you can. Doing this may seem a little awkward or silly at first, but it is a useful exercise. It is one way to tune into the forces within you that allow for a sense of control in your life. Not surprisingly, the picture of the inner warrior that most often emerges is an idealized version of one's self.

This is why it is important to lead active, heroic lives. In the gay and lesbian community, there are plenty of ways to affirm our fortitude — to tap into that warrior energy. First, channel your feelings of anger and hurt through activism or service. By giving time to the local chapter of ACT UP, or AIDS information-line, or the dozens of other gay and lesbian agencies and groups that now exist in nearly every community across the nation, you are contributing to yourself as much as others. If you don't see something that you would like to do, then decide what would be meaningful and create it. Actively seek out plans for positive change; otherwise, discontent turned inward can lead to depression and defeatism.

You might also want to find a spiritual basis for healing the things that haunt you. If organized religion — and, in some places, that can run the gamut from Zen Buddhism to the Metropolitan Community Church — is not to your taste, then discover the alternatives. Queer people (as some of us call ourselves these days) have a lively sense of faith, as we do humor, and that includes participating in everything from Wiccan circles to the Radical Faeries, tantric practices to twelve-step programs. One-on-one counseling with a compassionate, gay-affirmative therapist is also an advisable route to personal reclaiming. This is an excellent way to understand the dreams, memories, and personal myths that shape us.

Whatever path you choose, remember that what has been lost to you can be regained. It is a difficult, often frustrating process as I can candidly attest. But through conscious effort, and by demonstrating the inner work you do with social action, a newly strengthened sense of self is possible. And this, I believe, leads the way to the all-important task gay people have to do collectively in restoring balance and harmony to our lives. We must do this for ourselves. We must hold fast to the greater vision of who we are.

Always keep in mind: The mirror that was held up to you when you were young was a distorted one. The cracked image you saw could not honestly reflect who you were then — or who you are now. It is from that false picture that the whispers come past midnight to cast doubt where there should be pride and self-worth. The work of coming out inside is learning to honor the rightness of our struggle to love and be loved. True activism — the road forward — begins with such simple truth. By coming out inside, we learn first to love ourselves.

The Importance of Telling Our Stories

John Preston

When I was young I asked my father where I had come from. He's an engineer, he believes that all knowledge comes from facts. Following his scientific instinct he sat me down and drew diagrams and explained how physiological life came into being. I was a bit embarrassed, not by his explanation — I knew all that — but because he hadn't understood my question.

So I went to my mother and I asked her where I had come from. I remember that she was knitting, probably in a rocking chair while watching television. She put down her needles and nodded her head slightly, just enough to let me know that she agreed that this was an important question. Then she launched into a rich, complex answer that began with my great-great-grandfather and his brother, who had moved down to our hometown in Massachusetts from the Green Mountains of Vermont. They had wanted to make their fortune and had settled on our hometown as the place to do it after a few false starts in other villages.

We had lived here ever since, she explained. Anyone who married into our family moved to Medfield and settled here to raise their children, just as my father had moved to our rural community from Boston when he and my mother married and had me. This was where I belonged, she explained, because this is where I came from.

Now, that was an answer that a boy could understand! It was all the more appealing because the story was full of small details that brought the people in my history to life. The richest part was the names. My family was full of people with ancient New England names: the founding patriarch, my great-great-grandfather, was Raymond Blood, and his name has appeared in each generation since. Now I

21

understood how my uncle came to be called Raymond. My mother's father had been a Raymond Blood as well. Just to underscore how lavish that name was, he married a woman named Martha Honey, my grandmother. Blood and Honey, how much more elemental can a boy's heritage be?

When I first heard all of this, I think the idea of the family's journey from Vermont was the most exciting thing to me. I imagined my great-great-grandfather and his brother riding horses down from the mountains, or perhaps they came in a covered wagon; these were images that a young boy could cling to! My mother told me that they were always said to have been very close to one another; I could sense the fraternity between them as they camped out in tents while they built the first family house — it was over on Park Street, she told me.

My whole landscape became more alive after I heard this story. I began to ask more and more questions about the landmarks in our hometown. I wanted to know which ones my ancestors had seen when they first arrived in Medfield. I read town histories as soon as I was old enough, knowing that this was history that was meant for me, this was something that my family had made me a part of over the past two centuries. It was my mother's stories that gave me a sense of belonging.

A New World

When I was older, I discovered that I was entering a world where there were very few stories to give me that sense of belonging. I did read some strange psychological texts about homosexuality, but they were mainly about the dysfunction of a homosexual lifestyle. Their cold analysis gave me nothing, it didn't help at all to be called a sexual deviant. How could I create a life on that basis? Besides, I was *sure* there was something more to all of this than statistical tables.

But where was it all? It was the 50s and television certainly wasn't even acknowledging homosexual lifestyles. There were no political groups advocating our civil rights that I could read about in the newspapers. Magazines never carried any material about the lifestyle I was about to enter, unless it was a veiled hint at a terrible scandal. Who I was becoming was invisible to the whole world, and almost invisible to me. That's why I, like so many other young people at that time, thought I must be the only person in the world who shared these feelings. If there were others, wouldn't they be reported somewhere? Wouldn't their existence be recognized by someone?

I finally found a very few pieces of writing that hinted at another level of richness I might find. I read avant-garde literary magazines, the only source of information that seemed to have any texture to its portrayals of what it might be like to be a homosexual, but even they didn't really fulfill my needs. After all, I was a kid in a small rural town, doing well in school, expecting to go to college. I wasn't living on the cutting edge of society, I was right in the middle of it. How would this new intelligence about addicts and perverts fit into my life?

While I was in high school and later in college, I discovered a magic place, Provincetown, that started to give me the solutions I craved. Provincetown is an old beach resort at the very tip of Cape Cod. It has been an artists' colony for years. Because of its cultured reputation, and for some other reasons — maybe including the fact that it was the end of the world, the very edge of the country — I discovered that Provincetown had long been a center of homosexual life. Its very isolation seemed to allow the people there to construct an existence that fed themselves and gave them what they wanted. It wasn't perfect, there were many problems with being homosexual any place in the United States in the 50s, but it was a place where many gay men and lesbians would congregate.

I started to go to Provincetown as often as I could. I went there for the bars where I could find the men who hid in other places, but danced together and kissed right in public here. There's no question that there was a sexual thrill to being in Provincetown and taking part in all of its courtship rituals. But I also went there because it was one place where people were willing to tell their stories.

I would stand by the dance floor in bars, or lie on my blanket at the gay beach at Herring Cove, and I would listen to gay men and lesbians tell one another about their lives. They were often simple narratives about deciding where to live and getting along with a landlord, or about what it was like to work in a certain place. Yet they were sumptuous stories. They meant a great deal to me because they were telling me about how life could be, often they were dreaming about how it should be.

The stories I heard in Provincetown's restaurants and on its streets were often profound. There were tales about the horrors that gay life could mean back then, the cruelty that society could hand out to lesbians and gay men. The discussions I heard weren't just reports of how difficult things could be, there were also proposals on how to change things. Long before Stonewall there were many lesbians and gay men who were wondering how we could create a better life for all of us.

Those stories became as important to me as the stories my mother told me about my family, because they were also about my heritage and they were also about my place in the world. They were all the more important because there were so few other stories to be heard that could help me.

I became one of the people involved in gay liberation. I'm especially proud that I was one of the people who founded the first gay and lesbian community center in the United States; we called it Gay House, Inc., and it was in Minneapolis. One of the first things we did was to set up times and places when people of different types could come together and talk about their lives. We weren't necessarily trying to solve all the world's problems with our discussion groups, we were just taking advantage of a chance to finally talk to one another about what those problems were.

The circles were made up of many different affinity groups. There were times when lesbian mothers could talk to one another, other times when single gay men could have a chance to listen to each other. Then there were larger community meetings where everyone who used the place could get together. We all took different things from those meetings, but they were all essentially about learning to listen to one another to better understand how we had all gotten to this place of being lesbian and gay.

Of course there were many conflicts; we were entering new territory where no one had gone before. We often argued about what direction we should be pointed in — just the way gay men and lesbians debate those issues today — but there were at least as many times when there were feelings of goodwill and accord when we could discover our commonality and have a sense that there was a way for us to go forward together.

I continued to be an activist for a long time, more involved with setting up organizations and leading protests than in telling stories. But eventually the stories forced themselves onto me. I'm sure one of the reasons was my having seen how powerful it had been for people to share their anecdotes and yarns with one another. It was, I was sure, important to have even more chronicles and more points of view.

The Stories
By the time I became a writer, in the late 70s, there was beginning to be a whole body of lesbian and gay literature and it soon began to be available in bookstores in many places, not just the big cities. Where I had once found only texts on abnormal behavior that experts thought should be curbed by any means possible, there were now novels, poems, plays, and true stories about being gay and lesbian.

Not all of them told my particular story. It was a situation like those discussion groups at Gay House, Inc., where there were some conversations that were for just some people, and others that were for all the members. When I didn't find important legends and tales from my own life, I did the same thing I had done as a community organizer: I made my own.

The first novel I wrote was *Franny the Queen of Provincetown*. It celebrated the wonderful voices I had heard in that old resort community years earlier, the voices that had told me about the possibilities for my life and broke the silence of the world around me. There are lots of lovely parts to *Franny* that I enjoyed writing, but there were some parts that were hard to put down on paper. There should be fantasies in our lives, the charming stories that tell us about the happiness that's possible for us. The difficult stories need to be there too. They serve as warnings and cautions that let us know where there might be obstacles ahead: the external restraints like discrimination, and the internal ones like drug abuse.

I'm sure it's her own love of stories that led my mother to be very proud of *Franny*. She hadn't always been that happy that I was a gay man, but it seemed to make things much better between us when she was able to see that I was making myself an author out of the experience. She even hosted a party for me once, to show me off to her friends. She might never have promoted her son the gay man, but she certainly was willing to announce me as her son the author.

I've been a writer full-time now for over a decade. I've written many books, stories, and articles. My mother and the rest of my family have come to like the idea of my vocation. When I edited an anthology called *Hometowns: Gay Men Write about Where They Belong,* my mother was especially pleased.

One of my contributions to the anthology was an essay on Medfield, the legacy that my mother and I shared with one another. This was a book that she could truly be proud of. My mother is the town clerk of Medfield, an elected post that makes her a visible member of the community. She wanted everyone to know about the accomplishment she felt I had achieved with this new book and its essay on the town. So, she went out and bought a copy of *Hometowns* and donated it to the library.

There! she thought. Now anyone who went into the library would see this splendid book by her son. I imagine her sitting in her office in the town hall, smoking her unfiltered cigarettes and drinking her omnipresent coffee, pleased with the idea.

But there was a sudden cloud over her thoughts. What if no one ever took the book out of the library? What if it sat there for years in the stacks and someone came along and opened it to the back, where the circulation of the volume would be noted, and saw that the book had never been borrowed? That would not do! So my mother sent her friends over to the library, one a day, just to take the book out so it could be stamped at the back. It wasn't until she was sure that there would be enough evidence of its popularity that she relaxed again and went back to her cigarettes and coffee.

My mother's gift was very important to me because the Medfield Town Library is the place I had first gone when I was a young boy to look for stories about what it meant to be homosexual. There had been nothing but those dry scientific texts that had left me so alone and confused until I had found people to tell me stories about their own lives. Now, thanks to my mother, when there's another young gay man or lesbian in Medfield who goes to find stories to help her or him make sense of this life, they will at least find a copy of *Hometowns* and they'll be able to read about someone who had come before them and had lived in the same place, who had gone on and led a decent life, and had even written a book about it all.

That young person who finds the book is going to know how important it is for us to tell our stories to one another, because that person will feel the power of the story, the power that gives hope and destroys isolation.

The Changing Lesbian Social Scene

Robin Podolsky

In the decades between 1972 and 1992, lesbian social life has blossomed into a rich variety of communities and activities. Lesbians of color, religious lesbians, older and younger lesbians, lesbian art lovers, sports enthusiasts, parents and political activists are building and maintaining social bonds and organizations. There are lesbian associations built around hobbies and interests, which cater to wide cross sections of women: lesbian hiking clubs, professional women's networks, camera clubs and emotional support groups.

Our advances are evidenced not only in the mature and varied social life which exists by and for lesbians, but also in the extent to which lesbian social life overlaps many other worlds. Openly lesbian couples dance at high school reunions and compete in company bowling leagues. Some open lesbians are elected officials with high visibility at official functions and in the media.

The last decade has seen a broadening and an evolution within lesbian life, sparking more diversity than ever. There are at least three post-Stonewall generations now, with distinct styles and different needs. Some of the forms invented by lesbians in the seventies, such as women's music festivals, are still going strong, although under changing conditions. Also, the eighties and early nineties have given rise to developments such as the new nightclub scene and activist organizations which mirror larger social trends.

Cultural Activity

Invisibility as women, and as women who love women, has long been a major lesbian concern. Where gay men are likely to be demonized or falsely rendered in mainstream movies, magazines and books, lesbians are rarely seen at all. (Unfortunately, the popularity of the 1992 film, *Basic Instinct*, might change that situation temporarily by creating a vogue for lesbian slashers on screen.) Fortunately, independent lesbian film makers are on the rise. Their work may be seen at Lesbian and Gay Film Festivals and, increasingly, at art houses throughout the country.

Not surprisingly, one of the first manifestations of lesbian consciousness, following the watershed Stonewall Rebellion of 1969, was the proliferation of a lesbian literary scene which has grown from self-published chapbooks and audio tapes to the publication of lesbian novels and nonfiction by major publishing houses. Lesbian writers enjoy an active audience and appreciation of their work sparks important social activity.

Most major cities and university towns can boast at least one bookstore or coffee house that is oriented toward lesbians, lesbians and gays, or women. Often, such establishments host readings and performances by lesbian writers and artists. These programs, which are varied in style and, often, of superior quality, are major social events. Lesbians who want to meet other lesbians without going to bars can meet women with tastes and interests similar to their own — in an environment where conversation is encouraged and *audible*.

Bookstores, coffee houses and other lesbian-friendly businesses, such as San Francisco's women-only hot tub and sauna spa, *Osento*, provide community bulletin boards which advertise an array of classes, discussion groups and social gatherings, along with job offers and potential roommates. A visit to any gay and lesbian service center, college women's center, or women's bookstore will probably yield one community newspaper or at least a handful of leaflets which advertise the local goings-on. In fact, the national newsletter, *Lesbian Connection*, which can be found in most women's bookstores, offers a list of "contact dykes" from all over the country — and not limited to urban centers — who are available to take calls from lesbians who are passing through their region. The contact dykes serve as an underground chamber of commerce, offering entrée into local lesbian scenes and general tips on how to best enjoy a vacation in the area.

"Women's Music," which began in the early 70s, remains a staple of lesbian culture, albeit an evolving one. Those founding artists of the genre whose style is rooted in folk music, such as Chris Williamson and Holly Near, can still pack concert halls. So can such veteran Afro-American musicians as Sweet Honey In The Rock and Castelberry and Duprey, whose audiences include, but are not limited to, a faithful lesbian following.

However, a new generation of listeners has arrived with a taste for the sardonic, politerati lyrics and post-punk sound of bands like *Two Nice Girls* and *Girls In The Nose* — a delightful case of Women's Studies gone awry — or for bands like San Francisco's *Tribe 8* who take hard core rock out of the closet and into your face.

Fans of every style of music co-exist, more or less peacefully, at the yearly Women's Music Festivals which draw thousands of women, largely lesbian, from all over the country. The east, west and gulf coasts have festivals of their own and RhythmFest brings percussionists to the south, but the grandmother festival is still the one held yearly in Michigan which draws over ten thousand women to a week-long celebration. Most festivals are held in outdoor camping areas and feature nightly concerts, arts and crafts marketplaces, discussion groups, workshops and sporting activities. Most offer childcare, some to all children, including boys under ten, and some to girls only, although the girls-only policy has been a source of some controversy.

The festivals are often the ground on which new developments in lesbian self-definition are explored and conflicts are played out. There are fascinating, although sometimes difficult, yearly debates over such controversial issues as the admission to festivals of male to female transsexuals who consider themselves to be lesbian women, designated camping spaces for leatherwomen, and the admission of boy children to concert performances by lesbian separatists.

Daily Life: From Homesteads to Nightclubs

Daily social life within the many pockets of lesbian community throughout the country also displays diversity. From urban to rural, from defiantly open to discreet, lesbian friendship groups reflect a multiplicity of styles and interests.

Some lesbians choose to live on "women's land," buying or renting rural property to build private or collective homesteads. Often, lesbian land dwellers cluster together. The northwest coast and the Ozark mountains are just two of the many areas where "land dykes" tend to gather. Many communities, such as OWL (Only Women's Land) in Oregon offer lodging to women travelers in exchange for work or money. There are communities especially for lesbians of color, for women interested in earth-centered spirituality, and some for hardy individualists whose freeholds are miles away from everyone else.

Lesbians of color have also created their own urban spaces. Organizations like SalsaSoul Sisters in New York and Los Angeles' ULOAH (United Lesbians of African Heritage) and Lesbianas Unidas offer political and social autonomy to lesbians of color.

Also, some nightclubs and other more traditional social venues remain important to lesbians of color communities. An example is Jewel's Catch-One Club in Los Angeles. Jewel's, which serves a racially mixed and sexually diverse clientele, and may be the only bar which holds regular Alcoholics Anonymous meetings on its premises, offers a regular series of Afro-American lesbocentric events.

Younger lesbians and their friends have built an underground club scene. At such venues as New York's Club Clit, dancers in spandex and Doc Martins shake that groove thing for a crowd that runs from leather to denim to lingerie. Linked by an overt sexual charge, "alternative" music and a general affinity for radical politics, the underground clubs are also distinguished by their relationship to similar venues run for gay men. At least as interested in an all-encompassing "Queer" identity as a lesbian one, many underground scenesters mix easily with bisexual women and gay men, preferring an "outlaw" persona that unites people who live outside the heterosexual mainstream.

At swank women-only nightclubs, lipstick-loving lesbians can find unabashed glamour. The go-go dancers at Washington, D.C.'s Lesbo A-Go-Go and other more upscale clubs are likely to sport MTV garb and mixed drinks are served in a neon-and-firepit atmosphere.

Women with disposable income and a large appetite for romance and adventure can now sail on lesbian-only cruises to vacation spots that have hitherto symbolized heterosexual *amour,* such as the Bahamas and the Mexican Riviera. Olivia on the east coast and Robin Tyler Productions in the west are the largest producers of such excursions.

There are many lesbians of all cultural backgrounds, for whom the club scene holds no interest. Social networks abound among lesbian women who prefer dinner and movie excursions or entertaining their friends at home. Many older and professional lesbians are becoming homeowners whose dinner, cocktail and pool parties keep them busy every weekend.

Other lesbians prefer daytime excursions. Social organizations like the west coast's Southern California Women for Understanding provide a comfortable atmosphere for lesbians who want to enjoy traditional leisure activities from volleyball to museum visits.

Traditional neighborhood bars, now that they're not the only game in town — and are no longer subject to constant police raids — have become more relaxed in their atmosphere. In many communities, the bars remain unofficial centers of lesbian life, sponsoring pool tournaments and softball leagues, and their "open mikes" are launching grounds for aspiring lesbian musicians.

Changing the Self in Community With Others
The bars, however, still hold their dangers, alcoholism being the most serious. In the last decade, a movement toward sobriety has become a transforming force among lesbians. Recovery meetings, based on the Twelve Steps of Alcoholics Anonymous have become a recognized part of lesbian culture. There are recovery meetings especially for lesbians who are battling alcoholism, emotional (co)dependency, eating disorders and other compulsive diseases for which all historically disenfranchised groups are at high risk. Soda water and other non-alcoholic beverages have become *de rigueur* at lesbian functions, whether or not alcohol is also served and, frequently, alcohol-free space is provided. The sober woman, no longer considered a party pooper, has become an example of self-empowerment.

In fact, socialization in the traditional woman's skill of emotional housekeeping, the outlaw's sense of her own freedom to reinvent her consciousness, and the hunger of the oppressed to understand their situation have combined to make lesbians some of the most self-improved people in the country. Lesbians of every ethnicity and economic background are signing up for affinity groups, workshops and therapy designed to examine and enhance almost every aspect of human life: from healthy relationships, to economic survival in troubled times, to anger management, to artistic fulfillment. This is both a source of internal humor and a source of pride. No one can accuse the modern lesbian of complacency about her own development.

Political activity is, for many lesbians, a source of social contact as well as a means of creating social justice. There are lesbian organizations and lesbian caucuses within larger gay organizations which range from Democratic or Republican Party clubs to Queer Nation chapters. Many cities have organizations representing Afro-American, Asian, Latino and Native American lesbians and gays. Often such groups combine activism with cultural events.

Most large campuses list lesbian and gay associations among their organized student groups. Such associations range from highly politicized organizations that demonstrate in favor of civil rights advances — i.e., freedom from harassment or equal access to married student housing — to the more socially-oriented clubs that sponsor mixers, concerts and film showings.

Religion and spiritual life bonds many lesbian friendships. There are gay and lesbian congregations in mainstream religious denominations, along with many religious membership organizations like Dignity for lesbian and gay Catholics and Affirmation for lesbian and gay Mormons.

A growing movement among lesbians and other people is the neo-pagan movement of earth-centered spirituality which personifies the life-force as a Goddess, and, sometimes, a God. Lesbians have been a visible part of the growing interest among many women in images of the Divine which are androgynous or female. Also, some anthropological research indicates that in early tribal societies who included goddesses among their deities, people of both sexes who adopted the behavior or dress of the other gender, or combined genders, were considered to be individuals of spiritual power, rather than deviants. Some young people who are interested in creating a distinct "Queer" culture are looking for ways to modernize ancient shamanic rituals involving gender fluidity.

New Kinds of Families

A new phenomenon of the last decade has been the Lesbian Baby Boom. Lesbians have been giving birth to and adopting children in record numbers, creating new social forms in the process. Some lesbian couples raise their children in relatively traditional two-parent homes. Often their children are conceived by artificial insemination by anonymous donors. In other cases, the fathers are known to the parents and will be known to the children as well. Many times, the fathers are gay men with lovers of their own, who want an active parenting role. Thus, a new kind of extended family is born.

Lesbian mothers become friends with each other through parenting classes and support groups. Sometimes, their children grow up with a bevy of lesbian "aunts" who form casserole brigades to assist the mothers of infants and create babysitting cooperatives or playgroups for toddlers and school-age youngsters. Lesbians who are considering parenthood may want to make contact with such a group to establish a social network of support in advance of pregnancy. (The nearest lesbian and gay service center may be a good source of information about parenting groups.)

So Much Accomplished, So Much to Be Done

It should be noted that not all lesbians have access to the rich social scene to be found in large cities and on lesbian land. Joan Nestle, founder of the Lesbian Herstory Archives in New York City reports that she still receives letters from lesbians who live in small towns and are isolated, harassed or completely closeted. There are still parts of the United States where not just one-religion, but one-denomination counties still exist. The runaway daughters of such communities can be found in the lobbies of lesbian and gay centers around the country.

In the face of our society's decidedly uneven progress toward equality for lesbians and gay men, the significance of stable lesbian social networks cannot be overstated. In their friendships with each other, lesbians find role models, support, and the consistent mirroring which tells them that there is nothing wrong with them, and that they are part of a vibrant section of society.

Some open lesbians have resisted and continue to resist lesbian-only friendship circles, not wanting their social being to be defined by one aspect of their lives. The choice to select friends according to personal affinity, rather than sexual orientation, offers individuals a chance for growth and risk. It also allows them to model successful lesbian lives, not only to other lesbians, but also to the community at large.

At the other end of the scale there are lesbians who choose to live separatist lives, reserving their emotional energy and personal commitments for other lesbians. Such women feel that the common life experiences that lesbians share create a bond deeper than any other. Also that, by virtue of having been written out of the dominant culture's narrative, lesbians are free, within the insularity of invisibility, to experiment with new social forms, and they want to avoid mainstream assumptions to the greatest extent possible.

Increasingly, the choice does not have to be either-or. Lesbian social life has become so rich that it is easy to participate in it without compromising other aspects of one's identity. Today's lesbian social groups are no longer the chance combinations of people who find each other in hiding, but are chosen alliances of people with positive mutual interests. Therefore they are not prisons. Women who attend a lesbian potluck on Saturday might join a crowd of friends from work for a basketball game on Sunday and be equally at home.

Perhaps our greatest victory is that we cannot talk about "the" lesbian social scene anymore. Lesbian connections are as exciting and unique as lesbians themselves. No matter what the newcomer to lesbian life is looking for, she'll probably find it. Or create it for herself.

The Changing World of Gay Men

Michael Bronski

One of the most common questions asked of people who answer gay helplines is "How can I meet other gay men?" The question may come from a seventeen year old high school student who is just coming out, a twenty-seven year old construction worker who has just ended a relationship of six years, or a sixty-five year old bank vice-president who has lost his lover to AIDS.

The good news is that after twenty-three years of the gay rights movement there are literally thousands of opportunities for gay men to get together: in self-improvement groups, at social and cultural events, and in community organizations that cover a myriad of purposes. What a change this is from the 1950s and 1960s when the only gay meeting places were bars, bathhouses, and other venues designed primarily for sexual contact. Such situations were often dangerous and not exactly uplifting to the people who sought them out. A few gay social/political groups did exist back then, the Mattachine Society and the Daughters of Bilitis, for instance, but their meetings were for the most part surreptitiously conducted and their membership, in a few large cities, was small in number.

Since the Stonewall Riots in June 1969, and the growth of the gay rights movement, there has been a ever-expanding array of groups, clubs, social activities, and political and recreational opportunities for gay and lesbian people to meet and initiate the friendships that form the community as we know it today.

There are gay and lesbian organizations for mountain climbers, for religious worship, for writers, doctors, lawyers, dentists, scientists, journalists, and police officers. There are gay men's choruses in most large cities, softball teams, country dancing classes, science fiction clubs, Frontrunner Groups, tennis clubs, and couples' groups. There are gay and lesbian film festivals, concerts, theater, rodeos, and the

Gay Games which attract thousands of gay and lesbian athletes and spectators from all over the world. Of course there are the endless fundraisers, and the opportunities to volunteer in the many organizations set up to serve the needs of people with AIDS. This is only a small representation of what is available today to answer the question, "How can I meet other gay men?"

I consider myself lucky to have had the experience of being "out" before Stonewall because I have had the opportunity to witness the enormous change that has occurred over the last two decades in the way gay men are able to make contact with one another. I knew I was gay from an early age and I felt very little trouble about it. When I got to college, the year was 1967, I sought out ways to meet other gay men on campus. Once in contact we formed a community, and even though we were just a short train ride from Greenwich Village, most of my early gay friendships, sex partners, and lovers came from the small social world of our campus gay community.

After Stonewall
After Stonewall, it all changed. Many of my friends and I became involved in the new, emerging world of gay politics. We joined the Manhattan-based Gay Liberation Front, and our lives began to revolve around our new identity as gay activists. One of the first targets of the Gay Liberation Front was the mob-owned gay bar. Straight mob bar owners, who cared nothing for the well-being of their gay customers, would routinely make arrangements for the police to raid their clubs as part of the "payoff" to stay in business. Of course we stayed out of the oppressive mob-owned bars as one part of our protest. We spent our time organizing picket lines, going to GLF dances, and socializing at planning committee meetings.

When I moved from New York to Boston a strange thing happened. I was amazed at the difference in the gay political scene. After long Gay Men's Liberation meetings it seemed nearly mandatory that everyone went out to the local bars and discos, even though it was well known that most of them were owned by one of New England's leading mob families. At first I couldn't understand this. Here I was conditioned to think of gay bars as one of the most oppressive institutions in gay male life and now I was part of a "radical" political group that thought it was fine to celebrate the proclamation of our freedom from straight oppression by patronizing establishments owned by one of our chief oppressors.

In a short time I came to understand that there was another side to the story. The gay bar was then, and continued to be for a long time, the place where a real community of men gathered. In those days, there were no gay newspapers, no newsletters, no gay media of any kind. The bars were where you found out what was going on in the gay world, where you discussed whether or not Ken Russell's *The Music Lovers* really dealt with Tchaikovsky's homosexuality, where you traded stories about what was happening in the streets, in the meetings, and in everybody's bedroom. The bars were not just places to drink, they were our community centers, our town squares, our back fences that we could hang over and gossip, our local bulletin boards.

I don't mean to romanticize bar life. Of course there is a downside to what goes on in bars, then and now, and many people are just not comfortable in the bar scene. But, I think it is important to understand that the bars were, in those days, the visible reality of our diverse community. The great change in the past twenty years is that the gay bar is no longer the *only* place where gay men can meet and be together. We now have real community centers with programs to serve our need for affiliation as well as the many other needs that gay and lesbian people bring to these centers. We have gay newspapers and magazines and cable television shows, and gay computer bulletin boards, and neighborhood newsletters, and all kinds of public forums to trade ideas and educate the nongay public about who we are.

The reason I've wanted to write about the realities of the "gay community" is that the idea of meeting other gay men should not be something separate from being a part of this community. We have all of these new opportunities for contact because we have, *as a community,* taken this social space for ourselves. We have created this world with our new freedom, our new strength, our new vision of what we can be to ourselves and to those who share our way of living and loving. It is all of this that has given us the emotional, psychological and social options that we didn't have before, the permission to raise our expectations to anticipate, and to build lives that are free and open and as productive as we want them to be.

The idea of "family" is quite central to the idea of community for gay and lesbian people. Our community is organized around our gay and lesbian families of friends and lovers. The ability to be open and public about who we are has created the opportunity to know one another, to form our diverse friendship networks, our circles of most intimate friends. Were it not for this ability we would find ourselves back in the dismal world of the 1950s. That is one important reason for more of us to come out, to be visible, so we can find each other in the light.

The Search for a Lover
But one must not ignore what is for many gay men a very crucial part of their social life, the search for a lover. The gay male culture sends some mixed messages regarding the desirability of being coupled, and these messages reflect the mix of signals sent out by the mainstream culture. On the one hand, the message is that everyone should be in a couple relationship. This is the only way to be mature and have a satisfying life. (*Ozzie and Harriet* and *Father Knows Best* are the models here.) On the other hand, there is the message that being single equals freedom, fun, and a frolicking good time. (Club Med commercials are the model here.) How does one reconcile these seeming contradictions? For many gay men this has caused some confusion. Add to the confusion the homophobic stereotype that gay men are not capable of making relationships work. This can be quite confusing, especially for gay men who have internalized this prescription for failure. The clue to what most gay men do want for their lives is embedded in the lament that is heard from barstools to therapists' offices to the quiet corners of gay male conversation every-where, "Why can't I find a lover?" For those who want to live in a coupled

relationship there are many ways to get help with that mission. There are now a number of books written to assist in clarifying just what one might really want in a lover, what to look for, how to form and build successful relationships. All of the events and organizations mentioned earlier offer opportunities for meeting potential lovers. Actually they also perform a selection service. If you meet someone at a Metropolitan Community Church event it is likely you will have interests and values in common.

A useful resource to finding compatible people in your city is John Preston's *The Big Gay Book* (Plume, 1991) which lists everything from clubs for gay stamp collectors to gay bowling leagues to gay veterans groups. Local gay and lesbian publications, many of them throwaways, list times and places of meetings. Also, many cities have gay helplines that offer information about what is going on locally.

I tend to think that the main trouble men face in meeting other men today is not so much a lack of opportunity as a confusion as to why they are doing what they're doing. Is it the social pressure to be part of a couple that drives one's "husband hunting?" Or, is there really a need and a readiness for permanent partnership? It is important to recognize that one may not be emotionally ready yet for a close relationship, and that is all right. There is nothing wrong with being single and having fun until you feel quite clearly that you are ready to settle down.

For someone new to the gay male social world it is probably more important to make friends before beginning the search for a lover. I believe there is a new ethic regarding this. As AIDS decimates our friendship circles, forming and strengthening friendships becomes as crucial to our emotional survival as finding a lover. Also, it is important to maintain ties with the larger gay and lesbian community because, with or without a lover, the community is for so many of us the wellspring of our self esteem.

AIDS and Coupling

There has been much written lately on the new inclination, since the advent of AIDS, of gay men to want to be in couple relationships. In part, this is most likely a reflection of how hard AIDS has hit our community. Somehow the image of two men, monogamously tied together, is reassuring to many. Early safe sex information emphasized the necessity of monogamy in the battle to stop the spread of AIDS. We have since learned very specifically how the AIDS virus is spread, through certain forms of sexual activity rather than by certain definitions of lifestyle. There has been a popular sentiment that if you are in a couple relationship you are safe from AIDS. I think it is important to say here that you are only safe from AIDS by practicing safe sex. Certainly monogamous relationships will eventually decrease the spread of this disease, but your decision about how to live your relationship life should be made on the basis of what you know about your own real needs and what you are actually ready to do about them.

The fact is that there have always been gay male couples. That was true before AIDS and it will be true after AIDS. What has changed is that there is a new sensitivity to health and emotional matters. AIDS has made us all more conscious of *thinking* about sex. What do we like, what does it mean to us, what part does sex play in our lives. These are all questions that don't get examined enough by gay or nongay people in our culture.

There has been much talk about the "new" rules concerning dating and sex in the gay male community. In reality these are not *new* rules but only the reassertion of common sense old ones. We all have sexual desires, sexual fantasies, our sexual likes and dislikes. One of the things that has happened during the AIDS epidemic is that we have gotten better at *talking* about all of these things. There is a new frankness in the way sex is talked about not only among gay men but in the mainstream media as well. When you hear explicit discussions on the afternoon talk shows of which acts constitute safe sex and which acts don't, when CBS anchorman Dan Rather is discussing, on the evening news, the distribution of condoms to high school students, you know we have reached a point of no return in the consciousness of the American public with regard to sexual issues.

Along with the new openness about sex comes sexual responsibility, taking the chance of asking your sexual partners for a frank discussion of their sexual history and being willing to share this kind of information yourself. This is not always easy since we have all been imbued with the romantic notion that it's the passion that counts in sexual encounters. Well, passion is a necessary condition for the most lusty sexual experiences but it is not a sufficient one for the formation of a relationship. Talking about sex, no matter how difficult this may be, is an expression of your willingness to be sexually responsible. It is also a sign that you understand that relationships don't just happen, they take work, vigilance, the ability to confront problems and the courage to stick around when the focus is on something other than passion.

New/Old Dating Rules

While there has been much made of the "new dating" rules — that is, gay men spending time with one another before they begin a sexual relationship — it's important to point out that this is not a *new* phenomenon. For decades now gay men have been forming relationships before having sex. It's just that this is not the part of gay life that gets attention. What has changed however is that now there are more social structures for doing this and, in a sense, more social permission. It's "in" to date, to talk, to go to the movies, to community events, to any of the multitude of gay venues that are designed to bring gay men together in a nonsexual way. Actually, when you come right down to it, the new rules are not too different from the old rules that have always applied to any two human beings forming a relationship: honesty, politeness, consideration and a feeling of concern for your partner's well-being, happiness and pleasure. These rules apply whether you meet at a church social or at a bar.

Several years ago I was speaking at a prestigious Eastern college and a young man came up to talk to me after my speech. He said that he had just come out and had told his parents he was gay. He said he was becoming more and more involved in the gay group on campus as well as some off-campus community organizations. He had talked to his parents about his new activist role in addition to disclosing his gayness. He said his parents seemed okay with his disclosure, but his mother — a noted sociologist — said she hoped he was not going to isolate himself in a *single* community. I laughed out loud when he said these words. He was surprised and asked what was funny. Through my laughter I explained the irony of his mother's remark. When I came out in the early 1960s my prevailing fear was that I was "the only one." That was the real and palpable isolation that I had to live with. Being "isolated" in a "community" is a long way from being isolated in one's singular loneliness.

In point of fact the community does not close one off to life experience. In this case the gay and lesbian community opens the door to the opportunity to experience life and love with a newfound honesty and freedom and that applies to life within and without the community.

In the changing social world of gay men, becoming part of the vibrant and challenging adventure of community-building should be as exciting as finding the one and only man to share your life with. The community provides the opportunities for personal and relationship growth that are necessary for a rich and diverse life. Successful relationships (of all kinds), in return, give our community the strength and stability it needs to continue to grow. They go together. It's a sign of how far we've come.

PARTNERING: THE SPECIAL ISSUES OF SAME-SEX COUPLING

Building Successful Relationships

Betty Berzon

Very few among us have been fortunate enough to have had homosexual parents who could model for us the ideal gay or lesbian relationship — caring, growing, fun, mutually supportive — in the context of a burgeoning gay culture. Most of us were stuck with mamas and papas of the heterosexual variety — good, bad or indifferent as mates to each other and parents to us, but no help at all in fashioning our gay love life.

Lacking marriage manuals, parental guidance and models of conjugal bliss on film and television, we've had to wing it when it came to putting together workable love and life partnerships. Intimate relationships are a tricky business at best. Without the sanctions and supports of society's institutions (no positive messages at all), same-sex coupling presents a special challenge to the courage and ingenuity of lovers trying to build a life together.

At times, that challenge involves the same hassles that bewilder every couple trying to make a go of it. At other times, it involves bedevilments seemingly reserved only for gay lovers in an uptight and intransigent straight world. We'll look at both in this chapter.

Same-sex couples? Unnatural, unsanctionable, unconscionable, immoral, sick and immature. Can't work. Won't last. Doesn't count.

Negative messages undermine, subvert and scare us into pale versions of our dream of love. Sometimes we internalize the messages and they work against us from inside: "I'm immoral. I'm sick. I'm immature. My relationship can't work, won't last, doesn't count." We undermine our own efforts by echoing society's baseless pronouncements about us. Too often we allow these cliches to become self-fulfilling prophecies. The prophecy of doom comes true, in turn, reinforcing the cliches and making them appear as truth. We swallow these nontruths and the cycle is complete.

If we are ever going to bring order, reason and sense to our lives as gay people, we must learn to interrupt that cycle. We must learn to identify our own homophobic messages. We must become alert to their presence in our thinking, to the ways in which we incorporate them into our view of ourselves and other gay people. "It was so *gay* of him," I heard someone say recently when describing a piece of inconsiderate behavior. We must catch each other at this, work together to break the vicious cycle. Only then will we be able to really honor our deeply felt need to love and affiliate with persons of the same sex. Only then can we learn to believe in the rightness of gay love relationships because they are, for us, the morally correct, emotionally healthy and socially responsible ways to live our lives.

Many nongay people would argue with that statement. Some gay people would argue with it. Going against prevailing beliefs is always threatening, even when doing so is ultimately to our advantage.

Why Couple?

Let's start with the motivation to be in a coupled relationship in the first place. Why do it? After all, variety is the spice of life. Courtship is exciting. Freedom and independence feel good. So why couple up? The reasons are very much the same in the gay and nongay communities and they produce the same problems. Being alone has never been a valued condition in American society, being paired is, and the pressure to do so is almost as great in the gay world as in the nongay.

So, people seek coupling because:

(1) *It's important to find a partner so others (and you) will know that you can do it.*

(2) *Searching is boring* — all that small talk, game playing, insincerity, superficiality.

(3) *Searching is risky.* You can get set up, ripped off, done in by strangers who don't know or care about you.

(4) *Searching is time consuming.* I could be building, earning, learning, planting, painting, . . . doing.

(5) *Searching is nerve-wracking.* You can be put down, found out, written off.

(6) *Singles are socially out of it* — unsafe to have around a carefully homogenized couples scene.

(7) *Loneliness feels bad.*

When the partner search is motivated by such pressures, chances are the selection process will be short and probably short-sighted. That's not a disaster, since the willingness to work on a relationship can overcome such a beginning. The real problem is that short-circuited partner selection too often results in the fallacy of "if only I had a lover, then . . . " turning into the folly of "now that I have a lover, I will . . . ": be loved, involved, safe, using my time constructively, emotionally supported, socially sought after and lonely no more. And then you aren't. At least not enough, not often enough.

You have invested your partner with enormous, usually unwanted power over your life. Few of us hold up under such a burden. If it has to be because of me that you feel adequately loved, meaningfully engaged, safe from the cruelties and crudities of boors and evil-doers; if it's because of me that you will be enabled to meet the intellectual and creative challenges of your own potential, feel comfortable in your dealings with the world, invited to the most desirable parties and freed of the pain of aloneness, well, I don't think I can handle all that responsibility. If all of this is happening in the underground of our relationship, we don't have a chance to deal with it, to become aware of it, to understand it, to express how we feel about it, to divest ourselves of the awful responsibilities of it. So, we have to find a way to make these implicit expectations you have of me explicit.

What we have to do is open up awareness of our own and our partner's expectations and learn to communicate about them. This is particularly important for gay and lesbian couples whose relationships have to be made strong from within, since the culture without contributes so little to their stability. So how do we open up awareness and communication between us? How do we get to our fantasies and illusions about each other? Here's one approach.

Personal Mythology

Each of us has a personal mythology. That is, we have certain uncritically held beliefs about life, the basis for which may or may not be ill-founded. (It doesn't matter.) These beliefs make up our view of the world. They shape our expectations. They guide us in our decisions. They influence the way we behave with other people. The myths themselves come from a multitude of sources: the folklore of our culture, ethnic group, family, or adopted subcultures. Our personal myths may come from books we've read, movies we've seen, stories we've heard, people we've known. They may be (and often are) amalgams of all these.

The myths we have about romantic love and conjugal relationships are very important influences on how we go about making these things happen in our lives. They often determine when we are successful and when we fail in our endeavors as lovers and partners. For that reason they are worth looking at. Here's a way to do that.

(1) On a piece of paper, write three uncritically held beliefs you've had about how it would be for you in a love relationship. The beliefs may be mainly about the relationship itself, about your partner or about the effect on your life the relationship would have.

(2) Rank order these three beliefs for their importance to you.

(3) Assess your present, or most recent, relationship (or partner) for the degree to which these beliefs are holding up. In those instances where the beliefs have not held up, think about the reasons. It may be useful to think about where these particular beliefs originated and how this influences their importance to you.

You may want to use this exercise to begin to sort out the contemporary person you are dealing with from the illusions and fantasies you've had about any partner you would have in a love relationship. Or, you may want to update your expectations, integrate them with what you know about life, your partner, or yourself.

One way to approach this is to think about the ways in which the myths you have about yourself and a partner have translated into unspoken agreements or "contracts" with regard to how the relationship is conducted. If I have always believed that I would be the strong, worldly-wise caretaker in a relationship, I will probably choose someone who needs this strong, worldly-wise caretaker for a partner. Or, at least, I will convince myself that this is what the partner needs. It may be only partially so. Or, the person with such needs may outgrow them. If I continue to operate in terms of my myth, without making room for my partner's growth, I am in trouble. This kind of trouble happens most often when two people in a relationship don't talk about what is happening between them, when their relationship is conducted mostly in terms of their "contracts."

We develop these contracts in order to short-cut discussion around issues of potential conflict. We all have a tendency to try to keep our relationships as safe and comfortable as possible. Sometimes we overdo it. For gay people there are particular dangers in heavily "contracted" arrangements. There are important areas of our relationships uncharted by traditional gender-role expectations. In the absence of such guidelines there is often a tendency to respond even more to our fantasies about how our partners should be. We need to keep communication open so that we are relating, as much as possible, to a real person in the partnership rather than an idealized image of a person.

Let's look at some of the issues that most often cause problems for gay and lesbian couples. Some of the following will have more relevance for couples who live together. Many of the issues overlap, but each is important enough, I believe, to be looked at separately. If you are part of a gay or lesbian couple, I suggest you and your partner use the device below to get at your unspoken "contracts." Remember, a "contract" in this use is an arrangement that has been arrived at either by mutual consent or by default, and which determines how things are done in the partnership. Consider the questions posed for each item before you describe the contract as you see it, and as you would like to see it.

On a piece of paper, write out your responses to the items in the contract. Each partner should do this independently.

THE CONTRACT

ITEM I. PLANNING JOINT ACTIVITIES
Question: How are decisions made about social plans, trips, home improvement projects, mutual community activities?
A. Right now I think the contract is:
B. I would like it to be:

ITEM II. TIME SPENT WITH OTHER PEOPLE
Question: How are decisions made about how much time is spent with other people, and which people the time is spent with (each partner's family, gay or straight friends, business associates)?
A. Right now I think the contract is:
B. I would like it to be:

ITEM III: SEPARATENESS AND TOGETHERNESS
Question: How much are activities done independently versus activities done together?
A. Right now I think the contract is:
B. I would like it to be:

ITEM IV: DIVISION OF LABOR AT HOME
Question: How are decisions made about who does what?
A. Right now I think the contract is:
B. I would like it to be:

ITEM V: FINANCES
Question: How are decisions made about how money is managed and how money is spent?
A. Right now I think the contract is:
B. I would like it to be:

ITEM VI. SEXUAL EXCLUSIVITY
Question: Is the partnership sexually exclusive?
A. Right now I think the contract is:
B. I would like it to be:

ITEM VII: DEALING WITH CONFLICT
Question: How is conflict usually dealt with (avoidance, fighting, discussion and negotiation)?
A. Right now I think the contract is:
B. I would like it to be:

ITEM VIII: PHYSICAL INTIMACY
Question: What is the usual pattern for physical intimacy in private, in public?
A. Right now I think the contract is:
B. I would like it to be:

When you have finished, compare your answers with your partner's. Where there are differences, discuss them. Say how it seems to you. Say what you object to. Say what you want to happen. Say what you'll settle for. Negotiate for yourself a "contract" that meets your needs, that feels fair to you, that makes you feel as if you've been heard and understood.

Don't be afraid to do this. All too often same-sex couples will close off discussion about what is happening between them because they fear the bond that holds them together is too fragile to withstand the confrontation. Usually just the opposite is true. In confronting your partner with your true needs and wishes, you are performing an act of trust in this person, an act that is binding in itself, because it acknowledges the importance of the alliance to you.

Every human relationship is flawed. A male friend who has been married and now lives with a gay lover told me when he was married to his wife he could see the flaws in their relationship but then he'd think, "Oh, well, that's how it is with married couples. It's amusing. Look at all the situation comedies written around marital discord. It's okay. It happens to everyone." Now with his gay lover he reports, "It's frightening to fight. Discord might be signalling the end of the relationship." (Can't work. Won't last. Doesn't count. And we're dancing to their tune again!) But turning away from conflict is turning away from reality.

Denying anger, until it explodes unexpectedly at a later date, is bewildering and potentially very damaging to a relationship. Dealing with it as directly as possible, when it is happening, is strengthening though it may be painful and frightening to do so. Fighting is a necessity in a thriving relationship. Fighting fairly and to the finish is essential to the continuing growth of any partnership.

Unfinished fights are usually aborted because of fear of losing or fear of exposing hurt feelings or concern over letting go of one's emotions totally. Most of us have experienced all of these fears at one time or another. But unfinished fights leave the participants tense and anxious. If you feel that way when you stop fighting, your fight is probably unfinished. You should continue trying to work through to the finish — that is, until the real, underlying issues are confronted.

In a good fight, the partners are aware that they are risking themselves and they are willing to experience the discomfort that brings to resolve the conflict. In a good fight, the participants trust each other enough to be honest about their feelings, about their grievances and what they want to be different in the future. The good fight ends in negotiation, with both parties being clear about what is being asked for in terms of change. There is accommodation on both sides. Nobody loses. Everybody wins.

To sum up the above points and to make a few more, I've composed the following list of "Do's and Don'ts for Couple Fighting."

DO'S

(1) *Do be specific about your complaints.*
("It's dropping your dirty clothes into the pile of dirty clothes already on the chair that I can't stand!")

And about the changes you'd like to see in relation to your complaints.
("I'd really appreciate it if you would walk a few more steps and drop those clothes into the hamper.")

(2) *Do send "I" messages, not "You" messages.*
("*I* feel ignored and put down when I ask you to do something and you ignore me. *Not "You* are an insensitive and uncaring clod!")

(3) *Do try to get to underlying issues and feelings.*
("I don't feel like an equal partner in this relationship when you ignore my needs. When that happens, I feel angry and hurt!")

(4) *Do finish the fight — Keep at it until the tension between you feels worked through.*

DON'TS

(1) *Don't get stuck in the past.*
("You never did before, why should you start now!")

(2) *Don't "kitchen sink" your partner.*
("And not only that, I also resent the way you . . . and the way you . . .")

(3) *Don't deliver sweeping condemnations.*
("You are absolutely incapable of understanding me.")

(4) *Don't abort the fight. Don't stop fighting while you still feel strong resentment or frustration or confusion.*

We must be willing to fight with each other to discharge the tensions that relationship building inevitably brings. We must be willing to fight in order to work through the control issues that are a part of every partnership. The more openly these issues are dealt with, the better chance the partners have for a lively, satisfying and enduring life together.

Much of what I have written about so far is applicable to both male and female couples, for that matter, to nongay as well as gay couples. There are some ways, however, in which liaisons between two women and between two men are unique. I believe these differences are, primarily, outcomes of the ways women and men are differently socialized in this society.

Effects of Socialization

Men are conditioned by the society to be strong, competitive, independent and sexually aggressive. Relationship skills are secondary to the ability to earn, win, achieve, make sexual conquests and show strength by not showing emotion. With regard to sex, men are taught to get all they can, that they should want it, that it is their right to have it.

The inclination is to do what we are taught. We tend to pay particular attention to the socializing lessons we learned early in life because with those lessons we usually learned that doing what we've been taught makes us okay. Good marks, good student, good person. At some level, we all need to experience ourselves as included, competent and loved (though some people have learned to deny these needs as a means of surviving especially harsh psychological conditions in their early life). At any rate, the early lessons stick, the early conditioning persists.

Two men in a couple tend to put a lot of energy into showing who is superior. The competition may be over physical strength, sexual prowess, intelligence, accountability, worldliness, earning power, social popularity, or it may be to see who is the most daring, most dispassionate, most evil-doing, or who is craziest. The revealing theme is *competition*, a competition that serves the dual purpose of providing a source of personal validation and of avoiding the intensification of intimacy in the relationship.

In the early socializing process, most males learned that nurturance, affection and caretaking were women's work, and that a woman would eventually do these things for them. Without that dream come true, where does the gay male look for those experiences? To another gay male? But how do you ask for love and tenderness from your competitor? Many gay males don't, even though they want to. They haven't learned how to ask for the nurturing they want, or how to adequately express the deep and tender love they might feel for their partner.

As a counselor working with gay male couples, I try to help them get in touch with the ways in which they compete in order to cover up the intimacy needs they don't know what to do with. I encourage experimentation with cooperation and mutuality rather than competition. I suggest they try to end up agreeing, rather than winning or losing. I encourage them to figure out a way to do it together, rather than arguing which one's way is better. I push for increased expression of affection, even if it's uncomfortable at first. I try to get them to give themselves permission to ask for and give love to one another in deeper, gentler, softer ways.

Lesbians, on the other hand, socialized as women, are rewarded early for the development of relationship skills. Typically, little girls take care of their dolls and play at being mothers. As adolescents, they dream about home, family and spouse. They are conditioned to equate being okay with acquiring and hanging onto a mate. They are trained and psychologically prepared to be nurturers. Little girls who grow up to be lesbians often do not deviate from their programming, aside from the gender of their partners. Much emphasis is put on nurturing in the couple relationship. Having and hanging onto a partner is usually critical to their sense of well-being.

While success at this makes for stability and continuity in one's everyday life, it does sometimes create an overdependency on the relationship for validation. Options for individual growth outside home and the partnership go unrecognized.

In counseling with lesbian couples, I encourage more outer directedness of their activities. I encourage a broadening of interests and of contacts. I encourage the development of individual as well as joint goals in life. I support assertiveness in the pursuit of personal growth. I applaud the evolution of independent frames of reference. This usually builds self-confidence in the partners, respect for one another's differing competencies and renewed interest in the partnership as a source of energy, strength and love.

We're on Our Own

To end where I began, we gay people must accept the fact that we're on our own when it comes to developing relationship arrangements that work the best for us. We have to help ourselves. One way we can do this is to read the relationship guides that are now available for gay and lesbian couples. At this printing, the selections listed below are noteworthy.

In the 1979 edition of this book I suggested that gay and lesbian couples get together to form self-help groups to talk with one another about common relationship issues, problems, and solutions. I encouraged the sharing of social and educational activities, the building of support networks to mutually enhance opportunities for growth in relationships.

I am pleased to see that a grass-roots couples movement has indeed taken hold. In cities, large and small, couples meet on a regular basis to share their lives. These groups are most often co-sexual, so gay men and lesbians are learning about, and learning from, each other's relationships. These affirming encounters go a long way toward building the tradition of success in gay and lesbian coupling that will eventually obviate the need to hide our relationships, disguise them, or, ever again, doubt our right and our ability to love one another.

Suggested Reading

Berzon, Betty. *Permanent Partners: Building Gay and Lesbian Relationships That Last*. New York, E.P. Dutton, 1988 (Paperback. New American Library).

Clunis, D. Merilee and G. Dorsey Green. *Lesbian Couples*. Seattle, Seal Press, 1988.

Isensee, Rik. *Love Between Men: Enhancing Intimacy and Keeping Your Relationship Alive*. Englewood Cliffs, N.J., Prentice-Hall, 1990. (Also available in paperback.)

Marcus, Eric. *The Male Couple's Guide: Finding a Man, Making a Home, Building a Life*. New York, HarperCollins, 1992.

Partners: Magazine for Gay and Lesbian Couples. Box 9685, Seattle, Washington, 98109. Phone: (206) 784-1519.

Lesbian Couples in Particular

Nancy Toder

Lesbian couples: who are we? Descriptions range from the traditional homophobic view that sees us only in terms of our sexual activities, to the liberal heterosexual view that we are "just like any other married couples" (and that therefore no special effort is required to get to know us or to recognize and correct the injustices we deal with every day), to one version of the radical lesbian feminist perspective which states that our relationships don't or shouldn't have anything in common with heterosexual relationships. In fact, I find that many of our daily experiences as couples, many of our joys and difficulties, are similar to those of heterosexuals. However, we also have unique experiences, both as gay people and as lesbians, and must cope with unique issues in our couple relationships. In this chapter I will discuss some issues of particular relevance to lesbian couples. Throughout, I will explore both the extra stresses that we face and the singular advantages that are open to us. It is my belief that our relationships in couples can be vastly improved by our learning to recognize and deal with our unique stresses, and to celebrate and maximize our special advantages.

THE LESBIAN COUPLE IN THE HETEROSEXUAL WORLD: THE COMING OUT DILEMMA

Perhaps one of the most difficult decisions we lesbians face is to determine in which areas of our lives we can be ourselves, and in which areas we must wear a mask. If we stay in the closet, we risk never being known as we truly are, never having intimacy with family and friends, and losing self-respect and any sense of power and control over our lives. On the other hand, if we come out, we risk losing the love and support of our family and friends, forfeiting our jobs or curtailing our promotions, feeling the isolation of stigma, and in some places even getting arrested. Nevertheless, the advantages of coming out are great: a wonderful feeling of freedom, an increase in self-respect and integrity, the knowledge that we are doing something that may improve the lot of lesbians and gay men everywhere, and the opportunity to create friendships in which we are truly accepted for ourselves.

The stress on the individual who must make these decisions is obvious; what is not so obvious is the stress these decisions place on the couple. Not only do the additional pressures on the individual tend to bring more anxiety, confusion, anger and fear into the relationship, but the decisions that each woman makes for herself will directly affect the partner.

Couples run into the most conflicts when the two women are at different stages of the coming-out process. Thus, a lesbian who has come out with her family, who perhaps is beginning to feel comfortable about her lesbianism and to whom openness and honesty are very important, will have great difficulty pretending to be "the roommate" when her lover's parents come to dinner or for a month's visit. For many lesbians, home is sanctuary in an unsafe world, and even those who have not come out professionally or with their family may deeply resent the invasion of their home by people who are ignorant or disrespectful of their love relationship.

What is the impact of such situations on the couple? As in a juggling act, things have a tendency to fall and get broken. What may suffer here is the trust that each lover feels for the other as well as for herself. A few years ago, a friend with an important professional job threw a party at her house for some of her co-workers. Very few people knew she was a lesbian, so her lover's clothes closets were carefully shut, books hidden behind other books, a few pictures put away in drawers and other precautions taken to ensure that nobody would guess the household was lesbian. In addition, her lover, who works in the same profession, was invited to the party but had to pretend that she didn't live in the house.

This is a particularly dramatic example of how our fears can negate each other and invalidate our relationships. This happens all the time, usually in more subtle ways than we know. Chipping away at the trust, loyalty and respect that we feel for each other, these "little" betrayals can undermine the very foundations of our love relationships.

Problems with families — especially difficult around holiday time, when each member of the couple, seen as a single person, is expected to go home to her own family — do not automatically disappear when we come out to our relatives. Most family members react somewhere between the two extremes of horror and approval, and the lover often is not treated as one of the family, at least initially.

The couple may take out on each other the frustration and anger they feel in response to their families' treatment of them: "Why did you let her get away with that? Why didn't you confront her on the shit she was saying?" "Why didn't *you*?"

"Well, she's *your* mother." Many such fights revolve around disagreements on how to handle family. Each woman may feel torn between loyalty to the lover and fear of confronting parents or other relatives. Often the partner who is more open with her family will not be able to understand why the other partner is so "cowardly." The two lovers can become pitted against each other, making it more difficult for them to fight the real enemy: the homophobia in the world and in themselves.

Additional stresses in the relationship can arise from differences between the lovers' attitudes about being seen together publicly — as a function of different vulnerabilities in their work situations or different degrees of self-acceptance. These stresses range from inconvenience ("Can we go to the movies together on a Friday or Saturday night, or only on a weeknight?") to serious differences between the social and political activities the two lovers want to engage in: Does one lover want to go to the bars, while the other is afraid to be seen there? Does one lover want to become involved in lesbian/gay organizations, and is this a threat to the other lover? Again, these issues are a problem mostly for lovers who differ considerably in their attitudes and interests. However, even for a couple that shares similar goals and values on such issues as coming out, political activity and visibility in public, many conflicts can arise from smaller differences and from the difficulty of coping with such emotion-laden issues.

How can we deal with these conflicts? The lover who has come out more fully must be as patient and supportive as possible, trying not to put demands and pressures on the more fearful partner, yet at the same time encouraging her to take risks. Try to recognize that you and your lover are different individuals with different capacities, needs and circumstances.

The lover who is further in the closet must try not to be threatened by her partner's decisions and not to invalidate or belittle what is important to the partner. Try to keep some separation between your identity and your lover's identity, and try not to sabotage your lover's growth because of your own fears. If you are frightened that your lover's political activities will give her less time for you, that the two of you may eventually find your differences irreconcilable and have to separate, or that your lesbianism will be exposed as a result of your lover's activities, then express your fears to your lover, rather than attacking her with statements like "Gay liberation is stupid!" or "NOW meetings are a waste of time."

In situations where it seems impossible to come out, each lover can still show basic respect for the other and for the relationship. This means, for instance, not telling your mother about the fantastic (and invented) date you had last weekend when your lover is sitting with you at Thanksgiving dinner; it means making sure that people know your lover is important to you (even if you don't want them to know she is your lover) and that they treat her with respect and courtesy; it means avoiding situations where people who don't know about your relationship come to your house.

Our love relationships can be a tremendous support in separating reality from paranoia. By discussing the pros and cons of coming out in each situation, by role-playing (one lover plays the parents, boss, friend, etc. in a dialog intended to test the possible consequences of coming out), and by brain-storming for new ideas and strategies, the two lovers can be of great help to each other in making coming-out decisions. At best, each lover can give the other some of the courage that coming out requires and some of the support that dealing with the outside world necessitates. If desired, both lovers can be present in a potentially difficult coming-out scene, so that the one who is under fire will have support. In addition, each lover can help the other put things in perspective when something goes wrong, for example, in a family situation. We tend to be so vulnerable with our families that we have trouble sorting out craziness from reality, and our lovers can provide a voice of sanity and reason.

THE COUPLE IN THE LESBIAN WORLD

Some couples choose to remain relatively isolated from the lesbian support systems of friendship circles, bars and the political community. For many lesbians in rural locations and small towns, a peer group is not an option and isolation is chosen only to the extent that they chose to live in such a community in the first place. I think that choosing isolation often reflects homophobia ("We just don't find other lesbians *interesting*") or fear of losing one's lover as a result of exposure to other potential partners. In such an isolated couple, the two lovers often will become over dependent on each other, the homophobia of each will tend to reinforce the homophobia of the other and the resulting self-hate can lead to alcoholic pacts and other self-destructive and couple-destructive activities.

I firmly believe that some connection with the political lesbian community is essential to our individual and collective mental health. It takes an incredible strength to combat the homophobic pressures we deal with daily. Much of that strength comes from our inner resources and from the love and support of our partners. But within the couple relationship it is very easy to drain these resources and to feel overwhelmed by the huge obstacles we face.

The knowledge that there is a lesbian community, that our numbers are large and that we represent a positive political force is a great help in dealing with the fear and ignorance around us. It is through interactions with the lesbian community that we can begin to feel pride in ourselves and hope for our future.

I have heard lesbians say that going to their first meeting of a lesbian or gay organization, or marching in a gay demonstration, did more for their self-esteem than months and even years of psychotherapy. There is no equivalent for such an experience — for many of us, nightmares begin to recede and we begin to reclaim parts of ourselves that have been lost almost as long as we can remember.

Even in the healthy context of our own community, however, numerous pressures exist that can have an adverse effect on the couple. These peer-group pressures range from the pressure to stay together till death do you part (if all your friends are in couples — "How can you do this to us?" — or if you are seen as a model couple — "You two give me hope that someday I'll have a relationship like yours"), to the pressure in the radical lesbian community to be nonmonogamous and not to "act couple-y."

THE RELATIONSHIP ITSELF

Many lesbians are afraid to commit themselves to a relationship, not only because of a general fear of making commitments but also because of a more specific fear: that they are indeed gay. For those who have not fully accepted a lesbian identity, making a firm commitment to another woman cements the notion that they are actually adopting a lesbian lifestyle and must formulate a lesbian identity. This is no small step, particularly in our first same-sex love affair. In response to our fear, we may deny the implications of the relationship ("I'm not a lesbian, I just happen to be in love with this person and this person just happens to be a woman") or generally not believe in the viability of the relationship or fight for its survival against the obstacles that two women will encounter.

Money and Commitment
Money is likely to be a problem in a lesbian couple because of job discrimination against women. When money is scarce, there is more stress on the relationship than when it is plentiful; the two partners are generally more tense about financial matters, and each partner, frustrated by not being able to do or buy the things she wants, tends to blame the other.

I would like to devote most of this discussion, however, to an assumption that seems to be accepted without question in most lesbian couples: the assumption that money is not to be shared. In the heterosexual marriage, it is usually assumed that money will be shared. As many feminist writers have correctly pointed out, marriage is not a good model and is in many ways inappropriate to the lesbian couple. However, heterosexuals have one advantage in what is otherwise quite an oppressive package: the ease with which they can make a commitment to a love relationship by sharing their material resources. (Of course this is not always the reality, but generosity is supposed to be the spirit of the arrangement.)

The fact is that many of us who would not be opposed to the *idea* of sharing money with a mate, are actually very hesitant to do so with a same-sex lover. It is not uncommon for two women who have been living together for a number of years to keep strict accounts of who owes whom how much for what. Why is this?

Some lesbians argue that they need to have their own money; they want to know that they are financially independent and have a way out of the relationship if necessary. This seems reasonable. But sharing money with your lover does not necessarily mean that you cannot have your own checking or savings account. It simply means that the two of you share expenses in proportion to your income, either by pooling all your money or by working out a percentage agreement. ("I earn twice as much as you, so I'll pay for two-thirds of our rent, utilities, food, vacations, etc.")

Sharing money is not much of a problem when the two partners earn a similar income: each one pays 50% of the couple's expenses. However, when incomes differ or when an inheritance is involved, many problems can arise. Whose standard of living should be adopted? How can resentments be avoided? The less affluent partner often finds herself "owing" money to the other partner, and the longer the relationship, the less likely this debt will ever be paid off.

It is hard to imagine this happening in a committed heterosexual relationship. I think that lesbians are more cautious, more afraid of getting ripped off, less willing to trust in the durability of the relationship. In my opinion, this extreme cautiousness is often the result of internalized homophobia and the resulting fear of making a commitment to the lover.

Some may argue that keeping money and possessions separate makes it easier to divide things should the couple break up. I'm not sure that this is true. However, I am sure that never making the commitment to share money, always feeling on the edge of disintegration, may result in premature separation when problems arise. (In heterosexual marriages, the opposite is more often the case: the two partners feel that their lives and finances are so hopelessly intertwined that they stay together long after the time has come to separate.)

I believe the core of this issue is a question of family. When a woman marries a man, they become family to each other. The question is: When does a same-sex lover become family? Is it when you fall in love? live together? buy a house together? raise a child together? Is it when your blood family accepts your lover as a family member? We have no rules by which to answer these basic questions. And in this society, money is usually shared, if at all, only with family.

We need to ask ourselves certain questions: Is it my belief that two women in a committed relationship should share their money? If so, how and under what circumstances? If I am not living the way I believe, why is that? Do I have a good reason? For example, I don't believe my lover is trustworthy about money, or she doesn't work as hard as I do, or I don't believe we're going to be together much longer. Or am I responding to fears and deep-seated insecurities that may not apply to this situation, and in fact may be antithetical to what I want in this relationship?

I am not advocating that every couple share finances, simply that we look at our assumptions and attitudes about money, see whether healthy realism or unconscious homophobia is influencing our decisions and take responsibility for our financial choices.

Monogamy and Nonmonogamy

One of the most common sources of conflict in lesbian couples is the issue of monogamy vs. nonmonogamy. Most often, problems arise when one partner wants to open up the relationship and the other does not. This frequently happens when two women have been together for several years, and one partner feels restless, bored with the relationship, less turned on to her lover than before and attracted to others. (In the heterosexual world this is known as the *seven-year itch*.)

There are no right or wrong answers to the question of how to deal with such feelings. It is natural to feel attracted to others in addition to your lover and these attractions do not necessarily mean that something is wrong with your couple relationship (as many lesbians assume). Yearning for an affair with someone new or unexpectedly falling in love with someone new can reflect a healthy desire to recapture the intense passion of a new relationship or the desire to experience yourself in new ways through sexual or emotional intimacy with different partners.

The potential growth of the individual and even of the couple that can result from outside affairs must be balanced against the potential loss of trust and safety in the primary relationship. In addition, there can be some less-than-healthy reasons for wanting to open up the couple relationship: new affairs can be a way to avoid dealing with problems in the primary relationship, to keep from making a commitment to the relationship or to distract yourself from a boring job or frustrations in your work. By putting the bulk of your energy into numerous emotional involvements, you may be putting off the expression of your creativity in some other form and you may even be avoiding confronting a feeling of emptiness and meaninglessness in your life.

The general consensus in the radical lesbian-feminist community is that nonmonogamy is more liberated and healthy than monogamy. The basic argument is that heterosexual monogamy has been used to regulate women's behavior and to protect the husband's proprietary rights over his wife. In addition, monogamy is seen as fostering jealousy, possessiveness and dependency, and creating closed units of two, thus setting artificial and unnecessary limits on our relations with each other.

As a result of these ideas, a large number of lesbian couples have attempted to open up their relationships. In many of these situations, although the two women in the couple may have agreed on what they wanted, the results have been disastrous for the couple and sometimes for the individual. Why is this? I think the main reason is that many of us have been naive about just how emotionally complicated nonmonogamy can be.

Sex and love go together for most women in our culture. Even what is intended to be a relatively casual and unthreatening affair can quickly evolve into an intense and complex emotional involvement. Believing that as good feminists they should be able to handle nonmonogamy, many women have acted according to theory without having a realistic idea of their needs, the extent to which they would suffer from jealousy and their personal limitations in dealing with potentially ambiguous, frustrating or complex situations. I think that women in the radical lesbian community have drastically underestimated the damage that can be done to their primary relationship when they try to live nonmonogamously.

Furthermore, we women have been socialized to believe that our self-esteem comes primarily from our relationships with other people. We traditionally think of this self-defeating need as being acted out in a monogamous couple relationship, where one or both women may be building their lives around their relationship. A variation on this theme, however, occurs when a woman engages in multiple relationships. These relationships can occupy most if not all of her time, and her sense of worth and identity may come to depend on the success or failure of many relationships instead of one! The point is that nonmonogamy does not guarantee a strong sense of self and independence, just as monogamy does not automatically mean an overwhelming dependence on your lover or a severe limitation on your freedom and growth as an individual.

If you or your lover wish to open up your relationship, it is very important to create conditions that will make this new "state of affairs" acceptable to both of you. Condition number one for most couples is the knowledge that the couple relationship is top priority and that any outside affairs are secondary. Then it is important to specify details of the arrangement so as to consider each other's needs and feelings. For example, how much time and which blocks of time will you spend with others; what time will you spend together? Do you want to hear about these affairs or would you rather not? Are any special conditions important to you (e.g., that your lover not relate sexually to anyone you know or that she not bring anyone into the house you share)? Once you have opened up the relationship, be sure to meet frequently to make sure that things are still feeling okay to both of you and to work out any additional conditions that either of you is discovering to be necessary.

The Effects of Sexism and Misogyny

In addition to dealing with homophobia, lesbians must also cope with discrimination against women and with misogynist attitudes. These pressures range from the more subtle and covert forms of antiwoman stereotypes to the more blatant misogynist acts of rape, economic discrimination and sexual objectification of women on the job, in the streets and in advertising. All these pressures tend to keep women in a second-class position in the society.

As can happen with any stress, our anger and frustration tend to spill over into our love relationships, and our lovers become the easiest target for our rage. In addition, misogyny and homophobia are internalized by all of us, and can have a devastating effect on our self-esteem and identity as lesbians, thus creating problems in our couple relationships.

Most of us have been taught from an early age that a woman needs a man — to be a real woman, to achieve safety in the world and to complete her identity. These messages sometimes linger long after we have begun relating to women and they make the formation of a positive lesbian identity very difficult. In a society that labels a "real woman" by her attachment to a man, lesbians are by definition not "real women."

Having internalized this message, many lesbians continue sexual relations with men even after finding more meaningful relationships with women. Long periods of bisexuality are often a reflection of this conflict. Feeling that desirability is determined by their ability to attract a man, many lesbians find it necessary to prove to themselves that they could have a man if they wanted. This is almost always a losing battle, for as long as she believes that a woman without a man is not a real woman, the lesbian will not be at peace with herself, no matter how many men she attracts. The real question is not "Could I get a man?" but "Why on earth would I want to?"

Many women depend on men for protection. Because many men respect the notion that a woman is a man's property, and because men generally expect a man to fight back, a woman in the company of a man is much less likely than a woman alone to be attacked or bothered. Lesbians are most often not in the company of men, so we can feel particularly vulnerable on the streets. Worried that our lovers cannot protect us and insecure about our ability to protect ourselves and our lovers, we sometimes feel resentful and cheated. Underlying these feelings is fear, a fear accentuated if we live in high-crime areas.

Women who have lived with men and experienced a sense of physical security in their presence often feel that being with a woman is a disadvantage: "A woman can't protect you; a woman can't make it easier for you in the world." In fact, women who live with men often have a false and dangerous feeling of security. Married women are raped as frequently as single women, and probably more frequently than lesbians. A woman who is dependent on a man may be more vulnerable and less prepared if she is attacked when her man is not around. And if her man is abusive, who protects her from *him*?

Breaking away from traditional notions of what women are or should be is simultaneously frightening and liberating — frightening because we are moving into uncharted territory, liberating because we are breaking free of stereotypes and because we are now engaged in the most challenging and exciting process we can experience as women: generating new definitions of ourselves and creating a woman-identified culture to support our new consciousness.

Internalized misogyny often sabotages our attempts to build a women's culture and to make satisfying relationships with each other. For example, most of us have difficulty feeling good about our bodies, partly because of the rigid standards that our male-dominated society imposes on female beauty and partly because our misogynist environment has taught us that our genitals are dirty, taste bad, have an offensive odor, etc. When you add into the bargain that we are seen as both sexually insatiable and frigid, it is no wonder that some of us have sexual problems! All of these negative attitudes influence our ability to express our sexuality freely with our lovers.

Role-Playing in the Lesbian Couple

Role-playing has its roots in traditional heterosexuality. There is no more extreme role-playing than that which occurs in most married couples. Why have lesbians sometimes imitated this distorted notion of normalcy? It is no accident that in the "old days" there were many more butches than femmes. Role-playing is rooted in misogyny, and lesbians, who have always been aware of the raw deal that women get in this society and who were rebelling against the limitations of the prescribed female role, frequently chose to be identified instead with the male. The butch role in a lesbian couple is an attempt to cop some of the power and privilege that men get in the world. Because lesbians do not get that privilege in the outside world, home becomes the most important arena for acting out the wish for male privilege.

Wanting to be strong, independent and competent is not in itself a sign of role-playing or misogyny; on the contrary, it can be an important aspect of developing one's identity as a woman. Role-playing and misogyny come into the picture when a woman assumes that her strength must be pitted against the relative weakness of a femme lover or that her strength means that she is more like a man than like a woman. Underlying these assumptions is the association of femaleness with weakness and inferiority, and thus a self-hate and disdain for the lover who is identified as more female.

In my opinion, the lesbian community is the best cure for internalized misogyny and the best defense against external misogyny. By talking with other lesbians about these issues (either informally or in consciousness-raising groups), by participating in the development of a woman-identified culture and by organizing to fight sexism, misogyny and homophobia in the outer world, we can take real pride in ourselves as women and as lesbians and we can bring this pride to our couple relationship.

Overloading the Couple

Because we feel alienated from and feared and attacked by the outside world, many lesbians in couples band together fiercely against the rest of the world. Our lover can become the only person to be trusted in an otherwise hostile and condemning environment. The additional fact that as women we have been socialized to believe that our principal worth comes from our love relationships further augments our tendency to make our lover the center of our life.

These forces put a tremendous load on the couple relationship, particularly the couple that is geographically or emotionally cut off from the lesbian community. Each woman in the couple is expected to meet all of the other woman's intellectual, social, and emotional needs. If one or both of the women are unhappy, they assume that something must be wrong with or missing from the relationship. The basic, unrealistic premises are that a good relationship guarantees individual happiness and that one person can meet all of another person's needs.

Because the world is perceived as an enemy, and because our lesbian realities and values are daily ignored or contradicted, we often feel an extra need for our lover to validate our perceptions and beliefs. Any disagreement between the two women may be seen as a deadly threat; after all, it is only through the support of the relationship that many women feel they can tolerate their extreme isolation and alienation. Consequently, even tiny cracks in the couple's unity may precipitate major anxieties and major conflicts until consensus is reached. Because so much is at stake, the process of reaching consensus may involve bitter fighting, and the women may seriously compromise their individuality in order to achieve equilibrium in the relationship.

Individuality and growth may be severely limited in such a closed and rigid relationship. For this and other reasons I feel it is essential that we must reach out to other lesbians and develop friendships and resources outside of our couple relationships. Doing so not only removes stress from the couple relationship but also helps to build a stronger, more autonomous sense of self.

Motherhood and Shared Parenting

Many lesbians have had children before discovering or becoming ready to act on their lesbian feelings. Being a lesbian mother is difficult not only in the straight world but also in the lesbian/gay community. Until very recently, child care was not provided at most lesbian/gay events and the level of consciousness about the special needs and problems of lesbian mothers was low. Being a single parent is hard enough; lesbian motherhood has additional complications, of which the constant threat of losing one's children is only the most dramatic.

Some of these complications are eased and others accentuated when a lesbian mother becomes involved with a lover. The first issue that comes up is, generally, how much responsibility will that lover take for the children? Most mothers want their lovers to share this responsibility, and some women who do not have their own children are pleased to be able to relate to children without having to bear them or take on the responsibility that the blood mother usually has. In some situations, being a couple can be mutually beneficial; some of the strain of mothering is taken off the mother, the lover gets the opportunity to share in the raising of a child, and the child benefits from the attention of two adults rather than one. In the case where both women have children, moving into a single household can greatly improve the quality of both women's lives and those of their children.

Many couples run into problems, however. Most typically, the needs and expectations of the mother diverge from those of her lover. The mother, who for years may have been assuming total economic and emotional support of her child, may count heavily on her lover to ease her responsibilities and in effect to become a second parent. The lover, on the other hand, may have no desire to assume such responsibilities. I have heard women say, "If I had wanted children, I would have had my own." The lover often feels that she "fell in love with the woman, not her child," whereas the mother often feels, "Love me, love my child." It is important to air these feelings rather than harboring resentments. The two women must negotiate a balance between their different needs.

Of course, each woman's attitudes toward mothering may change over time. The lover may grow fond of the child and want to assume more responsibility, or the mother may discover that she wants primary responsibility for her child. The change in the lover's attitudes will often correspond to a change in her feeling about the relationship: if her lover (the mother of the child) begins to feel like family to her, she is more likely to feel that the child is family, too.

Jealousy is another common problem when one of two lovers has a child. The mother is put in a pivotal position, with the partner and child feeling like competitors for her attention and affection. The age and dependency of the child and the maturity of the lover will greatly affect the degree of resentment between the child and the mother's lover. Many women, especially in the early phases of a relationship, hate the idea of anyone else getting the attention they want all to themselves. In addition, the presence of children usually means a considerable cramping of the couple's style: a babysitter must be found before the two women can go out, the child must be picked up at school, etc. A woman who never wanted children for exactly this reason may feel angry and bitter about having to take a child into consideration now.

Getting close to the child poses a series of dilemmas for the lover. What if she and the mother break up? She will not only lose contact with the woman she loves, but very likely with the child, too. She knows she has no legal rights in this situation, and even if she has helped raise the child for years, the child will go with the mother. There are no simple answers to these fears. All loving involves risks; at some point a risk is worth taking.

As in any family, once two women agree to assume mutual responsibility for the child, there may be disagreements about the details of child rearing. For the lesbian household, however, there is the additional question of how to present the relationship to the child. Of course, the age of the child will affect what and how much is said.

A surprisingly large number of women never discuss their lesbianism with their children: the two women live together, sleep in the same bed, but say nothing to the child to clarify what this means. Even some lesbian-feminist mothers avoid talking with their children about their love relationships and even about feminist issues. This reticence is usually a sign of internalized homophobia (although there are certainly practical considerations, too, such as the possibility that the child will get into trouble at school by mentioning the mother's lesbianism and even the possibility that the father will use the child's knowledge of the mother's lesbianism as a point in his favor in custody cases).

As lesbians we are often accused of proselytizing and even of molesting children. Many women overcompensate in response to these false accusations. They try so hard not to influence the sexual preference of their children that they give no information at all about lesbianism. Such behavior springs from hidden pockets of shame. In fact, if we look at the behavior of heterosexuals, we find that they are proselytizing all the time; not only do they individually laud the advantages of their way of life but they have even gotten the major institutions of society to present their message. By providing a healthy understanding of lesbian relationships, and letting your child experience the love between you and another woman, you can do some little bit to counterbalance mainstream propaganda and give your child something approaching a free choice.

Rearing a child in a nonsexist and nonhomophobic household can be a most challenging and valuable experience. It is wonderful to be able to offer a child some of the wisdom and freedom that most of us have attained only in adulthood, and with tremendous struggle at that. In sharing this process, a couple can greatly enrich their individual lives and their relationship.

ADVANTAGES OPEN TO LESBIAN COUPLES

The fact that we have no images or models for the "successful" lesbian relationship, though it causes anxiety and confusion, may really be a blessing in disguise. Once we break free of the vestiges of heterosexual imagery, we can experience a marvelous sense of freedom. Uninhibited by the narrow restrictions of cultural acceptability, we can create our own structure and values. For example, the fact that we are in a same-sex relationship means that the predetermination of roles by gender, sometimes so destructive a force in heterosexual relationships, is not relevant to our lives. Each member of a same-sex couple is free to act from individual interests, predilections, and skills, rather than having to choose between conforming to or rebelling against the cultural norm. We are able to see the mainstream culture from a greater distance and a healthier perspective. This means that we know that many of the oppressive messages of the culture are inapplicable to us, and that others are simply false or distorted. Thus, we are able to circumvent much of what is jokingly referred to as "The Battle of the Sexes" — really, no joking matter at all. Ironically, it is the same-sex couple that can most clearly see itself as being composed of two human beings, whereas the heterosexual couple is constantly having to deal with the coercive personae of Man and Woman.

In many ways, we have an easier time of creating a truly egalitarian, mutual and mature relationship. In fact, some researchers are now beginning to look at the same-sex couple as a model for helping heterosexuals to create more human relationships.

In contrast with heterosexuals, who often feel alienated from their mates, we need only look inside ourselves to know much about our lovers. We are able to relax with each other in a much more trusting way than can most straight couples. The inequities in our relationships are individually made ones, for the most part, and not a function of historically sanctioned power imbalances that have created the fear and hatred in which many women and men coexist today.

In a lesbian couple, both women can freely develop strength and competence. In addition, having been socialized as women, we have been trained to be interpersonally sensitive, nurturant, gentle and compassionate. In a heterosexual relationship, these qualities are used primarily to serve the man and to oppress the woman, who often must bear full responsibility for the emotional quality of the relationship. These same attributes, however, can create a miraculously high-quality relationship when shared by two women who are matched in their capacities to share and to love.

FAMILY RELATIONS: FRESH PERSPECTIVES

Telling the Family You're Gay

Betty Berzon

On September 22, 1975, in San Francisco's Union Square, a woman moved out of the crowd, raised her arm, leveled a chrome-plated gun, and pulled the trigger. A man standing nearby saw the movement and pushed down on the gun barrel. The bullet missed its target by five feet. Oliver Sipple had just saved the life of the President of the United States. His quick action made him an instant hero. The President wrote him a letter thanking him. Over 1000 other people wrote to him praising him. It should have been a moment of triumph for Oliver. Instead it was a nightmare. "Within 24 hours, reporters had also learned that the ex-Marine was involved in the San Francisco gay community, and the story became page-one — and wire service — copy." (*The Advocate*, Oct. 22, 1975). *The Chicago Sun-Times* called him a "Homosexual Hero" in a headline. The *Denver Post* referred to him as a "Gay Vet." Oliver went into seclusion to avoid the media. He was so distressed at the prospect of his mother in Detroit reading about him as a gay hero that he all but declined to take credit for saving the life of the President of the United States!

This story poignantly illustrates the enormous apprehension so many people feel regarding the disclosure of gayness to family. It is for many an immobilizing fear that clouds judgment and prevents the kind of decision-making and planning about disclosure that could enhance family relationships. Because so much of the gay person's thinking about disclosure is conditioned by fear, it is important to understand better why this fear is so pervasive and what might be done to alleviate it.

Nearly every gay person with a family has been concerned about this issue at one time or another. It doesn't matter who the person is, what age, what socioeconomic status, what education, what occupation, there is a fear of disclosure and a pressure to disclose. Sometimes the pressure is just at the level of "I know I can't but I wish I could." More often it is stronger, and so is the fear. Stalemate.

Why is this such a problem to so many people? We live in a family-oriented culture. Given the prolonged period of dependency on family in our society, the family becomes a highly influential force in our lives, from the cradle to the grave. We are trained to look to the family for sustenance. We are trained to *need* our families. We are also trained to take on the values and attitudes of our families because it is more than the species the family is supposed to perpetuate, it is the value system of the culture supporting the nuclear family arrangement. So, the family is seen not only as the main source of sustenance but as the source of the values we live by.

Our families also give us a link with our past. They knew us when we were forming as the people we have become. Much of our identity is rooted in the family's expectations of us. These expectations get built into our hopes and dreams for ourselves, in either a positive or a negative way. I am drawn to a particular field of endeavor because it is one that is valued in my family. Or, I avoid same because I am rebelling against the values and attitudes of my family. In either instance I am acting in response to my family's expectations of me. Even when I reach adulthood and have developed my own ideas about how to live my life, the internalized values and attitudes of my family operate in me and must be contended with in one way or another. Families are hard to get away from.

In one crucial way gay and lesbian people do not fit family expectations. I believe the initial turmoil young gay people go through is in response to the internalized expectations from family training. From early on, being gay is associated with going against the family.

It is not surprising then that fear of confronting the family with the news of one's gayness is so strong in the minds of so many gay people. The fear is especially strong if the person has not adequately worked through the process of individuation from the family, carrying over into adult life too many feelings of childhood dependency. Then the fear of abandonment by the "needed" parents is a strong motivator in concealing from them anything that might displease them. Sacrifices are made in the person's own life to avoid giving parents any reason to remove their approval. But when the sacrifices are as destructive to one's emotional life as concealing one's basic orientation to love and affection, the details of one's lifestyle, the true nature of one's primary relationships, reassessment of the situation is in order.

FAMILIES, WHO NEEDS THEM?

As an adult, what do you really want from your family? In light of the drastic compromises with life many people make to spare their relatives the knowledge of their gayness, this is a question that all gay and lesbian people should ask themselves. I think most would answer that they want the family's love and support, validation for accomplishments, comfort in the face of failure, and attention to their struggles with life's dilemmas.

I have two questions to ask at this point: (1) are you getting these wants met enough to warrant concealing your true self from them? and (2) do they care enough about you to not withdraw their interest and support, not punish you, not abandon you because of any difficulty they might have in accepting your gayness? If the answer to the first question is yes, and you are quite sure about it, you may not want to read further. If the answer is no, I hope you *will* read further. If the answer to question two is no, there's nothing to lose in disclosing to them, is there? If the answer is yes, there's everything to gain, isn't there? Not that simple, you say? Of course not, and then again, it really is.

WHY DISCLOSE?

As a therapist I hear over and over the reasons people give for not disclosing their gayness to their families, especially parents. "They're too old, they won't under-stand." "They're in ill health, it might kill them." "Everything is going so well for them, I don't want to spoil it." The basic themes, with many variations, are that being gay is not understandable and is so heinous a truth that it might be lethal, at least toxic, in its effect. Such protestations are, of course, impossible to check out without making the actual disclosure. Fear thrives in an information vacuum. The unknown is unnerving. I have found, however, that in the majority of instances the fears are either unfounded or exaggerated, and that which was feared is taken care of by careful preparation for and judicious handling of the disclosure experience.

Let's look at the positive side. Why disclose? What constructive purpose does it serve?

For the Discloser
Disclosure can serve to bring the family into your life in a more real way. It opens up communication. It makes subterfuge and pretense unnecessary. Disclosure can strengthen the family bond. It can deepen love. It can help you become a homophobia fighter rather than a homophobia victim.

For the Disclosee
Disclosure can clear up the mysteries that are so typical of communication custom-ized to conceal the fact of gayness. It can bring children and parents closer, provid-ing opportunities for mutual support and caring. Parents often need validation from their children, though offspring have a way of neglecting this. The open communication that disclosure makes possible enhances the opportunities for parents to get the attention they might need from their children. In an emotional climate in which children are holding themselves back from their parents for fear of

loss of approval it is less likely that either is benefiting as much as they might from the relationship.

Assuming you decide to disclose, there are some things you should know.

GUIDELINES FOR DISCLOSURE

Basically, you are creating a learning situation for whomever you are disclosing to. As in any learning situation you can set up the conditions for learning but you can't learn *for* the person. You will want to set up conditions to facilitate learning about your gayness in the best possible way. When, where, how, what to say, to whom, what to say about a lover if you have one, whether to include your lover — these are all things it is best to think through beforehand. In the following suggestions I will emphasize disclosure to parents since that is the situation gay and lesbian people usually worry about the most.

Before You Disclose

It is important to spend some time with yourself doing two things. Examine your own attitudes about being gay. If you have mixed feelings, talk about them to someone you trust. If you have strong negative feelings, they will be conveyed and the disclosure will probably be a bad experience. Read some of the excellent gay-affirming books now on the market. Try to get straight about being gay before you talk about it to family.

Clarify why you are disclosing at this particular time. If, for instance, you are angry with your parents, try to deal with that anger somewhere else before you talk to them. If you bring anger into the disclosure you are likely to obscure the main message you are there to deliver and the occasion will be remembered as a negative one for everyone. Try to get in touch with the positive reasons for your disclosure and keep those in focus.

When to Disclose

The time to disclose is as soon as you are ready, taking into account whatever else is going on in the family situation. If possible, don't make your disclosure when other events are likely to co-opt the attention and emotions of the people you are disclosing to: your brother's wedding (tempting though it may be), your grandmother's funeral (you wish you'd been able to tell her because she had more sense and sensitivity than anyone else in the family), your parent's 25th wedding anniversary (you want to thank them for teaching you to love as beautifully as they do). Your disclosure is an important occasion for you and it deserves all the attention it can get.

Where to Disclose

I suggest that gayness be disclosed in a quiet, private place where you are unlikely to be disturbed or distracted, so that plenty of time is available to adequately deal with questions, discussion and reactions.

How to Disclose

Prepare the persons you are disclosing to by stating beforehand that you want to have a serious conversation about something that is very important to you both. Present your information in the most positive light possible. For instance, you would *not* want to begin by saying, "I have something terrible I want to tell you" or "You're not going to like this, but . . ." A better beginning would be, "There is something about me I want to tell you because I care about you and I want to be able to share more of myself with you."

What to Say

You've said you're gay and you've survived the moment. Now what? You might tell how you feel about being gay and how you hope they will feel about it and about you. Be prepared for the many questions parents usually ask, though they may not ask them directly at this time. You may want to bring them up yourself. Think through your answers to these questions.

1. How long have you been gay?
2. Are you sure you are gay?
3. When did you first know you were gay?
4. Have you tried to change?
5. Have you tried being involved with (a person of the opposite sex)? What happened?
6. Does this mean you hate (are afraid of) men/women?
7. Don't you want children of your own?
8. Are you happy?
9. Do you think you'll always be gay?
10. What is your gay life like?
11. Have you told anyone else?
12. Who else do you plan to tell?

At this time or later you may want to get into more abstract explanations regarding such questions as the following, which parents usually think about.

1. *What does being homosexual mean?* It means being predisposed to seek out same-gender persons as love and sex partners.

2. *What causes homosexuality?* It develops through the same complex process as heterosexuality. Experts increasingly agree that sexual orientation is primarily biologically based, occurring through some combination of genetic predisposition and prenatal influences. It is not a matter of choice and it is not amenable to change.

3. *Can homosexuality be cured?* According to research studies and to the official positions of the American Psychiatric Association and the American Psychological Association, homosexuality is not an illness, therefore it is not meaningful to talk about curing it.

4. *Can a person who is homosexual become heterosexual?* Most experts agree that basic sexual orientation is unchangeable. A person may choose to suppress behavior that is expressive of a homosexual orientation. Sometimes that can be done successfully, sometimes it can't. Nearly always suppression seriously inhibits a person's ability to be emotionally spontaneous, since there must be constant watchfulness over homosexual feelings being experienced too strongly.

5. *Why do you use the word gay?* About 50 years ago *gay* was a code word to disguise references to being homosexual. Gay people have long since adopted the word *gay* as a self-descriptive term replacing the more clinical *homosexual*.

SPECIAL ISSUES

Following are some special issues to think about in relation to disclosure. They are generalizations and do not apply to everyone. You know your own family and you are the best judge of how to use these suggestions for yourself.

Is It Better to Tell Parents Together or Separately?
Use what you know of your parents, the way each relates to you and how they relate to each other, to decide on this issue. If they tend to support and comfort each other, it might be best to enable them to share this experience. If you have reason to believe that one will be more supportive of you, tell that parent alone first and have that good experience behind you when you tell the parent you are more doubtful of. If your parents tend to compete with one another, you may create a problem by telling one before the other. Try not to get into playing one parent against the other in any way. Tapping into your parents' anger at each other might seriously distract from the very important message you have to deliver. This is especially significant if your parents are divorced and you have no choice but to tell them separately.

Don't Make the Other Person Say It for You
"There's something I have to tell you. You know what it is, don't you? It's . . . you know, don't you . . . ?" Ashamed to say the words? If so, you are not ready to make this disclosure. What counts here is the *affirming experience* of saying with your own voice, in your own words, to the face of someone important to you, that you are gay. If you have to force someone else to say the words for you, the impression you give might well be, "I can't say these awful words myself," which certainly is not the kind of tone you want to give to the disclosure of your gayness.

Should Your Lover Accompany You?
The presence of a nonfamily member could make it more difficult for those to whom you are disclosing to be as free to ask questions and comment as they might be with you alone. If you feel you need your lover present for support, weigh the advantages of that against the difficulty it might pose for your family. It may be easier, particularly for parents, to deal with your gayness in the abstract, before confronting them with your real-life lover. This might be true even if the family already knows and likes your "friend," who has now been significantly redefined for them.

"You're Gay Because of Your Lover"
Sometimes, in an effort to comprehend something that feels alien and disturbing at the outset, parents will attempt to explain their child's gayness by blaming it on a lover. "It's ____. If it weren't for her/him, this would never have happened to you." It's important to establish that your gayness is not something someone *did* to you, but something that expresses your basic nature, that you would be gay even if you were not in this relationship.

Parental Guilt
"Where did I (we) go wrong?" This question is often heard from parents struggling to understand the news of a child's gayness. You are, of course, much of what you are because your parents directly or indirectly created the circumstances in which you grew up. Therefore it is not surprising that they would be concerned about what they did to make you gay. No matter how good a job you do in presenting your gayness in a positive context they might initially relate to it in terms of their own homophobic conditioning. In response to this question, first reassure your parents that there is no wrong involved, that it is unnecessarily self-punishing to think of your being gay as a failure in their parenting. It is also inaccurate since the determinants of one kind of sexual orientation versus another are as yet not clearly established, though there is growing conviction that the direction of one's sexuality is primarily determined before birth. What is important is that good parenting does produce the ability to love others and if you have that capacity you should be grateful to your parents for making it possible. Let them know.

Counterpersonal Family Culture
In some families it is the custom to avoid dealing with anything of an intimate nature, especially if it is sexual. To introduce information about yourself that tells family members more than they want to know about your personal life is going against family "culture." As much as anything it is often this countercultural behavior that brings a negative reaction. If this is the case with your family, recognize this and take it into account when you are making your disclosure. The fear that they are going to hear something sexual about their children is very strong with some parents. In the face of this kind of obstacle to communication it is best to

reassure in some way that you are not going to expose them to the graphic details of your sex life in discussing your gayness with them. Not doing this effectively could make it impossible for them to listen to you at all.

Disclosure to Children

Sometimes the family members you want to disclose to are children, your own or nieces and nephews with whom you want to have as honest a relationship as possible. Many would disagree with me, but I advocate open discussion with young people about being gay. With the coverage homosexuality is being given in the media, it is unlikely that any youngster who can see, hear and read is going to escape knowing that gay and lesbian people exist and that a lot of attention is being paid to them these days. In the absence of accurate information, the young person may well get inaccurate information from homophobic sources and develop the same antigay attitudes that prevail in much of the rest of society. If that young person is in your own family it is in your best interests to make sure, if possible, that his/her attitudes toward gay people are enlightened ones. Listening to your 12-year-old nephew tell "fag" jokes and mince around in parody of effeminate men is not likely to brighten up the family occasion you've been looking forward to. It is likely to create tension between you and him and he won't even know why. In the meantime he goes right on thinking of gay people as strange creatures out there somewhere who have nothing to do with him or his family. It does not serve you, him, the family, other gay people or society to perpetuate his antagonistic and punishing attitudes by remaining silent about them.

How do you talk to children about being gay?

First, the youngster's age should determine the level at which you talk. Obviously you aren't going to talk about sexual behavior to a very young child. If you talk about it at all to a teenager, do so with sensitivity to the struggles that young person may be having to understand and feel comfortable about his/her own budding sexuality. In the latter instance, ask questions as you go to determine how much the young person knows already and how comfortable he/she is with what you are saying. The best approach, I believe, is to talk about being gay as loving and caring for and having a close, important relationship, like marriage, with a person of the same sex. Talk about familiar concepts such as marriage, and personalize what you are saying as much as possible.

Sometimes adults are reticent to discuss homosexuality with youngsters because they don't want to unduly influence the sexual orientation of the young person. While we don't know exactly what determines sexual orientation, we do know that one does not become gay by hearing about it, or by talking about it with someone who is gay. On the other hand, young people do become honest, courageous, open and direct in their relationships by seeing others behave that way toward them.

Seeking Professional Help

Sometimes the family will try to push you to seek professional help in order not to be gay. You, of course, will gently let them know that you do not need or want such help. However, if they are having particular difficulty accepting your gayness, you might think about referring *them* for help. If you should decide to do this, take time to find gay-affirmative professionals who are understanding and supportive of gay people and who are unlikely to reinforce whatever homophobic ideas your family already has. If you live in or near a large city, consult local gay and lesbian organizations for the names of such counselors.

Useful resources are the following books which list Gay and Lesbian Community Centers, and Hotlines, by city:

The Big Gay Book. Edited by John Preston. Published by Plume/Penguin Books, 375 Hudson Street, New York, N.Y. 10014.

The Gayellow Pages. National Edition. Published by Renaissance House, Box 292, Village Station, New York, N.Y. 10014.

PREPARING FOR DISCLOSURE

I believe disclosure works best when it is prepared for well. There are several things you can do to prepare yourself. First, read gay-affirming literature for information about homosexuality and gay life since you might need to answer questions and talk knowledgeably about the topic. Second, use the "Letter of Affirmation" below to work out what you want to say in the disclosure. Third, get one or more friends to role-play the disclosure experience with you so you can try out different approaches and explore solutions to problems that might arise.

Letter of Affirmation

Dear

There's something I want to tell you. It's difficult for me to tell you this, but it's important to our relationship that you know.

I'm gay/lesbian. I have been for _____.

The way I feel about being gay/lesbian is:

The way I want *you* to feel about it is:

The way I want you to feel about *me* is:

Before closing, I want to say to you:

AFTER THE INITIAL DISCLOSURE

If your family did not know you were gay, you have told them something that is probably very unsettling. If they did know but weren't facing it, you have broken the contract of silence and changed the rules for the way you all relate to this important fact. In either case they'll probably need some time to adjust. And different people adjust in different ways. Some do it silently, some noisily. Some do it in a thoughtful and reasoned way, some go crazy. Some will blame you excessively, some will blame themselves excessively. Some will be sad, some angry, some punishing. Some will badger, some will withdraw. Some will be hungry for more information, some will not want to hear another word.

Give them time and understanding, but don't let the conspiracy of silence take over again. Keep your perspective. You have done this to improve family relations. Disclosure is a courageous act and it is an expression of your willingness for your family to be an important part of your life. You are offering them an opportunity to deal with you as the person you are, not the person they imagine you to be. You are offering the gift of yourself. Don't lose that focus.

When the opportunity comes, begin to normalize the topic of your gayness. Don't harp, but talk about it naturally, as a part of your life. For those involved in gay and lesbian community activities, that subject is often an easy vehicle for talking about being gay. If it is feasible, invite your family to meet your friends. Recommend reading, and bring them the books yourself. Let them know when there is a gay-affirmative film or TV show or magazine story. Encourage them to talk to other relatives and to friends about your gayness. You'll probably meet with a lot of resistance to this initially. It is important that they have someone to talk to. The more they keep their feelings to themselves, the less chance there is of the normalizing process happening.

Remember, though, it is a very hot potato you've handed them. The gay family member often hears, "It's okay that you've told me (us) but don't tell your father/mother/Uncle Joe/Aunt Ida." Be prepared for this reaction. It may anger you at first because it seems to be saying, "Don't tell anybody else this terrible thing." In a sense it is saying that, but it is saying more about the person speaking than about you. Very often the notion that father/mother/Uncle Joe/Aunt Ida won't be able to handle your news is inaccurate. The real issue is usually a fear of guilt by association. "What will they think of *me*?" Your disclosee has not had time yet to work through, or even work on, this issue. Be understanding. Don't argue the point, but don't make promises of keeping the secret for the future either. Helping your relative (especially a parent) learn to handle the hot potato comfortably and gracefully is one of the most important things you can do as a part of your coming out. The disclosure for you probably has been the culmination of a lengthy process of preparation. It's a relief to have it over with. The people you are disclosing to are just beginning the process. Help them. Keep communications open. Use your creativity to find ways of introducing discussion of your gayness in ways that will inform and enlighten.

Another way to help your family adjust to having a gay member involves participation in a peer support group, if one is available. If your family lives in or near a large city, there might be a chapter of Parents and Friends of Lesbians and

Gays (P-FLAG) they might visit, or join. Or, they might be willing to talk on the phone to a P-FLAG member nearby. (See the listing of P-FLAG groups at the end of the Fairchild chapter in this volume.) Often these groups have "hotlines" which a parent can call anonymously.

Remember, both you and your family are common victims of antigay prejudice. You can help one another.

IF THEY DON'T ACCEPT YOUR GAYNESS

It happens. Some parents refuse to deal with what they have learned about their children and it doesn't get any better over time. That is the chance one takes in deciding to make the disclosure. Actually, it is not as chancy as many choose to believe it is. There are, after all, clues from past behavior as to how parents are likely to deal with the disclosure. Parents who have always been loving will, perhaps with time out for a period of adjustment, continue to be loving parents. Parents who are rigid, demanding and punishing do not deal well with any news that does not fit their agenda for their children. They probably won't be any more accepting of this than of anything else that conflicts with their fantasized version of who their children are.

Sometimes it is necessary to let go of a family who simply do not or will not try to understand. It is sad. It is extremely frustrating. But it is the best course of action for your own growth, when the passage of time has not mellowed the angry response or softened the rejecting attitude. Gay and lesbian people who allow such a rejection to color their own self-image or burden their spirit are ignoring one of the most impressive truths there is regarding human growth: it is possible to grow beyond your own parents' capacity for dealing effectively with life. Even in the saddest of times this is a phenomenon to celebrate and be thankful for.

FINALLY . . .

Recently I heard a woman member of Parents and Friends of Lesbians and Gays in Los Angeles talk to a group of lesbians about her experience of learning that her teenage daughter is gay. After a period of feeling upset and then coming to terms with the news, she began to chauffeur her daughter to the Gay and Lesbian Community Services Center to attend lesbian rap groups. As she described driving her daughter to the Center and waiting for her while she participated in the raps, most of the women in the group she was addressing sat open mouthed. The image of this pleasant-looking woman sitting in the lobby of a gay community center while her child was inside learning to feel better about herself as a lesbian was obviously mind boggling. There was a silence and then someone said, "I can't believe this. You sat and waited for your daughter while she went to lesbian raps?" The woman smiled and said, "Well she wanted to go there and she couldn't drive, so what else was I to do?"

I thought of the painful early years I'd spent, so alone, trying to understand what my strange and disturbing feelings were all about. It was unimaginable to speak to my parents about them. Unimaginable to have a place to go to learn what it all meant and that it was okay. Unimaginable to be taken there by my parent.

How things have changed for some, and will for many more, as we learn to open our lives to those around us, those who are perhaps waiting to know us better and love us more fully if only we can give them the chance.

Suggested Reading
Excellent books on the topic of relating to families continue to be published all the time. For a selection current at this writing see the list at the end of the next chapter.

For Parents of Lesbians and Gays

Betty Fairchild

Along with the gay rights movement in the 70s, a related endeavor emerged across the country. Starting in 1972, individuals in two or three locations started working with parents of lesbian daughters and gay sons to help them understand their child's sexuality, and homosexuality in general. This much-needed work proliferated, independent groups formed, and in 1979 there emerged the Federation of Parents and Friends of Lesbians and Gays (P-FLAG), which by early 1992 had more than 270 chapters and contacts in the United States and several other countries. In this unique support and educational organization, with its ever-increasing scope of activities, the primary work still remains very personal. Geared to the individual needs and concerns of parents, it has been successful in eradicating the sense of isolation, the grief and pain, the guilt feelings and the fear, hostility and anger that many thousands of parents have experienced and helping them understand what being gay or lesbian means to their children and to others. The advent of AIDS in the early 1980s, has of course complicated the picture — and the work of P-FLAG — tremendously. Right from the start the prime movers in this support work have been parents themselves — backed up by their children, other lesbians and gays, and numerous professional advisors.

I myself am one of those parents. Back in 1970 when my son told me he was gay, I was as isolated and as uninformed as most such parents were then, and still are. Fortunately, over the following years, I learned a great deal and gained a new and positive outlook on my son's life. I would like to share this viewpoint with you who are in similar circumstances.

THE PROBLEM: HOMOPHOBIA

Even today, more than 20 years after the emergence of the gay liberation movement, many of us in western society still believe the tired old stereotypes about homosexuality. And because we know so little of the reality of this sexual orientation, we tend to *fear* it, whether we consciously recognize that emotion or not. This fear, called homophobia, leads us to reject, hate and even attack homosexual men and women irrationally. However, when we consider new information and are able to let go of unjustified beliefs and attitudes, we come to understand human sexuality in a new light. In so doing, we parents draw closer to our gay sons and lesbian daughters; we get to know and care about our children's friends and lovers; and we find our own lives immeasurably enriched in the process. I am convinced that the same benefits are possible for you.

Few of us respond easily to the revelation that one of our children is lesbian or gay. Some of us react in ways that are less than helpful to our children or ourselves. But even as sincerely concerned parents, we find ourselves beset with questions and anxieties about this new phenomenon in our family: What does this mean to our child? to us? How can we deal with our feelings about it? What should we *do* about it, if anything? Where do we turn for help?

For many years, it was almost impossible to find much information that did not add to our fears and worries. Today, however, there is a wealth of helpful information — hundreds of excellent books, pamphlets and videotapes, well-informed advisers, and, of course, numerous P-FLAG chapters across the country. (Check resource information and suggested reading at the end of this chapter.)

Homosexuality itself is not terrible or disastrous. Nor are you, as a family and as parents, destined to face it in utter isolation. When you take into account that at least 10 percent of our population is primarily homosexual, you will realize that many thousands of mothers and fathers are dealing with the same issues as you. At present, you may not know any such parents; you may think you don't even know any gay men or lesbians. As a matter of fact, though, we all do; most of us are simply not aware that some of our most respected associates and friends — and perhaps relatives — are homosexual.

The truth is that lesbian and gay people exist, function well, and lead normal and rewarding lives everywhere. Gay men and lesbians contribute to every profession and occupation, at every economic and social level — in fact, there is no community in this country (or elsewhere) today that does not include homosexual women and men. And this has always been true, although we hear much more about it these days. Again, the problem is not homosexuality but *homophobia*, society's irrational *fear* of homosexual persons.

PARENTS' RESPONSE — AND RESPONSIBILITY

Once we recognize and then overcome our fear of homosexuality and realize that it has existed throughout history as a variant of human sexuality, we can go on to understand its place in the lives of our children. And although it *has* a place, it is only one facet of that person's makeup. Unfortunately, when we learn that someone — particularly our own child — is lesbian or gay, we tend to forget everything else we know about that person or think that there is nothing more to know. But listen to what young people so often say, in hope and despair, "I am the same person I was before you knew. You loved me then; I hope you still love me now."

Indeed, *reassurance of your love is the initial and primary thing your daughter or son needs.* For most lesbians and gays, the decision to tell their parents was a long and agonizing one to make. Although it is their wish to share this part of their lives with their families, it is still tremendously difficult to do so because of their anxiety about their parents' response. Rather than confronting your child, as some parents do, with accusations, threats, anger or rejection after this revelation, how much better to immediately affirm your continuing love and concern. Since many of us feel *responsible*, in some unknown way, for making our child this way, our reaction to the news may be guilt or shame. ("Where did we go wrong?") But as Ruth Simpson has put it in *From the Closets to the Courts*:

> *The larger part of the burden of providing security, comfort, and love in a parent-child relationship logically should rest with the parent. That a child is homosexual does not make the parent retroactively "unfit"; a parent of a homosexual child becomes unfit, in the true sense of the word,* only if ignorance and prejudice drive the parent to ignore or degrade the homosexual child. *(Emphasis added.)*

When you have affirmed your love for your child, it is vital to keep open lines of communication. It is helpful to be honest about your feelings — being careful not to express them in an accusatory manner. Ask questions and then listen to what your child has to say. Sometimes, of course, it's difficult to articulate your questions, but do acknowledge your need to learn. Too many of us start out by providing answers on a topic about which we know very little.

How much information your child can provide will vary. Adolescents are often not yet familiar with the larger issues of homosexuality, but they *do* know how they *feel*. If your daughter says: "I really care for Gini," believe her. When your son says: "I've known for years that I'm attracted to other men," don't dismiss this statement, as some parents do. An older daughter or son will be better informed, particularly one with a background of activism, perhaps having worked (unbeknownst to you) for months or years for equal rights and greater understanding. Along with this continuing interchange of feelings and experiences, you will probably want to seek other information, to get a more complete picture of what it's all about, and to hear what others have to offer in the way of comfort and information. Reading good books and finding a P-FLAG group (or individual parent) to talk with are among the most effective things you can do.

BEING GAY: IT IS NOT YOUR FAULT!
IT IS NOT A CHOICE!

If you are like most parents, you have assumed a heavy load of guilt and shame. "Where did we go wrong?" you ask. "If only we had known sooner, perhaps we could have done something." "*Why* is my child gay?" "We really tried to bring our kids up right but somehow, with Barbara (or Jack), we must have failed."

There are good answers to these questions, although they may not be the ones you expect.

First, regardless of what "causes" homosexuality, a lot of energy is wasted in agonizing about the past. Rather than focusing on *why* and *if we had only known*, you might better devote your energy to more constructive questions: "Where do we go from here? What can we do *now* — for ourselves (to learn more) and for our son or daughter (to support them helpfully)?" Second, as you learn to understand homosexuality as a natural variation of sexuality, you realize — with a sigh of relief — that there is no blame, and your feelings of guilt will probably disappear.

From studies of the lives and backgrounds of thousands of mentally and emotionally healthy homosexuals we can derive no facile answers as to why one person in a family develops a homosexual orientation and another a heterosexual one. Although theories abound, it is not definitely known to what degree the family situation contributes to a child's development of sexual preference. However, it is clear that the time-worn reference to such characteristics as "dominant mother/ weak father" does not hold up, since lesbian women and gay men come from all kinds of home situations, including warm, loving close-knit families. When you no longer regard this sexual orientation as bad, the causes, while they may be of some scientific interest, are of much less importance to you and your family.

I have known parents to ask: "How can you bear to live this way?" as if their child has deliberately *selected* a homosexual way of life. Some will say: "Well, you've chosen this lifestyle, but please don't bring your friends here." Or, "If you choose to live this way, I suppose there's nothing we can do." Whether we mistakenly attribute our child's sexual orientation to our own failing or to their choice, many of us start out, as I did myself, with the assumption — and great hope — that our gay or lesbian children can change if they want to.

The reality is quite different. (Ask yourself if you could change your sexual orientation on request.) By the time our young people came out to us as gay or lesbian, they will have been aware of being attracted to the same sex for some time. Although they may have denied this to themselves at first, they know by now that they feel closer to their own gender than to the opposite. With the tremendous societal pressures to be heterosexual, our children often find that coming to terms with their *own* sexuality is difficult and troubling, but ultimately unavoidable: it is not a choice. (How many of us would *choose* to encounter the disapproval and rejection with which our heterosexual society greets anyone who dares not to conform?) Thus, our expectations, demand, or hope for change are simply unrealistic. The sooner we recognize this, the sooner we move toward understanding.

The important question is not "Why can't they change?" but "What do I need to know about my lesbian daughter as she sees herself right now?" or "How can I better understand my son and what being gay means to him?"

THOSE WRETCHED STEREOTYPES!

How well we know the outmoded, old stereotypes of homosexuals: the effeminate man (who wants to be a woman); the tough, muscular woman (who wants to be a man); the ineffectual weaklings who couldn't hold down a job — or shouldn't be allowed to. Then there are those unwarranted fears that homosexuals are out to *get* heterosexuals, that they attack children, that they will somehow contaminate us if they are allowed to work or live among us (which, of course, they already do), that they should not be allowed to become ministers or teachers — not to mention the interesting argument that our future world population is in jeopardy if we "permit" homosexuality.

Many of us fear that our own gay and lesbian children will never have a good home, family life or children, that they will never know real love, that they will automatically be excluded from a successful career or that they will be outcasts and misfits, harassed and looked down on all their lives, ending up lonely and unhappy. The irony of all this is that if those projections were to come true, it would almost surely be the result of society's oppressive attitudes and behavior toward homosexual persons and not because they are lesbian or gay.

The majority of lesbians and gay men do not fit these stereotypes. In fact, you will find far fewer differences than you imagine between your gay son or lesbian daughter and your other children. Review the "fears" expressed above, and reflect on how often young people today, of whatever inclination, decline to live out our parental hopes, standards and expectations. Furthermore, there are many encouraging and even exemplary aspects to the homosexual person's life.

RELATIONSHIPS

It can be a great source of comfort to learn that our lesbian daughter or gay son has formed a loving relationship with another person. To many nongay people, homosexuality equates only with sex, and even today, a good many of us believe that at least male homosexuals will only have a life of promiscuity and fleeting contacts, to say nothing of degradation and illness. This is far from the truth.

I remember how, many years ago, I first became aware of *love* as a part of my son's life when he broke up with Seth, a man I knew and liked. His obvious genuine heartbreak was distressing to me, but I also realized that his feelings of loss were identical to those of his sister when her heterosexual love relationship ended. I was somehow comforted, as I thought, with a kind of sympathetic shock: "Why, he really *loved* Seth!" and this opened up for me a whole new dimension of such relationships. It seems that many gays and lesbians are surprised to learn that their parents are not aware that love is possible between two men or two women.

"But we are not different from anyone else in this respect," they reiterate, "except in whom we love." Many writings by women indicate that the pleasure and rewards of lesbian associations and relationships are far more complex than simply "being in love with another woman." I myself found this material very instructive in appreciating my own women friends.

Like many other parents, I have had the privilege over the past couple of decades of becoming close friends with a wide range of lesbians and gay men, and time and again I have witnessed the deep, caring relationships between two women or two men. I am always inspired by the scope of commitment, love and concern shared by these couples, including a genuine enjoyment of each other's company and a sense of fun that seems to be missing among many nongay relationships. Moreover, in this age of AIDS, the devotion of gay men to each other and to their friends, as well as the caring love expressed by lesbians (and nongay women) for their male friends, has been an inspiration to all of us who are aware of it.

There is frequently a remarkable absence of traditional role-playing by a gay or lesbian couple. The old question: "Which one is the woman and which the man?" is meaningless to most such lovers. In the past, with the force of heterosexual impact in our culture and the lack of visible and strong homosexual role models, couples often assumed a pattern of dominant/submissive relationships but today, most couples incorporate an exemplary model of equality.

Thus, there is indeed a strong potential for a loving, supportive relationship for the lesbian or gay man. If it does not last forever (although I know couples who have been together 50 some years), it is after all not so different from the marriage/ divorce picture in our straight society.

A word more about relationships: some parents deprive themselves and their children of great happiness by refusing to acknowledge that their daughter or son has a lover and simply ignoring that person's existence. Hopefully these parents are in the minority. Many of us get to know our child's lover, come to care deeply for that person, and welcome him or her as a member of the family. And even if we find little to like in our child's choice of lover, as sometimes happens, it is not much different and certainly no worse than how we might feel about another child's spouse.

As you welcome your child's partner into your home and your lives, you may at first resist accepting their expressions of affection. Some parents insist they will always be extremely uncomfortable with even the most casual interaction between their child and a lover — an embrace of greeting, a loving arm around the other's shoulder as they chat with the family, hands held at parting — and God forbid two men should kiss! While the nongay world's aversion to men's affectionate gestures is probably greater than to women's, there is still the mother who says: "It's OK for that woman to visit, but I can't bear to see her touch my daughter."

I contend that, apart from our general sexual uptightness, much of this distress is based on our *unfamiliarity* with affectionate behavior between members of the same sex. Our eyes are not used to it, our minds are not used to it, and our negative emotional response is deeply ingrained (but not ineradicably) by outmoded taboos against same-sex affection. And yet, if you are trying to understand what it means to your child to be gay or lesbian, an open attitude toward reasonable expressions of affection is part of the process. Few of us are comfortable in the presence of heavy lovemaking between any two people, but once you see simple affection for what it is, it is no harder to observe between your son and his friend than between your daughter and her husband or boyfriend. At that point, you may find, as I did long ago, that a tender embrace or even a quick kiss between two men or two women can be very endearing.

As parents, we must see that it's a matter of adjusting *our* viewpoint, and not of expecting others to conform to our rigid and uninformed standards. Life itself can be either a narrow confinement that keeps us critical, discontented and impoverished in spirit or it can be a continuing growth process for us, to our enhanced pleasure and enrichment.

HOME AND CAREER

Many of us believe our gay children will never have the good things in life. I have not found this to be true. With or without a loving relationship, comfortable, attractive, and sometimes luxurious home surroundings are common among both gay men and lesbians. It is classic stereotypical thinking to assume this might not be true.

If a successful career is what your gay or lesbian child wants, he or she can no doubt achieve it. Within recent years, laws have been passed in many communities prohibiting discrimination on the basis of sexual orientation. While this does not completely eliminate discriminatory practices, the picture is increasingly more positive as more men and women are unwilling to pretend to be something they are not. This refusal does not mean wearing a sign saying "I am lesbian" or "I am gay."

It does mean refusing to leave a lover at home during office social functions, or to talk vaguely of "dates" or to refer to one's lover as a roommate, or to live in fear that one's participation in various gay or lesbian activities will become known at the office.

Of course, there are still gay men and lesbians, especially in public life, who are unwilling to be so open. This had led to the argument by some activists that remaining closeted is detrimental to societal acceptance and understanding by continuing to deny the reality, as mentioned, that gay men and lesbians presently work successfully at all levels of every field. (Whatever the merits of this argument, as parents you will surely want to discern and comply with your own child's wishes in this regard.)

GAYS, LESBIANS AND CHILDREN

If you have reacted to your child's revelation with the stricken thought: "No grandchildren!" you have lots of company. (Keep in mind that even your nongay child may choose not to have children these days, and while this may not comfort a wishful grandparent, it does point up once more that your gay or lesbian child is not so very different.) But aside from this, increasing numbers of lesbian and gay couples are becoming parents through adoption or biological parenting, as well as those who have offspring from a former heterosexual marriage. The old fiction that homosexuals could not or should not have children is long outmoded. It has been shown time and again that lesbian mothers and gay fathers do as well by their children as any of the rest of us, and far better than some. Children of parents who have defined their own sexuality clearly as gay or lesbian are usually open to the wide range of sexual variation, and are not forced into a mold of either hetero- or homosexuality. I have never known a gay or lesbian parent to influence their child to be homosexual. They often say: "If they are, they know they'll get understanding from us. If not, we'll understand and support that, too."

Moreover, children of lesbian or gay parents usually come to accept having two moms or two dads — and often enjoy the unique qualities of these special situations.

And finally, potential grandparents who may resist the idea of their lesbian or gay offspring having children are usually won over when the grandchild arrives!

AIDS IN TODAY'S WORLD

Since the early 80s, AIDS has become a worldwide issue and one of particular concern to parents of gay sons — although we know that the disease affects other men, women and children as well. Certainly, thousands of fathers and mothers and their families have been touched personally and painfully by this disease. Almost *all* parents are deeply concerned about it, and many desperately fear that their gay son has, or will contract, AIDS.

The truth is that *not every gay man gets AIDS* or even becomes HIV positive; that not everyone who is HIV positive will face the same future, and that many people with AIDS continue to lead normal productive lives for many years. I myself have many gay friends who are *not* HIV positive and others who learned of their HIV positive status many years ago and who have not had a single symptom of AIDS. And I continue to meet and hear about the long-term survivors: men who were diagnosed with AIDS more than three years ago — some, *many* years ago, but who remain well. So the picture is not as bleak as a parent new to all of this might imagine it to be.

As concerned parents, then, we should not assume that because our son is gay, he "will die of AIDS" — nor should we continually question him (as some parents do) to find out something we don't want to hear! What we must do is educate ourselves about the realities of AIDS — what it is and is not — and at the same time, prepare ourselves for a sympathetic and knowledgeable response to critical news if it should come. Here, of course, is where extensive reading comes in: numerous excellent books are available. Furthermore, in most P-FLAG groups, AIDS information and compassionate support are there for the asking.

And what if we *do* learn that our son (or daughter) has AIDS, and is not well? Of course, many young people hesitate to tell their parents of their HIV positive or AIDS condition because they fear their response. So with this, as with all news of a critical nature, we do best by offering our love and support, not condemnation or fearful rejection. Here is one place where educating ourselves about AIDS is essential: when we truly accept the medical testimony that AIDS is not easily transmissible, that in ordinary contact, it is virtually impossible to pass on, our fears of being near, or touching or embracing and kissing, a person with AIDS will vanish. And when those fears are gone, we are less likely to condemn or accuse.

When you offer your son love and support, I believe you will find that good things follow, even in the midst of possible illness and loss. For beyond the deepened relationship with your beloved child — which almost surely ensues — you are likely to become aware of the numerous women and men — lesbian, gay and straight — who devote their time and energy to taking care of their friends with AIDS or volunteering support to others who need it. I know scores of parents in this situation who have suddenly realized how "wonderful" lesbians and gay men can be.

One mistake otherwise caring parents sometimes make is in suddenly coming in and taking over the care of their son (or daughter) who is ill. In so doing, they simply ignore or dismiss the presence of a lover or of close friends who have been devoted to providing loving care to this young man or woman. But as has been shown time and again, when all are sensitive to each other's feelings and goals, close lasting bonds are often formed between parents and other caregivers.

You may well find that your child, after diagnosis, has changed in some positive ways. People with AIDS (as with other life-threatening illnesses) often take a look at their lives and their values, and many set a different course. Some will leave unsatisfying jobs, determined to spend their time in more rewarding ways and not wait to do the things they have always dreamed of doing. Some also volunteer to support other people with AIDS, or work to increase AIDS understanding and support from the public and the government — all too frequently a frustrating endeavor, and one which we as parents would not want to further obstruct. Almost all people with AIDS realize that the greatest aspect of life is *love*, and that their relationships with their family, lovers and friends are far more important than prestige, possessions or wealth. I believe that you will be proud of such changes as you observe them in your child.

Although we emphasize that death is not an immediate "given" for someone with AIDS, you may need to prepare yourself for this possibility. Many people nowadays view death as a transition, a passage, or another step on the continuum of existence. Whatever your current beliefs about this experience, you might want to explore new viewpoints and attitudes. Stephen Levine's books, among others (see suggested reading), have proven exceedingly helpful for those who face the death of a loved one. If it is possible to talk this over with your son or daughter, it may be a great relief to both of you and will give you the opportunity of learning what your child's thoughts and feelings are about life ending, and what his or her wishes are in that regard. In a time that naturally is filled with sadness and grief, it can be wonderfully comforting to speak of things all too often left unsaid.

NOT AN END BUT A BEGINNING

As you consider these new aspects of a homosexual life style, you will realize there is much more to know than I can offer here. You will need to give yourself time to absorb these ideas; none of us achieve a different way of looking at life instantly. And if you do experience distress and anxiety about your lesbian or gay child, acknowledge that but don't *stop* with those feelings.

I was able to overcome my negative feelings (which were fairly intense) by talking with my son and his friends, by reading widely, by talking with other parents, both in and outside of parent groups; and perhaps as much as anything by getting to know scores of lesbians and gay men.

I hope that you will make the effort to find others who share your concerns and can help you — friends, relatives, counselors, and certainly other parents. Probably the best way is to find the nearest P-FLAG group in your area. Write or call P-FLAG head office (shown below), and be assured that all personal information is kept strictly confidential. Again, I emphasize the importance of reading extensively, and of meeting lesbians and gay men whenever you can.

But most of all, be open with your own gay or lesbian child. All our children are precious to us, I know, and surely we are willing to work toward knowing each one of them as honestly as possible. If at times this seems difficult, look forward to the rewards of deeper, more loving relationships with your children, of a family more closely united. It will be more than worth the effort, I promise you.

Federation P-FLAG Head Office:
Federation of Parents and Friends of Lesbians and Gays, Inc.
P.O. Box 27605
Washington, DC 20038-7605
(202)638-4200

Suggested Reading

For Parents

Borhek, Mary V. *My Son Eric*, New York, Pilgrim Press, 1979.

A mother tells the moving story of coming to understanding and acceptance of her gay son.

Borhek, Mary V. *Coming Out to Parents: A Two-Way Survival Guide for Lesbians and Gay Men and Their Parents.* New York, Pilgrim Press, 1983.

Self-explanatory title.

Fairchild, Betty and Nancy Hayward. *Now That You Know: What Every Parent Should Know About Homosexuality.* A Harvest/HBJ Book. New York, Harcourt, Brace Jovanovich, 1989 (Revised Edition).

The authors, parents of gay children themselves, present accurate, comforting information, anecdotes, and helpful suggestions. This updated edition deals with AIDS and the family. Considered a classic guidebook, this is often suggested as the best "first book" for parents.

Griffin, Carolyn Welch and Marian J. and Arthur G. Wirth. *Beyond Acceptance: Parents of Lesbians and Gays Talk About Their Experiences.* New Jersey, Prentice-Hall, 1986.

As the title implies, this excellent book goes beyond the first stages of dealing with homosexuality, commenting on and offering numerous first-person statements to illustrate the spectrum of phases, feelings, levels of understanding, and sometimes activism experienced by various parents (and their gay offspring). Includes moving "afterwords" by the authors' own gay sons.

Muller, Ann. *Parents Matter.* Tallahassee, FL, Naiad Press, 1987.

While most literature on homosexuality describes gay males, this book draws evenly from stories of parents' relationships with both lesbian daughters and gay sons.

Rafkin, Louise. Ed. *Different Daughters.* Pittsburgh, PA, Cleis Press, 1987.

Addressing issues of family, community, religion and politics, 25 mothers of lesbians trace the growth of their relationships with their daughters.

About Death and Dying

Levine, Stephen. *Who Dies? An Investigation of Conscious Living and Conscious Dying.* New York, Anchor Books, 1982.

An outstanding book likely to be of interest to everyone. Offers a positive and open-hearted approach to dying and has much of value to offer about living. Eastern approaches made useful to Western people.

Levine, Stephen. *Meetings at the Edge: Dialogues with the Grieving and the Dying, The Healing and the Healed.* New York, Anchor Press, 1984.

Another valuable book from a man who has worked with the dying, and the living, for many years.

Levine, Stephen. *Healing into Life and Death.* New York, Anchor Press/Doubleday, 1987.

An exceptionally fine book, in which the author defines healing as an ongoing life process. Several meditations along with a wise, tender, and heartfelt approach of benefit to all of us.

PARENTING: THE CHALLENGES CHILDREN PRESENT

On Being A Lesbian Mother

Diane Abbitt and Roberta Bennett

Once we were just mothers. We concerned ourselves with the typical problems of child rearing — what diaper to buy, when to toilet train, which school would best suit our children's needs — and nobody noticed. We were just two out of millions of concerned women doing our best to make the right decisions in raising our children. Then five years ago everything changed — and nothing changed. Now we are still just two concerned women raising our children, but our child-rearing practices are of great interest to other people. Why? What wrought this miracle? What has brought us to the attention of those we meet? What has given us the honor of having these words published? The answer is one simple seven-letter word that precedes the word *mother*: *lesbian*.

We are two women, ages 35 and 34, living in a typical middle-class neighborhood with our four children — two boys and two girls, ages seven, eight, nine and ten — two dogs, three cats, two parakeets and a fish. The only thing that sets us apart from the families of our middle-class neighbors is that our family has no father and one spare mother.

Five years ago we combined our respective families. The decision to do so was easy. Carrying it out has proven to be the most difficult yet most rewarding undertaking of our lives. It's hard to trust another person to help raise your children and the transition to "our" children has been a very slow process.

The hardest concept for our children to accept was our definition of *family*. Over and over they would ask, "How can we be a family?" And time and again we would answer, "A family is people who live together and love and take care of each other." We knew we were winning when the children started teasing strangers about their being siblings. A few months out of every year our two oldest children

93

are the same age. They would put people on by saying they were twins (they look nothing alike) and then confuse people further by giving their birth dates (five months apart). With humor came acceptance. For instance, one of the most touching moments we have shared was when our oldest boy, who calls his mother "mom" and his spare mother "aunt," handed us a picture he had drawn in school. On the bottom was lettered, "To mom and mom."

Like most lesbian mothers there is a small part of us that worries and has doubts about what effect our lifestyle will have on our children. At the same time, intellectually, we realize that our children will turn out just as good or just as rotten as children being raised in a traditional family. But for that small part of us that does doubt and have fears, we appreciate the few studies and articles appearing so far which conclude that children raised by lesbian mothers fare just as well psychologically as those raised by heterosexual mothers. We feel encouraged and validated by this.

We find ourselves, individually and as a couple, spending an inordinate amount of time discussing our children. We have been told that we are overconcerned, too strict, too permissive, too rigid, too loose, overprotective, underprotective, etc., all of which is probably true at one time or another. What distinguishes our neurotic fixation on our children's development from that of our nongay sisters is our ever-present awareness of the future. Should we succeed in our effort to raise four fantastic, productive, responsible, contented human beings, it will be a statement to those who condemn the lesbian mother as unfit, solely on the basis of her lesbianism, that they are wrong. In reality, we know there are those who would say that our success had occurred in spite of our lesbianism. We most certainly know that if we fail it will be blamed on our lesbianism.

The Custody Issue

One fear surely shared by almost every lesbian mother is that of losing her children in a custody battle. Such a court battle not only risks the loss of her children, but adds a humiliating debasement of her person when insensitive, uneducated judges order her, over the objections of her attorney, to describe the intimate details of her sex life with her same-sex lover. It is impossible to adequately describe the effect of this degradation on women who have experienced it. For the individual mother who anticipates this "Armageddon" the question becomes one of how to handle her fear of it and how to best prepare for it.

The manifestation of this fear can often be seen in the aforementioned perfect mother/perfect child syndrome. After all, a little voice inside says, "The more perfect my children, the more perfect I am as a mother, the better my chances in court."

The best advice for a lesbian mother anticipating a custody fight is to stay out of court if possible. Custody is decided in the "best interest of the child," which the judge usually equates with "better" or "normal." Since judges are most often white, older, middle-aged, straight men enforcing their own value system, a lesbian goes into court with two strikes against her before anyone says a word.

There are a wide variety of "bargains" that can be arranged with your spouse so that you can get custody of your children and not go into court. For example, you may be willing to take less in the way of a property settlement or you may grant extensive visitation rights to your spouse. Child custody arrangements are a complex area of the law and we have touched on it only briefly and superficially. If you have problems in this area, consult an experienced, sympathetic attorney and follow her advice.

How Open To Be?

All people struggle with the question of how much of their private life they are willing to expose to the world. The lesbian mother knows that her decisions will have far-reaching repercussions for her children as well as herself. The decision to tell or not to tell her children of her lesbianism usually determines how much she is willing to tell the rest of the world. Some lesbian mothers never tell their children; others are completely open about their lifestyle, and the rest fall somewhere in between.

The lesbian mother who chooses not to reveal her lesbianism is usually motivated by fear — of psychological damage to her child, of her child's rejection of her, of losing her child. Or she might be concerned about her child telling others. This could result in job loss for her and/or rejection by her family, friends or neighbors. She might also fear her child being hurt by her/his peers upon disclosure to them. These women lead a double life, a particularly difficult arrangement for the woman who lives with her lover.

Our approach, from the beginning, has been to be completely open with our children, to encourage discussion and to answer their questions as honestly as possible. We decided to do this after a careful discussion in which we weighed the pros and cons of remaining in the closet. The key word was *honesty*. We pride ourselves on being totally honest with our children and encourage telling the truth to the point where severe punishment is handed down for lying. What would hiding our lesbianism do to our family's value system? We decided that when the children found out (as surely they must), two things would happen. One, they would lose all belief in us and in everything we had attempted to teach them, and two, they would think that we were ashamed of who we are and they might buy into that shame.

We believe that if we have a positive attitude about our lesbianism and impart it to our children before they reach the age where peer pressure molds their thinking, that they too will have positive attitudes and will be better equipped to handle some of the problems that may lie ahead.

This doesn't mean that we will be surprised if at some point in the future one or more of our children withdraw from us emotionally and think that we are awful. Looking back at our own adolescence and speaking with others has made us realize that most children have to find fault with their parents at some level so that they can become separate individuals in their own right. As teenagers most of us "hated" our parents because they were poor or rich or ugly or fat or Jewish or black or Republican. We fully expect to go through this with our own children. It's a part of growing up and children have an uncanny way of seeking out their parents' most sensitive spot and exploiting it. Our children aren't going to have to do a lot of searching to find our spot. We only hope that when our time comes we can be as objective as we are now. It will still hurt, we know that; just because you expect something doesn't necessarily make it easier to deal with when it happens. However, knowing that if there weren't lesbianism, there would be some other "spot," should make it a little easier. Perhaps one of the most difficult aspects of motherhood is the fight to keep a sane perspective and reasonable expectations of one's children.

What the Children Understand

Right now, the children being of "tender years," it's hard to know exactly what they think of our lesbianism. They can all verbalize a proper definition of the word: "A lesbian is a woman who loves another woman." What this means to them still is not quite clear.

It appears that the word *love* is the key. On our way home from a conference once, our oldest son expressed it well. We were all tired and cranky, being stuck in traffic at the end of a long day, when our eight-year-old daughter popped up with the comment that she was a lesbian. Our oldest son, not to be outdone, looked at her and said, "I'm a lesbian too." Scornfully she replied, "You can't be a lesbian! A lesbian is a woman who loves another woman." Said he, "I love my Daddy." With that the other two joined in and within 30 seconds, we were busy giving a lecture on different types of love and where lesbianism fits into the broad spectrum of things.

We encourage these types of discussions, no matter how they arise, and answer specifically and as fully as possible the questions asked — no more, no less. Their questions tell us how much they are ready to learn and we are anxious that they grow at their own pace.

We have tried to explain to the children that some people think that the way we live is wrong. We discuss prejudice, using blacks, Jews and other minorities to illustrate our points. We have never told the children not to tell anyone about our lesbianism. We have left this decision up to them, reminding them of the possible repercussions such as ostracism and teasing.

So far we have only one child, our eight-year-old, who has come out of the closet. She accomplished this feat in a most unusual way; coming out in her classroom during "Show and Tell." She announced that she was being raised in a lesbian family, that her Mommy was "chief" of the lesbians (we do a lot of movement work) and that she got to go to a lot of lesbian conferences. Now mind you, this was a first grade class. One of her peers told her it was "inappropriate" for women to kiss each other. We found out about the incident one day when we were kissing good morning in the kitchen while the children were having breakfast. She turned to us and said, "That's inappropriate," and then told us the whole story. The teacher's reaction? "We have got to learn to respect the differences of others."

Three of our four children have had this first grade teacher, an older woman with a reputation for being a conservative, tough, no-nonsense person. We wanted our children to be in her class because we felt that they would get a better education, even though we suspected that she would not understand or approve of our lifestyle. We have never talked with this woman about our lifestyle, even though over the last three years we have met with her fairly regularly. She has always been warm, kind, interested and concerned when we discussed the children, their problems or our problems with them. She expects and accepts that we will both show up for parent/teacher conferences or that one of us will pop into her room to ask about our nonbiological child.

We hope that in some way we have been instrumental in raising her consciousness about lesbian families. We know she has raised ours. We no longer automatically pigeon-hole any nongay person we meet as having nothing in common with us or as a nonsympathetic bigot to be avoided. We now show up together at all teacher/parent conferences and we haven't had one bad experience yet.

Expressing Affection and Parental Roles

In keeping with our attitude of openness and honesty with the children, we are also openly affectionate. Affection is a very important part of loving and we want our children to know not only how much we love them but how much we love each other. Many people have disagreed with us, telling us that we should reserve our expressions of affection with each other for the bedroom and not expose the children to a sexual contact between two same-sex adults. We feel that it is essential to differentiate between affection and sex. This isn't done in many heterosexual households. Who knows how many people have grown up without seeing their parents kiss? We believe that what is important is growing up with affection, not the sex of the people expressing it. It is only by seeing and being involved in warmth and loving that children grow into giving, loving adults. We agree — keep sex in the bedroom, but affection, never!

Many people ask if one of us is considered the daddy by the children. The answer is an emphatic *no*. We have divided child rearing much the same way we have divided the other chores of maintaining a home and family. Each does what is most comfortable. One of us gets physically ill when a child vomits, so the other takes care of the children when they are sick. One of us used to be a primary-school teacher, so she's in charge of homework time. One enjoys bathing the children, the other drying their hair. This has worked out pretty well. A problem arises only when neither of us enjoys or wants to do a necessary task, for example, chauffeuring the children around — to school, from school, to and from friends, and so on. In this example we split the load. Of course, natural talents and abilities enter as well: The mechanically inclined one usually fixes the toys; one cooks and the other does the dishes; and so on.

We are both strong disciplinarians and for the most part run a tight ship. We have found that this is necessary for survival with a family of six. It helps when everyone knows what is expected of them and this includes the children.

An interesting problem arises from this discipline: each set of children fears and respects their stepmother more than their mother. This presents an interesting problem. We both acknowledge that our own children "have our number" and we are thankful that the other is there to step in when the situation gets rough. On the other hand, there seems to be an inevitable resentment by the biological parent of the disciplining nonbiological parent, even when we both agree that the discipline is appropriate.

Community Involvement and Friends

Working within the gay, lesbian and nongay communities to change attitudes and to achieve equality and full civil rights for gay people is very important to us. To this end we are active in many organizations, we lead workshops, we give lectures, we do radio shows and speak with legislators, counselors, therapists and attorneys. Having children affects the way we handle our activism. We do not give magazine interviews as lesbians nor do we appear as lesbians on TV. We adopted this policy to encourage the children to decide for themselves when and whom to tell of our lifestyle. Sometimes this is not easy to follow, and there have been times when the policy has been slightly bent, but overall we feel it has worked. When the children are older and capable of fully understanding why it is important for us or people like us to give interviews and to be on TV, and if we *all* agree that this is important and something we want and are willing to do, then we'll do it.

In the gay community, children and parenting are not common phenomena. We have found people who just plain don't like kids, as in the heterosexual community. However, most of our gay friends enjoy being around our children and talking with them. For many of our lesbian and gay male friends, our children provide the only real opportunity they have to relate to the world of children. We are surprised at how often our children are included in gatherings with our friends, and how genuinely disappointed our friends are when we don't bring them. Of course, the other side of the coin is our friends' distress when they don't want the kids and we can't find a babysitter.

Friends often volunteer to take the children for a day or a weekend, which provides immense enjoyment for us and them. We think our gay male friends have a particularly interesting reaction when we share our children with them. It's as if some part of these men has bought into the myth that they can't be trusted with children and they are touched that we would share and trust our children with them. We have watched them talk with the children, rough house with them, calm them when they're scared and pick them up and soothe them when they are crying. We love the caring and warmth our male friends display around the children.

We like men and so do our children. We feel it's very important for men to be around for the children to interact with; just as important for our girls as for our boys. We feel fortunate that the majority of the men our children relate to have a feminist consciousness and we hope, despite peer and social pressures, that we will end up with four fine feminists. (Right now we think the odds are 50/50.)

We are often asked how we would feel if one or more of our children were homosexual. We believe the scientists who tell us that our children's sexual prefer-ence was already decided before we got together. However, we're not sure that this is something we could have consciously influenced even if we had wanted to. After all, most parents raise their children assuming they will be heterosexual, yet it is estimated that between 10% and 20% of the U.S. population is gay.

We want our children to be happy and to accept themselves. If this means being gay, then that's fine. We have discussed the societal pressures our children will have to endure if they are gay. It's not easy in our country to be a member of a minority, and like all mothers, we don't like envisioning our children in any kind of pain. We hope that the next generation of gay men and lesbians will have less pressure to deal with and be even better equipped to handle it.

What you have just read is our truth. Mothering is a very personal experience, a very individual experience, and nothing in this chapter is meant to reflect on mothering in general, lesbian or otherwise. We must all learn to trust ourselves, our abilities and our insights. While the experts can give us advice and help us use our own skills and wisdom more effectively, it is up to us, ultimately, to do the job of raising our children. We hope sharing some of our thoughts and experiences is helpful to you. You are not alone. Good luck!

Thirteen Years Later

This past decade has held so many positive changes for us and for the gay and lesbian rights movement, we hardly know where to begin. More and more gay men and lesbians are becoming parents. No longer are gay and parenting mutually exclusive concepts. A measure of the growing incidence of parenting is the practice now of offering child care at many gay and lesbian conferences, church and temple services, and other community events. A few states are beginning to approve same-sex *couple* adoptions as opposed to the more traditional single-parent adoptions gay and lesbian couples had to accept before.

Many municipalities and corporations are now offering medical insurance for spousal equivalents and family care and bereavement leave for significant others. We believe this is truly the beginning of legal recognition and social validation of our familial status. Judges are now attending seminars on gay and lesbian families. More gay attorneys and judges are being open about being gay and are educating their peers in the process. And as lawyers (we both are) with family law as one of our specialties, we see parents no longer losing custody as often or being denied visitation solely on the basis of their being gay or lesbian. At least this is true in the larger cities of the country.

Now, to us and our own children. Of course they are no longer "children." They are 23, 22, 21, and 20. One is married, one is a parent, one just graduated college, and the "baby" is a junior in college. They are each wonderful and unique in his/her own way. We have two staunch feminists, three environmentalists, and two vegetarians. All experimented with drugs very briefly, two are extroverts, one is shy, one is a loner, and none are bigots. They are close and loving, and have given us the ultimate compliment by saying they hope they can be as good parents for their children as we have been for them. However, interesting to note, the child who turned us gray before our time says he will not be as lenient as we were. There is no doubt that they believe we are a family. Somehow, it all worked.

Although we are sure of the fact that our adult children were raised by lesbian mothers had some effect, some influence on them, we are not sure exactly what that influence has been. While they would be judged by anyone's standards to be pretty "normal," they are very different from one another in their psychological makeup. So far, none of them has announced that they are gay or lesbian.

We think each of our children at some point struggled with our lesbianism in terms of their own sexual identity — embarrassment over being different, angry over all sorts of things. But, our worst fears were never realized, not even close. Except for the usual dilemmas of adolescence, our children's teenage years were pleasurable, for them and for us.

Our children are very accepting of us, our friends, and our activism. They have a generally positive view of what the gay and lesbian community is all about. We believe that this is due to the fact that we never lied to them. We were open and honest and we always took their concerns seriously and responded to them as fully as we could. As to whom they chose to tell about us, we always told them when they were growing up that they could tell or not tell their friends.

When the children were 17, 16, 15, and 14, we moved. We had lived in the same house for nine years, and our cul de sac had ultimately accepted and befriended us. Moving to a new community created a certain tension, but based on our past experience we were optimistic about what would happen.

As moving day approached, the family shared their concerns over dinner. A few days later, our youngest son came home and announced that no one had to worry about the neighbors knowing our story because he had "told" his friend who lived around the corner from our new house, who, in turn, told his friends and parents. He said he was sure that within a few days the entire neighborhood would know about us. Of course, he was right, but so were we — no one seemed to care.

You may have noticed when you read our original chapter that we did not include our children's names. This was intentional. When we were asked to write the chapter, we discussed it and decided that we did not have the right to come out for our children. In addition, we were afraid at the time of the possible discrimination they might experience. Today, each of them comes out to their friends, their classmates and their workmates with great pride in their family and in themselves.

We are equally proud of them and of ourselves, and so it is with deep gratitude that we thank Christine, David, Allison, and Danny for the opportunity to write this chapter, for being the delightfully unique people they are, and for sharing with us the new, wonderful and, at times, terrifying frontier of lesbian motherhood.

Suggested Reading

McPike, Loralee. *There's Something I've Been Meaning to Tell You.* Tallahassee, Florida, Naiad Press, 1988.

Mothers tell their children about being lesbian.

Pies, Cheri. *Considering Parenthood: A Workbook for Lesbians.* San Francisco, Spinsters Ink, 1987.

A manual, with shared experiences for women and men considering parenthood.

Schulenberg, Joy. *Parenting: A Complete Guide for Gay Men and Lesbians with Children.* New York, Anchor Press/Doubleday, 1985.

Covers issues of coming out to children, co-parenting, adoption and foster parenting and the impact of AIDS.

Note: An excellent series of pamphlets on parenting issues is available from the National Center for Lesbian Rights in San Francisco. (415) 621-0674.

On Being A Gay Father

Jeff Carron

"You're going to adopt a *what*?" my family and almost all of my friends asked incredulously when I told them about my plans. "You're gay, you're unattached, you're nuts!" ...

And so it began. Of course, once Jenny was born it changed.

In my life, at least, it seems that once I have gotten past the "I'm going to" stage and into the "I'm in it" stage people have come around. But I had my fears and my doubts, too. I just felt in my heart that I had to, I wanted to, be a father. It turned out that it was a great decision.

Jenny changed my life. I was a fairly "out there" gay man prior to adopting Jenny. I wasn't closeted and I had a supportive family and friends, both in and out of the gay and lesbian community. I am a bandleader and have been for twenty years, performing at private and corporate parties and having a pretty successful run at it. I was (and continue to be) healthy. I had been in a long-term relationship for 8 years that had ended 2 years earlier and I was very happy in my "singleness" — but something was missing.

I grew up in a close-knit family in Brooklyn, and I missed that ambience in my own life in Los Angeles. I wanted to have the "continuity" that I felt only a family of my own could bring.

I asked myself what I thought were the crucial questions: "Will I be able to meet all of this child's needs as a parent?" "Will she/he be able to understand and accept who I am?" "Will she suffer discrimination because I'm gay?" I realized that the first question is one most conscientious parents-to-be ask of themselves. The answer to the second question would depend on the quality of our relationship and I intended to make it as open and honest as possible. That's the kind of person I am and the only kind I'd like to be with her. Also, the foundation for what happens between us would be in the context of that loving relationship. I would be the person who made her life secure and happy. I believed that everything else would fall in line with that.

The third question bothered me the most until I thought about children born to minority parents. No one tells people of color not to have children because they might be discriminated against. They prepare their children to deal with that possibility and when it occurs, they give the children support and understanding. That is exactly what I would do. After all, how much can you or *should* you protect a child from life? None of us really escapes that.

I was also concerned ... very ... about a child being in the world without a mother. However, many children experience different parenting arrangements, don't they? There is divorce. Parents die. Single parenthood is more and more common. And, I had many women in my life who would, of course, adore my child. I think children have to deal all the time with difficulty ... being too tall, too fat, wearing glasses. None of this equates with the mother issue in importance, but the bottom line is they cope. We would cope together.

I came to realize, about this time, that there were many reasons to hesitate about becoming a gay father. I could spend all my time being overwhelmed by the questions or I could decide to do it because I really wanted to and I knew in my heart I could do a good job. I am so grateful that I did not persuade myself to back out.

Getting Jenny

Getting Jenny, after the "decision" was not an easy task. At that time, several years ago, it was much more difficult than it is today. Attorneys, believe it or not, did not jump at the chance to represent me as a potential father who was gay. However, I found one (who had to think it over a bit before making a decision) and she was wonderful to me.

Jenny's birth mother was five months pregnant when we agreed that I would adopt the child-to-be. She was unable to provide for a child and wanted to find a loving, caring home for him/her. I think she was intrigued by me and my "story" and, although she had moments when she wavered, it didn't ever appear to be for any reason other than her own.

Jenny was born two months premature. She weighed less than four pounds at birth and remained in the hospital for a month as they tried to get her weight up. During this time, her birth mother had a chance to waver some more, which made for a very insecure month, believe me! Nonetheless, I visited every day and fed her and changed her and talked to her and then went out and shopped for her. I was in heaven. A very nervous heaven.

Finally, the day came and we waited for the birth mother to sign the papers that would allow me to take Jenny out of the hospital. (Ordinarily, this is done ASAP, but since she was in the hospital for a long time, it was postponed.) As soon as the social worker came in with the papers, I took Jenny and drove home. Many of my friends were there helping to "get ready" and what a day it became! And, it has only gotten better since then.

It really did not take very long to get into the rhythm of caring for a baby. When a baby needs changing, you don't have much of a choice . . . you just do it! Same with crying, holding, bathing, feeding and all the rest. It was "interesting" to see how unbelievably fast you can fall in love with another human being and totally forget what life was like before.

To me, the point was (and still is) that I thought I'd be a terrific parent and any child that came to me would be very, very loved.

From the first, Jenny has been a warm and loving and spectacular addition to my life. Being needed 24 hours a day was a new idea for me. Up until then I only had to think of what I wanted to do . . . where I wanted to go. Now, I had bottles, formula, diapers, carseats, playpens and *many* changes of clothes to take with me each and every time I went out. Until I got the hang of it, I looked like a gypsy running around with packages and bags and a baby on my back trying to stuff it all into the car. Believe me, I figured it out quickly.

Being a Parent

Being a parent is being a parent, folks. Gay or straight doesn't matter when your child needs changing, feeding or wants to be held. It's wonderful, it's exhausting, it's thrilling and it's very consuming of your time and your emotions . . . no matter what your sexual identity.

The issues, I have found, really lie within *us*!

I have been accused of being a Pollyanna when it comes to "being accepted" into the mainstream of society as an openly gay man. I realize that I am very lucky to be living in a major city. I also realize that unless we, as gay and lesbian people, are open and honest with the people we meet, no matter where we may live, there will never be an "easy" time for us. We can easily be "invisible" and no one would know anything about us. People can meet us, become our friends and work with us, without ever knowing that they even *met* a gay or lesbian person. When that happens, though, people that have all their preconceived ideas about who we are and what "we" look like, have no basis to change that view. Because they don't even know that they have met us . . . they cannot go home and tell their husbands or wives (or . . .?) and say, "Honey, you won't believe this, but you know that guy that we sat with at the company picnic? . . . Yes, the one with the baby. Do you know that he's gay? I know . . . we really liked him. What do you think . . . he sure isn't like I expected a gay man to be!"

So, in my life with Jenny, I have been very upfront with people. In "baby gym" and in nursery school and in kindergarten and pretty much wherever we have ventured.

In addition to my own strong views about this subject, I also felt it would be very wrong of me to lie . . . because I would never want Jenny to grow up feeling that I was in any way ashamed of who I was. How could I hope to bring up a child who could respect everyone's choices and just like them (or not) based on who they were . . . if I was lying to people about who I was?

When Jenny was three months old, my luck showed itself once again and I met and fell in love with a wonderful man, Spencer Howard. He was thrown into a brand new relationship and a brand new baby . . . and, I guess he liked it, because he is still here and is now Jenny's other dad.

I believe I was lucky because having a baby is not every single gay man's idea of a wonderful time. There were some guys that I met early on who were very interested in me, but when they found out about the infant in the crib they sort of turned pale. (Actually, there was a time when I was on a very nice date and we were in the living room and the music was soft and the candles were flickering along with the fireplace and we looked into each other's eyes and . . . you guessed it! . . . diaper time. So much for that date!)

Having been single for a few years, and liking it fine, I really wasn't looking. You know the old saying? When you don't look, there it is. Well, there it was!! And Jenny and I have been very lucky indeed to have Spencer join our family.

Spencer Howard is an only child and he was brought up by his mother, after his father left. I have a brother and a sister and their respective spouses and several nieces and nephews . . . and a myriad of cousins and aunts and uncles. We're a very noisy family. Spencer is a fairly quiet sort. Spencer really had a lot to get used to!

All relationships take time to grow, and ours did as well. But Jenny seemed to hurry things up a bit. Our "courtship" was unusual. Instead of lots of moonlight dinners and dancing until dawn we had Gerber dinners and bottles through the night. (No breast feeding jokes, please . . . we've heard them all!) It was unusual . . . but it was fabulous. I wouldn't have believed it then, but I *miss* getting up at night. It's a great time.

Being a gay parent did involve a period of adjustment for many of our friends who were clearly not used to the idea of having a baby around. When we were invited out, we had to decide when it was appropriate to go alone and when we didn't want to leave Jenny. Although most new parents go through this, too, they usually have many more friends in the same boat . . . we did not! So, if we were going to a casual dinner or brunch, we made sure it was alright for Jenny to be there and when it was a night out . . . we didn't. Still, imagine being invited to a casual "during the week" dinner . . . with 6 or 8 single friends. Ready to dish and gossip and then . . . in we come with a portable playpen and toys and bottles and blankets . . . our friends went through a lot. (I think they loved it!)

All of the fears and all of the questions seemed to take care of themselves. As we got more used to being parents, so did those around us.

It's amazing how quickly you learn what to do. You have no books to study from . . . you just wing it. And you get *lots* of advice from your family and your married friends, as well. And just as in the rest of your life, some of the advice is welcome, and some of it . . .!

Travelling out of the country with Jenny for the first time was quite a challenging experience. I had been cautioned about the possibility that someone might think I was one of those dads fleeing from a custody decision with my stolen child. I carried a notarized statement to the effect that I was Jenny's sole legal parent and that I didn't need spousal permission to be travelling with her. Trying to board the plane for France, I was stopped and almost refused entry because I hadn't done the papers "correctly." They apparently needed to state that she had been adopted only by me and that there were no other "claims" for custody. I hadn't thought that was necessary. I also was supposed to bring a copy of her birth certificate for the same reasons. Eventually, the supervisor came out, and after much negotiation he was convinced that I was telling the truth, and we were allowed to board. I was certain, after that, always to have it "correctly"!

Once in France there were other incidents. One hotel keeper demanded to know where the mother was. In very limited French, I tried to explain *le adoption*. Then he wanted to know if we were "sure" we wanted one big bed instead of twin beds. We looked at him, smiled, and told him we were sure. And then, "whose baby is this again?" We weren't sure if he really thought we were kidding him or not. (Those *crazee* Americans!) His face was a study in perplexity. Where's the camera when you need it?

Entering School

When the time came for Jenny to enter preschool, we chose a school that was very good and very near our home. I had to go and interview with them and I went alone. I was surprised at how nervous I was.

After the tour of the school was over and I was sitting across from the woman in charge, I knew it was time. I told her the "story" and waited. She said it was a "first" for this school, which is a Jewish preschool, but she had no problem with it. She also said she would be happy to talk to the teacher of the class Jenny would be in. I said I thought I should do that. So, I did. No problem again.

Was it all going to be this easy?

The answer was yes, and no. Although there was to be no negativity shown toward us by anyone, the first announcements are always hard and very nervous-making. Take our first Parent Association meeting, for example. Both Spencer and I were apprehensive as we prepared to get dressed. I remember asking him if he thought all parents felt this way. We decided we didn't care if they did or not. We were nervous. Period.

We had an "ally" who was vice president of the parents group. Fern is an attractive, married woman who runs a very successful theatrical casting agency. The older of Fern's (and Larry's) sons was in Jenny's class. He was adopted, also. We became good friends early on. She was our anchor that night as all the parents were seated in a circle. We were asked to introduce ourselves and tell our child's name and the class they were in . . . it began: "Hi, I'm Colette and my son Evan is in Carrie's class" on to "Hi, I'm Gary and Evan is my son, too" to "Hi, I'm Linda and my daughter is . . . and Hi, I'm her husband." You get the idea. Then, "I'm Jeff and my daughter, Jenny, is in Carrie's class." Followed by, "Hi, I'm Spencer and Jenny is my daughter, too . . . in Carrie's class." The sudden looks were flying around the room like flies.

The meeting broke into discussion groups. The main group was centered around our friend, Fern, who was heard to exclaim "What do you *think* they meant? Use your imagination!" And the ice was broken and from then on Jenny started her schooling with lots of friends coming over for play dates. With our increased parent involvement, we became friends with several of the couples.

As Jenny continued on into elementary school, we continued to encourage friendships with the other parents. Our feelings were that we very often may have to initiate the relationships more than we might ordinarily, but we found that all the kids and their parents were just as happy to get together with us as we were with them. So, again, we have had a lot of fun meeting new couples and getting together.

Life With Jenny

It also is important to us to socialize with other gay/lesbian families. Although this may be harder to do in some cities, it is becoming more and more common to find gay men adopting and lesbians either adopting or having children biologically. Jenny needs to see other kids in situations like hers to make sure she doesn't get the sense of being totally unusual. (Just a little unusual is fine, we think.)

My family was very welcoming to Jenny and she is as much a part of all the cousins, etc., as anyone else in our family. We speak openly to all my nephews and nieces (we do, however, speak to whatever age level they are at, of course) and they all know she is adopted and that Uncle Jeff and Uncle Spencer are her two dads. When they ask us questions, we try to answer as honestly as possible. My siblings have generally left it to our discretion when we talk to their kids.

Taking Jenny to the park, to museums, to plays and really, just about anywhere, really has become the "special times" in our lives.

Having a daughter is an indescribable joy. Having been single when I adopted Jenny, it seemed a miracle that I was able to actually do that. Being a gay couple with an unusual twist has been an extraordinary experience, fun, satisfying and *never dull!*

If you are Gay or Lesbian be proud and live your life as honestly as you know how. You can have a family or not. But it is your choice. If you ever thought about adopting a child and you felt it was "not in the cards" because of your sexuality — think again. It's possible. It's wonderful. It's worth it.

AGING: A SEASON OF GRACE

The Older Lesbian

Del Martin and Phyllis Lyon

Aging is evolutionary. Sometimes it creeps up on you, despite the usual reminders: at 30 you are "over the hill." "Life begins at 40." Over 50 is "no-person land." Over 60 it's "down-hill" all the way.

Del first became aware of her own aging when at 30 she was editor of the *Daily Construction News* in Seattle. Her staff, all in their early 20s, thought she was "ancient." As a couple we became aware of our aging when we read Jess Stearn's book *The Grapevine* in 1964.[1] It came as a jolt. He referred to us as two "middle-aged" women who had founded the Daughters of Bilitis (DOB), the first national lesbian organization in the United States.

Lesbians in our current age bracket (late 60s and early 70s) grew up in a time when sexuality was never discussed — let alone homosexuality. In isolation, thinking "I am the only one," most of us struggled with our sexual identity. Once we acknowledged we were gay or lesbian to ourselves we then had to struggle with self-acceptance. It wasn't easy to maintain one's self-esteem when all the literature available described "perverts" who were supposed to be like you but with whom you couldn't possibly identify.

While there were never any laws against homosexuality per se, there were laws against certain sexual acts. The church declared us immoral and psychiatrists said we had a personality disorder. With those three strikes against us, many, as a matter of self-preservation, burrowed underground, pretended to be heterosexual, lied about having lovers of the opposite sex, met furtively in gay bars or hoped that "the one" you cared for would surreptitiously convey that the feeling was mutual. If you

---

[1] *Jess Stearn*, The Grapevine. *Garden City, New York: Doubleday, 1964.*

111

were exposed as gay, you might lose your friends and family, your job or career. There was also the ever-present threat of blackmail.

In response to our book *Lesbian/Woman*, first published in 1972,[2] we received hundreds of letters from isolated and lonely older lesbians who rejoiced in their new knowledge that there were others like themselves. Some had rejected the gay life for the more respected and accepted heterosexual family life only to find that as the years went by their longing for a close woman-to-woman relationship seemed almost unbearable. Many of these wives were waiting until their children grew up and left home, or their husbands died, in order to fulfill their own needs and desires.

A couple in Utah wrote: "We are in our fifties, have been together for 18 years, but have never declared our love for each other in front of a third party. When we shut our doors at night we shut the world out. We have no gay friends that we know of. We are looking for friendships and support, but in the lesbian organizations we've contacted we find only badge-wearing, drum-beating, foot-stomping social reformers. They consider our conservative life `oppressed,' and we think of their way of life as `flagrant.' There must be more like us, but how do we meet them?" The invisibility of closeted lesbians prevented their meeting each other. We put a lesbian couple in touch with another couple in Kansas. It turned out that two of the women already knew each other — on the job.

Other mid-life lesbians also wanted to know how to meet their peers. We suggested starting a group for older lesbians. "But how can you do that when you don't know any other older lesbians?" asked Ev Howe, an old time DOB activist. So in the mid 1970s we agreed to convene a meeting at our home and invited every San Francisco Bay Area lesbian we knew over 45 years of age.

The trouble began by setting the cut-off age at 45. The 40-year olds were upset they weren't included. So the age was dropped to 40. Then the 39-year olds complained. Eventually the age limit was lowered to 30. Probably the younger ones cared more about being left out than the "preference for older women" that they claimed. The group also rejected the name "Older Lesbians." Slightly Older Lesbians (or SOL) lives on in various groups around the country.

After that we began to receive requests to write and speak on the subject of "older lesbians" — presumably from our own experience and perspective. When Betty Berzon asked us to write a chapter for the first edition of *Positively Gay* we fit the category, but had little overall knowledge of the topic.

Our personal observations in that edition were: "Admittedly we were reluctant to apply the term `old' to ourselves. It is used to compare people and it has a lot more to do with mind-set than wrinkles or gray hair," we said. "Turning 50 — the half-century mark, had given us pause, however; the years left are definitely fewer. Death took on a reality it never had before — not necessarily ominous or fearsome. We believe in everlasting universal consciousness and we believe that death is a

---

[2] *Del Martin & Phyllis Lyon*, Lesbian/Woman. *San Francisco: Glide and New York: Bantam, 1972.*

transition. But we are much more aware of our time left on earth, of financing our retirement, of protecting the other financially when one dies, of the many things we still wish to accomplish.[3]

We had our wills made when Del's daughter was a teenager. When she reached mid-life and our grandchildren adulthood, we decided it was time to update our wills. We also drew up powers of attorney for decisions regarding health and financial matters in case one or the other was incapacitated. And, we attended a seminar on "How Not To Be a Bag Lady in Your Old Age" sponsored by San Francisco's Community College. One topic of concern was how to protect the other if one of us was stricken with a catastrophic illness. A lawyer from Legal Services for the Elderly said, in the seminar, that a married couple would have to spend down to the limit of cash assets allowed before Medicaid would kick in. He assured that the family home would be left intact as long as the other spouse resided there. We asked "What about us? — a lesbian couple whose home is held in joint tenancy." He hadn't been asked that question before. He paused a moment, pointing out that, no matter the longevity of our relationship, legally we are strangers! "In your case you'd probably have to sell half the house," he concluded. That would be difficult to do with one bedroom, two cats, and no inside doors except to the bathroom. The other option, we learned later, is to keep telling the authorities that the partner in the nursing home would be returning home.

The Literature on Lesbians and Aging

Our search of the literature for the 1979 edition of *Positively Gay* showed scant attention had been paid to lesbian and gay aging. Most studies concentrated on the etiology of homosexuality, presumably with the idea of stamping it out. We found particularly interesting a study on 25 lesbians over 60 conducted by a young lesbian, Chris Almvig, as part of her master's program in gerontological administration at the New York School for Social Research.[4] Subsequently we have discovered three additional studies: Mina Robinson's sample of 20 West Coast lesbians over 50 for her master's thesis at California State University, Dominguez Hills,[5] in 1979; Monika Kehoe, Ph.D., who gathered a sample of 100 lesbians over 60 in a study begun in 1980 and completed in 1984,[6] and Jean Quam, director of graduate

---

[3] *Del Martin & Phyllis Lyon. "The Older Lesbian" in Betty Berzon and Robert Leighton (eds.) Positively Gay. Millbrae, California: Celestial Arts, 1979.*
[4] *Chris Almvig, "The Invisible Minority: Aging and Lesbianism." New York: Utica College of Syracuse University, 1982.*
[5] *Mina Robinson (now Meyers), "The Older Lesbian," Master's thesis at California State University, Dominguez Hills, 1979.*
[6] *Monika Kehoe, Lesbians Over 60 Speak for Themselves. Journal of Homosexuality Vol. 16, Nos. 3/4, 1988. Harrington Park Press, 1989.*

studies at the University of Minnesota's School of Social Work, who surveyed 80 older gays and lesbians, which she reported in 1991.[7]

All the studies suffered from small samples which were self-selected and thus not representative of the lesbian community at large, especially since the majority of the subjects were Caucasian. For example, Chris Almvig distributed 2,500 questionnaires to lesbians and gay men and received a little over 300 responses — only about a quarter of them from lesbians. The reason for the low return from lesbians, she surmised, was that older lesbians tended to be in close monogamous relationships, had a closed circle of friends and didn't get involved in gay community activities; thus they were unaccustomed to any kind of "public" revelations about themselves outside their limited social networks.

Another problem, almost non-existent among gay men, Almvig found, was that many women refused to see their homosexuality for what it is. "I know a lesbian couple who have been together ten years who know only two other lesbians," she said. "They don't call themselves lesbians. They hate the word *gay*. They think they're in some special category and they think it's just really unusual that they found a very special woman in their life. They're in love with each other and it has nothing to do with being gay. There are a lot of older lesbians in this category — that's how much oppression has affected them." We used to call such women *lace curtain lesbians*, a way of saying they were too nice to be lesbians and had thus drawn the curtain of secrecy that separated them from their selves, their would-be friends and any potential support group.

Despite their shortcomings, the four studies are valuable for providing more knowledge of old lesbians than had been available before. As with Almvig's findings, Kehoe had many closeted (or mostly closeted) lesbians in her sample with some still married. For all the women studied isolation was a problem. Robinson's conclusions found that how closeted a lesbian is impacts on her life by creating isolation where she could have had support groups. Quam found that those closeted "tended to be the ones who were much more frightened about their aging."

The majority of those sampled felt positive about their lesbianism. In Kehoe's study 71 of the 100 felt *very* positive. A not surprising finding was that many felt that young lesbians discriminated against them. As one woman put it, "young lesbians are too busy with their lives to be close friends to old lesbians." A high percentage of older lesbians were interested in their own age group as lovers and friends (95% of Kehoe's sample associated with those within ten years of their own age). Quam's subjects felt that being lesbian helped in the aging process since coming out and accepting oneself usually tends to enhance psychological and spiritual resources.

Almvig had a significant number of subjects with relationships of 20 years or more. Kehoe's sample contained 43 out of 100 who were coupled. Average length of

[7] Jean Quam. *Interview with Barbara Brynstad*, Equal Time, *October 25-November 8, 1991. "Age-Related Expectations of Gay & Lesbian Older Adults,"* The Gerontologist. *June 1992.*

relationship was 13.5 years with the longest 56 years. Twenty of her sample had had long-term partners who had died. The women in Robinson's group all had at least one major relationship and all said they would prefer to be coupled, although not all of them would want to live with someone or be monogamous. Robinson's sample was quite feminist in responses and many suggested alternative ways of living in their older years such as collectives or agreeing with a friend to live together if neither had a lover.

Quam found that many older lesbians showed they were comfortable talking about who they are and what they are about. "Older lesbians appear to be taking on partners or living with other women and tend to have a much stronger network than heterosexual older women," she said.

Almvig had expected that lesbians who predated the gay and women's movements would assume butch-femme roles in their relationships. Surprisingly, those who did turned out to be very much the exception. From our experience in the 50s these roles were common among lesbians, particularly those who frequented gay bars. Since these bars were the only place we had in which to socialize, many of us acted out such roles because the lesbian sub-culture at the time appeared to require it. However, we did not necessarily carry on this role-playing in the privacy of our homes. Knowing they will have to take care of themselves, usually without family support, many lesbians know how to perform tasks associated with either gender. Very few in any of the studies mentioned here were into butch-femme roles and seldom did any of the women go to gay bars.

Almvig's lesbians were not interested in gay retirement villages and those who were preferred living with both women and men. Kehoe's subjects, on the other hand, were somewhat positive to a lesbian retirement community but neutral to a mixed lesbian/gay community. Robinson's women were enthusiastic about a mixed gay, lesbian, women's retirement community. On the subject of nursing homes, most of the subjects were for lesbian only nursing homes although they really didn't want to deal with the idea of nursing homes at all. Quam's sample did, however, have "wonderful fantasies about how they would like an all-lesbian nursing home or some sort of alternative housing that was all lesbian or all women."

Robinson found her single lesbian women had more lesbian friends than the lesbian couples did, and few had any non-lesbian friends. In Kehoe's sample 61 had almost exclusively lesbian friends while 30 also had a few straight women friends. Few of the women had male friends. Sixty of Kehoe's sample belonged (or had belonged) to lesbian or lesbian/gay groups.

Sexuality was still alive and well for some of the women while for others the urge waned after 60. One woman in Robinson's group, a 73-year-old, said she had been in a relationship for 40 years with no sex for the last 30 years. In a new relationship now, she said she felt 35 and sexual again. Of the 100 lesbians in Kehoe's study, 66 were currently sexually active. Of those celibate, two-thirds said it was not by choice. In later years the women seemed to find sex an important part of their lives but not a main part.

Getting Together

Chris Almvig became the founder of New York City's Senior Action in a Gay Environment (SAGE) in 1979, the first center providing services for lesbian and gay seniors in the country. Because of our age and interest she put us on her national advisory board.

Mina Robinson was instrumental in creating the first West Coast Celebration and Old Lesbian Conference at Dominguez Hills, California, in 1987. Monika Kehoe was an old lesbian herself when she did her survey of 100 lesbians over 60 and her preliminary nationwide survey of 50 lesbians over 65 which was started in 1980 and completed in 1983. Jean Quam's study was reported on in late 1991. She found especially poignant comments written by women who came out in their 50s and 60s and were worried about how to tell their children and grandchildren.

In the 1970s we were invited to an early meeting of Gays Over Forty (G40+), a San Francisco group which was trying to establish a social network for older lesbians and gays and provide support for those who are bedridden or confined to their homes. The few lesbians involved had been closeted all their lives and had not been active in the gay community. Most were retired and reasonably comfortable financially. Though relieved of the pressure to be circumspect because of their jobs, they were still reluctant to mix with those they perceived to be too open and too militant. We suggested they might make contact with more older lesbians and gays by requesting that San Francisco's Downtown Senior Center schedule regular meetings for gays and that they be publicized among all other senior centers. A delegation from G40+ did approach the executive director of the downtown center but not unexpectedly he turned them down. They accepted this denial without protest. Unfortunately they refused to seek help from the organized gay community. Unaccustomed to being aggressive about their needs, a good idea went begging.

Services

It is difficult to reach, organize, advocate and provide services for lesbians who are invisible in the general population. By the 80s we thought it would be easier for older lesbians to come out. But when Del received the newsletter announcing her speaking engagement for OWL, the lesbian version of Older Women's League, she found herself referred to as the co-author of *Lesbian/Woman*. Even *The Ladder* published by the Daughters of Bilitis in the scary 50s used the "L" word. The magazine's contents were protected by the proverbial plain brown wrapper.

Carole Migden, now a member of the San Francisco Board of Supervisors, was, in 1980, executive director of Operation Concern, a lesbian/gay mental health agency. She took up the challenge of trying to develop services for senior lesbians and gays. She enlisted Del and others to take our case to the Commission on the Aging. After a couple of tries the commission, which controlled government funds allocated for seniors, came around in 1982. Gay and Lesbian Outreach to Elders (GLOE) became a project of Operation Concern which served as its fiscal agent. We were invited to serve on GLOE's Advisory Board. Thus began a new phase in our lives as activist aging lesbians.

We had political expertise to contribute to the group. The others had fascinating backgrounds and all sorts of talent to offer. Many older lesbians were service-oriented and knew the ropes of the social services bureaucracy.

Almost immediately we found discontent among our new colleagues. Young gerontologists, who were hired by Operation Concern, ran our program in accordance with government regulations required by the Commission on the Aging and their own academic notions of the needs of their elders.

Our first concern became having representation on the hiring committee. We figured that those over 50 should have an edge. It seemed strange to have twenty-year-olds running our programs. We were able, eventually, to have program co-ordinators in their 60s which felt much better to us.

Older vs. Old

Personally, we have traded the word older for old in referring to ourselves. We have had some excellent mentors in helping us come to terms with the realities of old age and ageism, for instance, columnist Page Smith said, "Old age is inevitably going to have the last word. What I'm counseling against is aiding and abetting it." He went on, "A temptation peculiar to old age is blaming old age for a host of things not necessarily connected with it at all. It is a vice indulged in, I suspect, especially by the `new old' men and women in their 60s and early 70s who are relatively inexperienced at being old. . . ."[8]

Smith used memory lapse as an example. Most people who are unable to recall a name or date readily would say, "It will come to me if I don't try. Just give me a minute. I feel so foolish." But when it happens to someone old, there seems to be an irrepressible impulse to say, "I can't remember, I know it so well, I must be getting senile." That's blaming old age, Smith pointed out. We are learning to say, "We have a lot more data in our unconscious mind's computer. Today it must be on overload. It will come to me."

The first West Coast Celebration and Old Lesbian Conference had an indelible impact on our lives. Shevy Healey started our attitude restructuring: "Such remarks as `You're only as old as you feel,' `You're in good shape for your age,' or `That makes you look younger' are not compliments, but are indications of ageism, of equating youth with beauty and desirability; old with sickness, ugliness and powerlessness."

Barbara MacDonald, author with Cynthia Rich of *Look Me in the Eye: Old Women, Aging and Ageism,* added, "Our own panic about what's ahead is the linchpin of ageism. We have become the old woman we have been taught to dread. But at each plateau of life, whether it be 40 or 60 or 70, we find it isn't here yet. What we are

[8] *Page Smith, columnist, "This World," Sunday supplement, San Francisco Chronicle, p.73, June 25, 1989.*

experiencing is the cumulative deposit of the uncertainty of life. Illness, being confined to a wheel chair, loss of sight or hearing are not inherent risks of old age, but rather inherent risks at any age." MacDonald also pointed out the tendency of younger lesbians to ignore the old. For example, she cited *Plexus* which referred to its readers as between the ages of 18 and 54.

The organizers of the conference established 60 years of age and over as old and participants proudly displayed their age on their name tags. The Steering Committee defined the conference goals: "To look at the unique contributions to the process of aging already made by old lesbians; to act politically coming from our own daring and dreaming; to look at how ageism affects each of us; to dispel the illusion of inclusion; to find our common voice, to define our own turf."

Since lesbians, like other women, have been conditioned to the "female preoccupation of age-passing" (as the late Baba Copper put it),[9] there has been a good deal of healthy controversy over the use of the word "old" before, during and since the first Old Lesbian Conference. Those who attended had their consciousness raised about ageism and began to reclaim the word old.

At the second Old Lesbian Conference, in 1989, at California State University, San Francisco, the recurring theme was "Old Is In — Ageism Is Out." Participants formed a national network, Old Lesbian Organizing Committee (OLOC), and signed petitions demanding representation (which was granted) on the Steering Committee of the National Lesbian Conference held in Atlanta in 1991.

OLOC sponsored a preconference seminar in Atlanta for old lesbians and hosted a dance open to all ages. A large contingent of old lesbians dressed in white with purple sashes marched proudly behind their banner into the opening plenary session of the national conference. The women, most of whom came out in their 50s and 60s, displayed an air of confidence and militancy as a group, saying in essence, "We are old. We are strong. Don't tread on us."

Baba Copper pointed out the contradiction between the interests of old women and those who earn their living from agencies that study or serve the old. "These agencies get their funds from politicians, foundations and individuals who must be convinced that the client groups are terribly needy — unable to take care of themselves, isolated, pitiful, helpless."[10] Ageism is built into the system. It perpetuates the notion that old age is little more than a terminal disease. Social services are linked too often with medical services, forcing old women into the role of patients. Senior Centers are designed exclusively for heterosexuals. But old lesbians, gays and bisexuals also need to find friendship networks, support groups and life-fulfilling programs, not just preparation for death.

---

[9] *Baba Copper*, Over the Hill: Reflections of Ageism Between Women. *Freedom, California: Crossing Press, 1988.*
[10] *Ibid. p.95.*

Inventing Our Lives

We have had to invent our lives as lesbians through its many phases: struggling with the isolation of being different; achieving self-acceptance despite societal hostility; defining our own relationships as couples; creating our own communities; media, institutions, national and international networks; opening our own space in the world.

Now we are inventing our old age — reclaiming the word old in its positive sense, just as we did with the terms lesbian and dyke. Old denotes chronological age, a stage of life which can be a beginning, tying up loose ends, learning and changing, doing things we had always wanted to do but never seemed to have the time, creating new endings.

Betty Berzon, editor of this volume, wrote in *The Advocate*, "I understand the fear of aging that runs like an earthquake fault under the lives of gay and lesbian people caught up in the cult of youth. But dismissing people who have aged is no way to buy a stay of execution from aging yourself. It should be working in just the opposite way. Integrating older gay people into your life could well be a counterphobic move. You conquer the fear of losing the youth that feels so essential by giving yourself the opportunity to find out that aging is one of nature's most valuable rewards."[11]

Despite the seeming separation of old lesbians in drawing the line at 60 and their militancy against ageist remarks and attitudes of the young, a strong pull still exists toward an intergenerational lesbian community. GLOE has ties to Lavender Youth Recreation and Information Center (LYRIC) and Lambda Delta Lambda, the lesbian sorority at San Francisco State University. LYRIC puts on an annual pancake breakfast, a fundraiser which brings together lesbians, gays and bisexuals across the age spectrum, and the sorority sisters are helpful at old lesbian socials and dances. Included in the program of the fourth annual Texas Lesbian Conference in Austin in 1991 was the workshop on "Our Youth: Baby Dykes: the Facts behind the Fiction." The panel of young lesbians age 17–21 talked about their lives and isolation. They said they look to older lesbians for information, history, socializing and mentorship.[12] This would seem a possible turning point in relations between younger and older lesbian women.

So now that 60 has been established as old, we find some "slightly younger lesbians" in their 50s counting the years until they can join the ranks of old lesbians. As we continue to invent our lives as lesbians we continue to bridge the generation gap.

---

[11] Betty Berzon, *"Why are older gays and lesbians treated like pariahs?"* The Advocate, Jan. 28, 1992.
[12] Del Martin & Phyllis Lyon, Lesbian/Woman (updated). Volcano, California: Volcano Press, 1991.

Resources For Older Lesbians

Organizations

GLEAM (Gay & Lesbian Elders Active in Minnesota). Get-togethers 2nd Sunday of month 1–4 p.m. at 1515 Park Ave., Minneapolis. Phone Margaret Dousett, 612/724-8021.

GLOE (Gay & Lesbian Outreach to Elders), 1853 Market St., San Francisco, CA 94103. Phone 415/626-7000. Old lesbian support group, dances, reading & writing groups, informational lectures.

OLOBA (Old Lesbians of the Bay Area), c/o GLOE. Tea dances, consciousness raising on ageism, activism.

OLOC (Old Lesbians Organizing For Change), P.O. Box 980422, Houston, TX 77098. National network.

Options for Women Over 40. 3543 18th St., San Francisco, CA 94110. Phone 415/431-6405. Lesbian groups for personal support and employment.

SAGE (Senior Action in a Gay Environment), 208 W. 13th St., New York, NY 10011.

SAGE, P.O. Box 4071, San Diego CA 92164. Phone 619/282-1395.

Publications

Broomstick, 3543 18th St., San Francisco, CA 94110. National feminist political journal by, for and about women over 40.

Golden Threads, P.O. Box 3177, Burlington, VT 05401-0031. Contact quarterly for lesbians over 50.

Wishing Well, P.O. Box 1711, Santa Rosa, CA 95403. Contact quarterly for lesbians of all ages.

Books

Marcy Adelman (ed.), *Long Time Passing: Lives of Older Lesbians*. Boston: Alyson Publications, 1986.

Barbara MacDonald with Cynthia Rich, *Look Me in the Eye: Old Women, Aging and Ageism*. San Francisco: Spinsters, Ink, 1981.

Jane Rule, *Memory Board*. Tallahassee, FL: Naiad Press, 1987.

May Sarton, *At Seventy*. New York: W.W. Norton and Toronto: George J. McLeod, 1984.

Video

West Coast Crones: A Glimpse into the Lives of Nine Old Lesbians. A Madeline Muir/Wolfe Video Production, P.O. Box 64, New Almaden, CA 95042. Phone 408/268-6782.

The Older Gay Man

Raymond M. Berger and James J. Kelly

We were sitting in the "blue room." We were authors of the first studies of older gay men, and now we waited to be interviewed by our television talk show host, for a segment on "Growing Older Gay."

We had carefully reviewed our findings about older gay men with the show's producer. We told him that: most older gay men were not generally alienated from family and friends; they continued to have satisfying sex lives with age-appropriate partners; they were not prematurely old; and, that adapting to the aging process was easier for gay men than it was for straight men.

As we watched the TV monitor in the moments before our appearance, we heard the following: "Gay men who grow old. They are lonely and isolated. Since they can no longer find lovers, they look to younger men, who are not interested in them. At forty, they are over the hill. As tough as it is for anyone to adjust to growing older, it is doubly difficult for homosexual men."

We learned a lesson that day: stereotypes die hard.

What we have learned is that negative stereotypes about the anguish of gay aging, can create negative expectations on the part of older gay men and those who care about them. For example, gay men who expect to be rejected by others, sometimes bring on that very reaction by their defensive attitudes. But, if negative expectations can bring on a lonely old age, can't positive expectations create a fulfilling old age? As gerontologists and as people who are aging, that has been the hardest lesson in our own lives. The ball is in our court.

We began to study older gay men by spending time with them. We both felt odd and out of place. We wondered if older men would accept us into their circles, and if it was possible for us, as younger men, to understand their worlds. When we

121

went on to study these men through oral histories, interviews and questionnaires, we did gain an understanding of their experiences. But it was an intellectual understanding, because we ourselves were not old. An outsider's view is always incomplete. As one older man described it: "it is like standing outside an oven door, looking in."

Then something remarkable happened. We too became older. We proved the aphorism that "older folks are the one minority group to which we all aspire." We think we might now have some of the insights of aging, that we always admired in our older peers. (We are both in our forties, admittedly with a lot of growing old yet to do.) So, now that we have joined the very group we studied, what do we think about gay aging? Do we still believe the things we said when we were in our twenties?

We believe we were right about some things, and wrong about others.

What We Know Now

We were right that those older men who project positive attitudes about their lives, create positive lives. We were right that there are some gay men who are resentful, bitter and utterly alone, but that these men are not typical. We were right that surviving the challenges of being gay and proud in our twenties, gave us an edge in being proud of who we are later in life. We were right that young gay men are usually less attracted to older men, and that deeper and more satisfying relationships happen when we value the soul and personality, in addition to the body. And we were right about one of the least advertised benefits of being older: we are happier because we care less about what others think, and more about how we feel.

We were wrong about some things too. We were wrong in advising older gay men who live in rural areas to move to cities in order to find support. Ray loves living in the country. He has no intention of giving up his country life because he is gay. And support can come from straight people as well as gay.

We were wrong in saying that coming out is easier for older gay men. True, older men, especially those over 65, have fewer worries about being "out" at work, or about failing to meet the expectations of parents. But being "out" about our sexual orientation is always a complex ballet, and depends more on our circumstances than our age. For example, a gay man who wants custody of his child or grandchild, or one who works in a homophobic environment, might want to be cautious about being "out" at any age.

Like everyone else, we underestimated the impact of health problems on the quality of our lives. The AIDS epidemic has hit hardest among the age groups who are in, or will soon enter, "middle age." For millions of gay men, this disease has radically altered expectations about being older. And it has made us realize that subjective age is as important in our lives, as is chronological age.

It is increasingly difficult to maintain our balance as we grow older, because our bodies seem less and less able to stand up to the effects of time. We believe this is because our modern way of life, with its pollution and stress, has damaged the immune systems of all of us. So, it is more common today for the "young old" — those of us in our forties, fifties, and sixties — to do battle with cardiovascular disease, cancer, and auto-immune disorders like diabetes. These challenges can be faced with positive attitudes and constructive adaptation. But surviving well into old age is as dicey now as it has ever been.

As young gerontologists, we were naive about the indignities of physical aging. We didn't know what it felt like to lose hair on the tops of our heads, only to sprout it in unlikely and embarrassing places on our bodies. Until we looked in the mirror and saw the coming signs of aging in our own faces, we didn't *really* know. Nor did we understand how difficult it can be to depend on others when we became incapacitated.

But we happened upon an unexpected discovery. It was best described by Ken, an 80 year old friend of ours, who does volunteer work with nursing home patients. He was sent to drive another elderly gentleman to a doctor's appointment. Apparently, Ken was not what the gentleman expected. With a gesture of disgust, the gentleman blurted out to Ken, "Why, you are nothing but an old man!" Ken responded, "Hey, don't judge me by this shell!"

We didn't know that our true self is spirit, and that our bodies are only vehicles for carrying that spirit. Experiencing the aging of our bodies led us to this understanding, and to a deeper awareness of our true selves and our place in the universe.

Research Findings

Historically, younger gay men have looked upon older gays with a sense of horror about their own futures. Arnie Kantrowitz described his impressions of an older gay man:

> *I never knew his name. He lived somewhere on the floor above us, rather anonymously . . . I only knew a few things about him. He wore too many rings. He liked cats and Mozart. He was gentle-mannered and fastidious, and he scared me half to death. That was because he was everything I was afraid I was going to be: an 'auntie.'*

In the course of our research we had the opportunity to interview scores of older gay men, and to talk to hundreds of others. We listened with fascination to stories about being gay in the 1920s, 1930s, and 1940s. Many of our respondents talked about the difficulties of being gay, of concerns about careers, relationships with family members, and the universally accepted requirement to conceal.

But with few exceptions, our older respondents spoke with satisfaction and calm acceptance of their lives. There were wonderful stories of passionate love affairs, the excitement of furtive social gatherings, the challenge of early efforts for gay rights in the 1950s. The Second World War was an especially important time for many of today's older gay men. With the nation's attention turned to fighting the "good war," and with an easing of traditional sex roles, as women back home turned to the war effort, homosexuals too, were granted a new sense of freedom. The military was a setting in which many of our respondents met new friends and lovers, had wonderful adventures, and attended openly gay social gatherings.

The post-war period led to the McCarthy era, and a return to repression. Some of the men to whom we spoke found themselves dishonorably discharged from the service, despite their brave contributions to the nation's defense. But the advances of the war period could not be turned back. Gay bars and social clubs began to appear in the large cities, and fledgling gay rights groups such as the Mattachine Society took root. A new community had emerged.

Today's aging gay man faces a world much different from yesterday's counter- parts. For the older gay man who wants involvement with other gays, there are almost endless opportunities. Most large cities, and many smaller ones, have social and political organizations for groups as diverse as retired teachers, couples, and those interested in leather clothing. And, as the gay population ages, and as the AIDS epidemic helps us to value each other more, older gay men are more easily accepted in most corners of the gay community.

It was this setting, in the 1970s, in which we began our research into the lives of older gay men. What did we find? And what were the findings of other researchers?

Although a few older men fit the stereotype of lonely and anguished souls, they were a small minority. On a broad range of measures of psychological adjustment — including self-acceptance and anxiety — older gay men were, on the whole, well adjusted, and on some measures, they even scored more favorably than younger gay men. On a measure of Life Satisfaction, their scores were indistinguishable from those of the general population of their age peers.

Older gay men were less active socially than younger gays, but this did not seem to diminish their psychological adjustment or sense of well-being. Rather, it is probably an indication of the "settling in," that is a part of growing older for most people, gay and straight. And less involvement in social organizations does not mean that these older gay men were social isolates. The great majority of our older respondents had close friends and were well integrated into social networks. Two- fifths to one-half had lovers.

The information we gathered about the sex lives of older gay men, predates the AIDS era. Most of the men in our studies had active sex lives: they had regular sex, and reported overall satisfaction with their sex lives. If they differed at all from younger gays, it was that they had fewer partners, and used a narrower variety of sexual techniques. These characteristics may have served them well, in minimizing risks associated with sexual activity.

Early social scientists wrote about the problem of "accelerated aging" among gay men — that is, the notion that gay men become old prematurely. Presumably this is due to rejection by society and peers. The idea was probably based on the belief that gay men were only interested in each other for their sexual appeal, and the observation that only young men were considered desirable among gays. In reality, there is no evidence to support the notion of accelerated aging among gay men. And traditionally, a number of younger gay men take a particular interest in older men, for love, companionship, guidance, and occasionally, for financial support.

A New Perspective on Gay Aging

For years, the "experts" warned us about the disadvantages of "gay life."

These messages came to us from heterosexual clinicians and researchers, who failed to understand the lives of gay people. For one thing, their conclusions were based on their experiences with gay people who had trouble in their lives: psychotherapy patients, those admitted to psychiatric hospitals, and those apprehended for criminal offenses. Also, heterosexual writers were outsiders looking in. Often they even failed to ask the right questions.

For example, in an otherwise thorough study of gay men, Kinsey Institute sociologists Martin Weinberg and Colin Williams, completely missed an opportunity to understand the concept of "lover," which is a feature of gay relationships understood by gays themselves. So, although they asked their gay respondents about ongoing sexual relationships, they never asked them if they had a lover. The results were predictable: a distorted view of gay men, incapable of commitment to a life partner.

When gay people started writing about themselves, a new perspective emerged. This trend was picked up by new experts — mental health professionals, psychologists, sociologists and social workers — who were influenced by more accurate views of homosexuality, views which took account of gay people's own perspectives. This was also true of academics who began to study older gay people, and to develop theories about them.

These newer theorists — and we were among them — suggested something startling. They suggested that being gay might actually be an *advantage* in coping with the aging process.

There are several reasons to believe that gay people have an edge on adjusting well to growing older. One of the most difficult aspects of coping with aging, is learning to master the stigma that our culture assigns to older people, who are seen as less attractive, less capable and useful, and therefore less valuable. Heterosexuals usually face this stigma for the first time when they grow older. But for gay men, learning self-acceptance in the face of societal stigma, is a replay. Every gay man has had to learn how to value himself — how to survive as a self-respecting human being — in the face of the sometimes overwhelming stigma of being gay. And this mastery process usually occurs by the mid to late twenties. So most gay men have a successful coping pattern which they can follow in mastering negative societal messages about being old.

Gay men may have other early life experiences which help them when they get older. In addition to mastering societal stigma, they also master what we can call a "crisis of independence." And again, this usually happens in early adulthood. Heterosexual men know that once they leave the protection of their families of origin, it won't be too long before they are supported within their own families of procreation. Except in unusual circumstances, they have no reason to believe that family and friends will abandon them. The world looks different to a gay man entering adulthood. He cannot take it for granted that social support systems will be there for him. He is less likely to marry, and even if he does, he is always keenly aware that his status as a homosexual, may jeopardize the support he has always relied on, from family and friends. Happily, this is changing, as societal attitudes about homosexuality have become more positive. Still, few gay men can take their social support systems for granted. That is why gay men so often become adept at caring for all their own needs — emotional as well as practical needs, from earning an income to decorating one's home.

As heterosexual men age into their 60s and 70s, they also face a crisis of independence. It may be due to financial needs, which become great when they find themselves living on fixed incomes. Eventually, if they survive, they will need to become more independent, as they lose other elderly friends and relatives, as well as their spouse. This transition is difficult for any older person. But gay men may be more experienced in mastering their own emotional and practical needs. After all, they had to do it much earlier in life.

Gay men are also more likely than straight men to be flexible in their "gender roles." Ray recalls a situation in his own family. When his mother was hospitalized for surgery, his father suddenly entered a crisis. The family discovered that Ray's father did not know how to prepare nutritious meals for himself, operate the washing machine, or manage the checkbook. He had always relied on Ray's mother for these things.

While such rigid roles are typical among many older heterosexuals, they are rare among gay men. Not being locked into traditional male roles, gay men go on to master all the things that need doing, from taking care of the car, to sewing a button onto a shirt. With the loss of spouse or friends who were relied on in the past, these skills become vital in adapting to advanced old age.

There is one heterosexual trauma that is rare in gay circles: the widow who is rejected by her still-married friends, who perceive her as a threat to their own relationships. Gay men with life partners are just as likely as heterosexuals to lose a partner to death. The AIDS epidemic has increased the phenomenon of "gay widowhood." But gay singles find easier acceptance in gay social circles where the concept of chosen family operates in a way it does not in nongay social circles.

AIDS

The gay and lesbian community's mobilization in the fight against AIDS has been nothing less than extraordinary. In a few short years, hundreds of efficient organizations sprang up to provide support services to those affected by the disease. Many other groups mobilized to help in other ways — for example, to disseminate information about legal rights, and the latest available treatments. Others formed into political advocacy groups to make our voices heard in the larger community, to fight for our social and political rights, and to lobby for research funding.

All epidemics end, and so will this one. When that happens, we will face the same situation as that which confronted the March of Dimes when polio ceased to be a public health problem. The March of Dimes turned its service, education and advocacy efforts to a new cause: conquering birth defects. What goals will AIDS organizations pursue after their current mission ends?

AIDS organizations will have a wonderful opportunity to redirect their efforts toward remaining needs in the gay and lesbian communities. Some of those efforts should be directed toward helping runaway youth, the chronically mentally ill, and other vulnerable groups. But one of the most important groups which can benefit from these efforts is the frail elderly. In serving persons with AIDS, the gay community has acquired experience in providing services such as friendly visiting, home-based meals, counseling, transportation, and case management (assessing needs and serving as an advocate for the client, with a variety of agencies). This experience can be readily adapted to the situation of older gays and lesbians who need similar services.

The Future

There is a great deal of anecdotal evidence which suggests that when gay men enter their last decades of life and become frail, the services they receive from mainstream agencies are often insensitive to their identities as gay people. For example, social workers may fail to understand that some of their older clients are gay, that they may have lovers, or they may be widowers (if their partners have died), or that they need the company of other gays. The experience of gay service agencies — such as Seniors Active in a Gay Environment (SAGE) in New York City — shows that gay people themselves are in the best position to provide supportive services to members of their community who need them. SAGE has been doing this since 1977, providing a full range of social services such as information and referral, transportation, friendly visitors, care management, support groups, and social events.

The Gay Helper Bank[1] is one strategy which gay community agencies should consider as a way to facilitate this process of younger serving older. Under this program, younger volunteers earn "credits" for providing assistance to their older counterparts in the gay community. Volunteers then "bank" these credits, and redeem them in later years when they themselves are in need of supportive services. Admittedly, this type of program requires a level of coordination and a long-term historical record, which gay organizations have not yet achieved, but it is something to begin to work toward. The Helper Bank will also require inter-regional coordination, or perhaps a national clearinghouse, so that today's volunteers can "cash in" their credits in their places of retirement, wherever that may be.

---

[1] *We would like to thank our colleague, Dr. Catherine Goodman, for alerting us to the concept of the Helper Bank.*

Along with a national clearinghouse for volunteers, we would also like to see a National Center on Gay and Lesbian Aging. This center, housed in a research university, would fulfill a number of functions. The Center would conduct basic research on the aging process for gays and lesbians. For example, there is a great need to collect historical material, including oral testimony, from "very old" gays and lesbians — those who grew up gay in the early part of this century. Since there are few places in which early twentieth century gay experiences are recorded, we must gather this information from surviving elders. Time is limited.

The Center could also originate and test innovative service delivery concepts such as the Helper Bank. It could train student professionals who will go on to serve or to study elder gays. As an established and legitimate voice, it could educate the general public, as well as the gay community, about the realities of gay aging — a much needed task, considering public attitudes about older gays. The very existence of such a Center would lend legitimacy and salience to the needs of older gay adults.

Older gays and lesbians have contributed to society in a way that has not been generally recognized. Older gays with financial resources and with few surviving family members, often bequest their estates to charitable causes. Ironically, some of those charities exclude needy gays from receiving their help.

Older gays and lesbians (as well as younger ones!) should consider these issues in allocating their bequests. For example, it could be very gratifying to will one's estate to gay service agencies (such as SAGE), or to gay-related programs such as a gay nursing home. The donor can sometimes require that mainstream agencies which receive bequests, allocate the funds in a way which guarantees that gays will not be discriminated against in service allocations. At the very least, this will alert charitable agencies to the existence of gays and lesbians.

Over the years, gay gerontologists have discussed the notion of a gay retirement community. In the past, when concealment was an inevitable part of being gay, moving to a mainstream retirement community and continuing to conceal, was taken for granted by gay men entering retirement. But many of today's middle-aged and older gays are accustomed to living open lifestyles. These folks may find that a gay retirement community provides the smoothest transition from their accustomed lives. It may offer a setting in which they will be accepted and supported, and where they may find others who share their perspectives and interests.

Gay retirement communities may not be appropriate for some older gays. The practice of housing segregation has its drawbacks — for example, it diminishes the diversity which can enliven one's later years. Still, in a society often marked by insensitivity to the needs of gays, older gay men and women should have the option of retiring to communities of their own design. We support the idea that older gay men should have as many life options as possible, including a full range of choices about retirement living.

The AIDS epidemic, gay social service agencies, assertive older gays, gay retirement communities — who would have thought our future would bring these developments. Will the years ahead bring more surprises? Almost certainly. But our development as an assertive, self-conscious community has guaranteed a few things. As gay men, and as older gay men, we will be increasingly true to ourselves in our work, family and leisure lives. Our ties to community will strengthen. Our social service and advocacy organizations will become more established. Our feelings of self-esteem and belonging will increase. We will weather tragedy and loss. We will know who we are and we will face our futures with grace and an appreciation of the gay spirit that has always distinguished us as special human beings.

Suggested Reading

Berger, Raymond M. (1984). *Gay and Gray: The Older Homosexual Man*. Alyson: Boston.

Berger, Raymond M. (1990). Older gays and lesbians. In Robert J. Kus, (Ed.) *Keys to Caring: Assisting Your Gay and Lesbian Clients* (pp. 170-181), Alyson: Boston.

Curry, Hayden, and Clifford, Denis (1990). *A Legal Guide for Lesbian and Gay Couples*. Nolo Press: Berkeley, CA.

Gwenwald, Morgan (1984). The Sage model for serving older lesbians and gay men. In Robert Schoenberg, Richard S. Goldberg, and David Shore (Eds.), *Homosexuality and Social Work* (pp. 53-61). Haworth: New York.

Weinberger, Martin S., and Williams, Colin J. (1974). *Male Homosexuals: Their Problems and Adaptations*. Penguin Books: New York.

Organizations

Seniors Active in a Gay Environment (SAGE)
208 West 13th Street
New York, NY 10011
Phone: (212) 741-2247
Social services, information, social support

Prime Timers
Midtown Station
P.O. Box 291
New York, NY 10018-0291
Social, recreational

Project Rainbow
c/o Gay and Lesbian Community Service
   Center
1213 North Highland Avenue
Los Angeles, CA 90038
(213) 464-7400

Center 55
The Center
2017 East Fourth Street
Long Beach, CA 90814
(310) 434-4455

The 39 Plus Club
P.O. Box 461324
West Hollywood, CA 90046-1324
(310) 281-1791

SAGE of California
P.O. Box 4071
San Diego, CA 92164
(619) 282-1395

Gay and Lesbian Outreach to Elders (GLOE)
1853 Market Street
San Francisco, CA 94103
(415) 626-7000

Mature Friends
P.O. Box 30575
Seattle, WA 98103
(206) 781-7724

Gray Pride of Chicago
2524 North Lincoln
Chicago, IL 60614

Older Lesbians of the Bay Area (OLOBA)
77 Waller Street
San Francisco, CA 94102
(415) 626-7000

RELIGION: RECONCILING THE SPIRITUAL DILEMMA

Judaism: A Time of Change

Rabbi Denise Eger

Judaism has undergone radical changes in recent years that have kept it a rich and vibrant, growing faith. Prominent among these changes is the shift in attitudes toward those of the tradition who are lesbian or gay. Once a taboo subject, homosexuality has become a priority topic for discussion as gay-affirming action is occurring in a variety of Jewish venues. The late twentieth century is indeed a rewarding time to be gay or lesbian and Jewish.

Beginning in 1972, a group of Jews in Los Angeles established a synagogue with a special outreach to the gay and lesbian community, a radical move for its time. Inspired by the efforts of the Reverend Troy Perry, who had founded the Metropolitan Community Church, they called themselves the Metropolitan Community Temple. But this title soon gave way to a name that was more expressive of their Jewishness, Beth Chayim Chadashim (House of New Life). The group received initial help from the Union of American Hebrew Congregations (UAHC) which is the Reform movement in Judaism and one of the most liberal movements. Visionary rabbis and some heterosexual lay people were instrumental in BCC successfully applying for actual membership in the UAHC. The consequences of this action would be far reaching. The issue of homosexuality and Judaism was forever out of the closet.

After much debate within the denomination, Temple Beth Chayim Chadashim became a full member of the Reform movement in 1974.[1] This was an historic

---

[1] *For further information on the debate surrounding BCC's entry into the UAHC see the* Central Conference of American Rabbis Yearbook. *84: 28-29 (1974) and* CCAR Journal 20:3 *(Summer, 1973) in which there are several articles about the formation of a homosexual congregation.*

moment for lesbian and gay Jews. A mainstream denomination of Judaism was acknowledging and legitimizing a group that had previously been stigmatized and excluded. Building on that success other lesbian and gay synagogues formed in New York, Miami, San Francisco, Chicago, Atlanta, Boston, Philadelphia, Dallas, Seattle, and Washington, D.C. Some of these synagogues became affiliated with the Reform movement, others with the Reconstructionist movement,[2] and yet, others remained independent of any denominational affiliation.

In recent years gay and lesbian Jews throughout the United States and Canada, Europe and Israel have continued to organize. European and Israeli gay and lesbian Jewish groups usually formed with a social and political emphasis. The ritual and worship aspects of Judaism seemed to be less important in these communities than in the American experience. In Israel the gay and lesbian group is known as the Society for the Protection of Personal Rights (no gay or lesbian in the title), and it functions more like a community service center. The SPPR also works within the political structure of the State of Israel to reform anti-gay laws and was instrumental in the repeal of the law that made homosexuality illegal in Israel.

Eventually, all of the various groups and synagogues around the world would gather for an event called the International Conference of Gay and Lesbian Jews. This gathering gave birth to the World Congress of Gay and Lesbian Jewish Organizations, which continues to sponsor a biennial international gathering as well as regional conferences.[3]

These meetings of lesbian and gay Jews offer a chance for networking by people from everywhere in the world. The conventions include workshops on everything from combating homophobia and sexism to political organizing, Jewish spirituality and increasing self-esteem. Such gatherings are particularly affirming to the struggle to integrate being gay or lesbian with Jewish life.

Some important mainstream Jewish organizations have adopted resolutions of support for gay and lesbian civil rights, among them are the American Jewish Congress, American Jewish Committee, the Anti-Defamation League of B'nai B'rith, the Rabbinical Assembly, The Union of American Hebrew Congregations and the Central Conference of American Rabbis.

During the summer of 1990, at their annual convention in Seattle, Washington, The Central Conference of American Rabbis (Reform) adopted the report of their Ad Hoc Committee on Homosexuality, concluding that openly gay men and

---

[2] *The Reconstructionist movement is the fourth denomination of Judaism and also a liberal movement. It is based on the writings of Rabbi Mordecai Kaplan. It includes synagogues, Haverot, smaller groupings of people who celebrate holidays and worship together, rabbis and a seminary.*

[3] *For more information on the World Congress of Gay and Lesbian Jewish Organizations, or its member groups, write to: World Congress of Gay and Lesbian Jewish Organizations, P.O. Box 18961, Washington, D.C. 20036.*

lesbians could be candidates for ordination as rabbis. This was monumental decision. The Reform movement of Judaism was not only welcoming openly gay and lesbian individuals and families as members of their synagogues but acknowledging that a homosexual orientation need not be a bar to serving as clergy.

The Reconstructionist movement was the first to ordain open lesbian and gay candidates as rabbis. In fact, in February of 1992 the Federation of Reconstructionist Congregations and Haverot[4] adopted an historic forty page report that reaffirmed the movement's positive position on gay issues. This report even called for the sanctification of same-sex relationships, recognizing them as valid unions on a par with heterosexual marriages! This was a first for any denomination of Judaism.

The Conservative Rabbinical Assembly has endorsed civil rights for lesbian and gay people and acknowledged them as synagogue members. In March of 1992, the Law Committee of the Conservative movement issued a report which denies admission to seminary and ordination to gay or lesbian rabbinical candidates.

The reluctance to accept gay and lesbian Jews as rabbis, cantors, Jewish educators and communal workers stems from the Biblical prohibitions listed in Leviticus in chapters 18 and 20. Leviticus 18:22, for instance, states, "Do not lie with a man as one lies with a woman: it is an abhorrence." The disapproval of a particular sexual act thus has been enlarged to withhold approval of gays in any position of authority in Jewish life. Further, several of the stories in the Book of Genesis, including part of the story of Noah and the story of Sodom and Gomorrah, are traditionally interpreted as being about homosexual conduct that is then vilified and severely punished. Lesbianism is not addressed biblically, an expression of the virtual invisibility of women in the Bible. However in later texts, such as the writings of Maimonides, lesbianism is an offense, though a lesser one than the offense homosexuality is in Jewish men.[5]

Orthodox Judaism, the most rigid denomination, continues to view homosexuality as a sin and heterosexuality as the only permissible life style within the Jewish faith. Were one to grow up in a traditional Orthodox Jewish household, these ideas would be strongly conveyed, reinforcing homophobic attitudes. It is often difficult for a lesbian or gay person who comes from an Orthodox background to break free of these bonds. Sometimes the gay or lesbian Orthodox Jew completely leaves their Judaism for a while. Later, as they have explored gay and lesbian life, they find ways to reintegrate their Jewish experience without the homophobic trappings and discriminatory point of view.

While the Bible has been used as the basis for many kinds of discrimination, that usage is flawed. There are any number of prohibitions in the Bible that Jews and

---

[4] *Haverot is a small network of people — an affinity group within, or in place of, a full synagogue.*
[5] *Mishneh Torah,* "Issurai Bi'ah" *(Laws of Forbidden Intercourse) 1:14, 21:8.*

everyone else, tend to ignore. In Deuteronomy, the text states that the rebellious son should be taken to the town square by his parents and stoned to death for his behavior. No one today would accept this as an appropriate solution when a child questions parental authority. We would call this child abuse and murder. Further, there are many passages in the Bible which support and uphold the institution of slavery. No one today would endorse the ownership of another human being as legitimate.

If we accepted only the traditional Biblical and rabbinical worldview concerning women there would continue to be serious barriers to equality for women in the Jewish life. However, in Reform, Reconstructionist, and even Conservative Judaism, women have moved from behind the dividing curtain in the synagogue to become rabbis. This is an example of how Judaism can change, widening its worldview, to embrace a shift in attitude reflective of contemporary knowledge and thinking.

For me personally, I hearken to Judaism's message of justice. In so many cases Judaism stresses how we are to treat individuals: with kindness and compassion. I find it difficult to reconcile that this same tradition which emphasizes these important, overarching concepts would oppress and exclude gay and lesbian people. It is in this context that I see the need for the Jewish community to fully correct and confront its denial of equal access of lesbians and gay men, and for gay and lesbian Jews to work vigorously to achieve this objective.

Further the Jewish tradition emphasizes a process of integration of self. In fact the Biblical statement in Genesis 1:27, that God created humanity, male and female, in the Divine likeness, teaches me that all human beings are made by God. This includes male and female, people of all colors and lesbians and gay men and heterosexuals as well. This acknowledgement that I, too, am created in the Divine image helps me to live as a lesbian and a Jew. So too, this wholeness of personhood is a goal of the *mitzvah* system, our Jewish system of responsibilities.

As I have struggled with my faith tradition and coming out process, I have relied strongly on my belief that the goal of the *mitzvah* system is for me to be the best person I possibly can be. That means that not only do I have certain obligations to make the world a better place, but it means for me to be happy, and well adjusted and caring for self and others. I believe that is what my God would want of me. Thus I live my life continuously trying to integrate myself and the cultures in which I live.

Finally, I believe that Judaism isn't a fixed process. Rather it is an evolving and growing faith tradition, just as we human beings are learning new things about ourselves and the world. Thus as we confront our past and ourselves, we must find ways to make this new knowledge and these discoveries a part of our spiritual traditions. We do so by acknowledging our sexual orientation and living both as Jewish and gay.

Thus those of us in the more liberal circles of Jewish life continuously struggle to incorporate new truths into our ancient value system. Sometimes this means confronting the old myths of the sacred texts. While the Bible condemns certain kinds of sexual conduct between two men, it is condemning of specific behaviors. The Bible does not have a concept of sexual orientation and this misunderstanding has to be confronted. Homosexuality is about a great deal more than sexual acts. It is, for instance, about loving relationships, and in some quarters of Jewish life this is being recognized.

As of February 1992, the Federation of Reconstructionist Congregations and Haverot do now sanctify same-sex unions. Many lesbian and gay couples are creating their own Jewish ceremonies of commitment. These ceremonies are often similar to the traditional Jewish wedding ceremony, utilizing symbols such as the *chupah* (wedding canopy), rings, a form of the *sheva brachot* (seven wedding blessings), and the breaking of the glass. For the gay and lesbian couples going though these rituals it is an opportunity to acknowledge their commitment and love for one another in the presence of family and friends, and in the context of their religion. Often the story of David and Jonathan is read from the Bible. When Jonathan dies, David laments that "your love was sweeter to me than the love of a woman."[6] Others read from the story of Ruth and Naomi who pledge their commitment to one another. Sometimes, couples who have been together for years go through such ceremonies to recommit their relationship in the context of their Jewish faith. Some rabbis are willing to officiate at ceremonies such as these, but as yet these ceremonies are not officially recognized by the state nor by most Jewish communal circles.

Some in the Jewish community point to passages in the Bible that condemn any sex act that does not fulfill the promise of procreation as a way to deny the gay or lesbian relationship. Yet, the Bible and other important Jewish texts provide a tradition that presents sex for intimacy as an important concept. Jewish tradition never viewed sex in the context of marriage as sinful. Sex was and is seen as the loving expression of intimacy between husband and wife. There are several places in the Talmud (the Jewish legal code) and other important texts which state that a husband must fulfill his wife's request for sexual relations, and emphasize the sanctity of human sexuality. This acknowledgement of loving, fulfilling sexual relations is not seen as "dirty," sin-based, unlike some other religious traditions. Thus, we can see how Judaism has a broader approach to sexual fulfillment. It is upon this basis that lesbian and gay loving relationships are seen as sanctified. Not to mention the fact that many lesbians and gay men are experiencing the *mitzvah* of parenting by having or adopting children.

---

[6] *See II Samuel 1:26. The story of David and Jonathan appears to be about two lovers.*

Another instance in which Judaism has had to confront its inherent homophobia involves the AIDS epidemic. For a long time the prevailing attitude was that Jews did not get AIDS. Just as there have been myths that claim Jews don't do all sorts of things, including, incomprehensibly, be homosexual. The staggering statistics in the American AIDS epidemic alone have forced acknowledgement that anyone can get AIDS including Jewish men and women, homosexual and heterosexual.

That acknowledgement demanded action and Jewish agencies and organizations responded albeit slowly. The Union of American Hebrew Congregations was one of the first religious denominations to publicly reject the homophobic notion that AIDS was God's punishment of homosexuals. UAHC has published a series of study guides and information packets designed to educate young people about AIDS. The UAHC has also established its own National Commission on AIDS that creates AIDS education programs for synagogues, creates services of hope, and remembrance for persons with AIDS and their families. To commemorate all the Jews who have died of AIDS, the UAHC has created a memorial panel for the NAMES PROJECT AIDS QUILT.

The Conservative movement as a whole has been slow to acknowledge that AIDS also affects Jews, but individual Conservative synagogues around the country have sponsored AIDS education projects and outreach programs for those with HIV disease. For the most part, the Orthodox community has done little in response to the AIDS epidemic. While some Orthodox rabbis have urged compassion for those who have HIV disease there have not been educational efforts or outreach to those at risk, or those already infected. The Orthodox community, for the most part, continues to see AIDS as a disease of homosexual sin and this homophobic view appears to overwhelm whatever compassionate response might otherwise be forthcoming.

The most aggressive effort to help in the AIDS crisis comes from local Jewish agencies who have developed effective AIDS assistance programs for Jews who have HIV disease and their families. In Los Angeles, San Francisco, and New York, these programs are part of Jewish Family Services. For information on available resources in, or near, your city call the nearest Jewish Federation office.

I can think of no better way to convey the energy and growth that characterizes gay and lesbian Jewish life than to list some of the many organizations that are serving its communal needs around the world. That list appears at the end of this chapter.

Now more than any time in Jewish history, lesbians and gay men have gained a measurable presence within the Jewish community. It is one more example of the Jewish will to survive. And every Jew should take heart from this movement that enlarges the window of Jewish life and creates an example for all people to embrace their tradition and heritage and make it their own.

The following is a list of synagogues and organizations worldwide who are members of the World Congress of Gay and Lesbian Jewish Organizations:

Agudot L'shmirat Zchuyot Haprat
(SPPR)
PO Box 16151
66161 Tel Aviv
Israel (3) 625-629

Am Segula
PO Box 271522
West Hartford, CT 06217
203-676-9245

Am Tikva
PO Box 11
Cambridge, MA 02238
617-926-2536

Beit Haverim
BP 397
75626 Paris Cedex 13
France (1) 4747-7855

Bet Haverim
PO Box 54947
Atlanta, GA 30308
404-624-3467

Bet Mishpachah
PO Box 1410
Washington, DC 20013
202-833-1638

Beth Ahavah
PO Box 7566
Philadelphia, PA 19101
215-790-0603

Beth Chayim Chadashim
6000 W. Pico Blvd.
Los Angeles, CA 90035
213-931-7023

Beth El Binah
PO Box 64460
Dallas, TX 75206
214-840-3553

Beth Simchat Torah
PO Box 1270
New York, NY 10016
212-929-9498

Beyt G'vurah
PO Box 8503
Minneapolis, MN 55408
612-870-1081

B'nai Shalom
c/o Jacobs
642 S 2nd Street #1004
Louisville, KY 40202
502-583-0528

Chevraya
1228 Bourbon St #D
New Orleans, LA 70116
504-525-8286

Chevrei Tikva
PO Box 18120
Cleveland, OH 44118
216-932-5551

Chaverot v'chaverim
Honolulu, HI
808-672-3026 or 808-924-8674

Chutzpah
PO Box 6103 Station A
Toronto, Ontario M5W 1P5
Canada
416-323-3564

Etz Chayim
19094 W Dixie Hwy
N Miami Beach, Fl 33180
305-931-9318

Hinenu
c/o LLGC
67-69 Cowcross St
London EC1
England UK
(71) 706-3123

Jewish Lesbian and Gay Group
c/o Greg Segal
PO Box 897
Bondi Junction
Sydney, NSW 2022
Australia

Jewish Gay and Lesbian Group
BM JGLG
London Wc1N3XX
England, UK
(71) 224-9037

Jewish Lesbian and Gay Helpline
BM Jewish helpline
London Wc1N3XX
England, UK
(71) 706-3123

Jewish Lesbian Daughters of Holocaust
   Survivors
PO Box 6194
Boston, MA 02114
617-321-4254

Jews and Friends
PO Box 1288
Dalinghurst, Sydney NSW 2010
Australia

Kol Simcha
PO Box 1444
Laguna Beach, CA 92652
714-494-3806

Lambda Chai
1401 St Andrews #122
New Orleans, LA 70130
504-566-1361

Michpachat Am
PO Box 7731
Phoenix, AZ 85011
602-249-3949

Michpachat Chaverim
c/o Emenitove
959 South 51 Street
Omaha, NE 68106
402-551-0510

Nayim
PO Box 18053
Rochester, NY 14618
716-442-3363

Or Chadash
656 W Barry Ave
Chicago, IL 60657
312-248-9456

Sha'ar Zahav
220 Danvers St
San Francisco, CA 94114
415-861-6932

Simcha
PO Box 652
Southfield, MI 48037
313-353-8025

Sjalhomo
PO Box 2536
1000 CM Amsterdam
The Netherlands

Tikvah Chadashah
PO Box 2731
Seattle, WA 98111
206-323-7795

Tikvat Shalom
PO Box 6694
Denver, Co 80206
303-331-2706

Va'ad L'milchama B'AIDS
84 Ahad Ha'am Street
PO Box 3602
61336 Tel Aviv
Israel
(3) 203-121

Yachad
P O Box 3027
San Diego, CA 92163

Yachad
PO Box 4781
Rivonia 2128
South Africa

Yakhdav
3617 Marlowe Avenue
Montreal, Quebec H4A 3L8
Canada
514-487-2880

NECHAMA: Jewish Community AIDS
Program
6505 Wilshire Blvd.
Los Angeles, CA
Temple Kol Ami
P.O. Box 5041
Los Angeles, CA 90209

Further Resources

The UAHC has also published several study guides about homosexuality and Judaism. Again aimed at young people, the guides clearly try to create an atmosphere of acceptance and tolerance for lesbians and gay men. Ask specifically for the issue of *Keeping Posted* magazine on homosexuality. There is also an excellent study guide about parent's acceptance of a child's homosexuality. All of these are available from the UAHC, 838 Fifth Avenue, New York, New York, 10021.

In the fall of 1989, a book called *Twice Blessed: On Being Lesbian, Gay and Jewish* was published. Edited by Andy Rose and Christie Balka for Beacon Press, this anthology included many wonderful articles on Jewish gay and lesbian life. Not only do lesbian and gay people write of their experiences but it includes parent's reaction to their child's coming out. It makes for a wonderful entry into this unique part of the Jewish community.

Along this same line, is a book called *Nice Jewish Girls: A Lesbian Anthology,* edited by Evelyn Torton-Beck and published by Persephone Press originally in 1982. This book delves specifically into lesbian Jewish culture. It is diverse in scope, covering issues about cultural Jewish lesbians and religious lesbians. It, too, is an anthology so the variety of authors and ideas covers a wide range of the community.

Theologically speaking, Judith Plaskow's feminist theology includes a section on sexual orientation that affirms lesbian and gay Jewish life. You can read more about this in her book *Standing Again at Sinai* (San Francisco: Harper & Row, 1990).

In the realm of fiction, there are a number of books written by lesbian and gay Jews that incorporate both themes into the story. These include the works by authors Lev Raphael, Alice Bloch, Ruth Geller, Harvey Fierstein, Adrienne Rich, Melanie Kay Kantrowitz, Irena Klepfisz, Gary Glickman and Jyl Felman. These authors are successfully able to weave ideas about Judaism and lesbian and gay issues together.

Protestantism and Gay and Lesbian Freedom

Rev. William R. Johnson

Growing up a lesbian or gay Protestant Christian is at best confusing, at worst, non-descript. North American Protestantism is an expansive, often confusing array of religious expression — a tree with many branches (i.e., denominations and sects) sprouted from numerous conflicts about theology and biblical interpretation. Hence, a "Protestant identity" is difficult to define. Neither a monolithic Protestant church nor a dogmatic Protestant belief system exists. Most of us grow up knowing with certainty only that we are not Jewish or Catholic.

Self-aware lesbians and gay men within the wildly diverse Protestant faith traditions experience everything from severe condemnation to openness and affirmation. Both extremes often exist within a single denomination. Though the "official" ecclesiastical positions concerning homosexuality of Protestant bodies are generally affirming of lesbian/gay civil liberties, homophobia is alive and sick within Protestant churches. Even though laypeople and church leaders may have less rigid attitudes than might be expected, too often the pro-lesbian/gay attitudes of all are sacrificed on the alter of image "for the good of the church." Still, undeniable fact is that as lesbians and gay men have become more visible and affirmed our sexual orientation and our emotional and spiritual lives, many church members have experienced significant changes in attitude.

There is no issue causing more discussion — sometimes even dialogue — within Protestant bodies today than the demand of lesbians and gay men for justice, equality and affirmation. The historic silence of lesbians and gay men within Protestant churches has been broken. Increasingly, we are speaking our truths as persons who affirm our sexuality, and the sexuality of others, and who celebrate our faith in the precepts taught and personified by Jesus of Nazareth.

Many of us are aware that the systemic oppression of our people is rooted in the patriarchal devaluation of the feminine, institutionalized in religious structures, the law, the culture and the popular mind of Western peoples. Many Protestants today struggle to change that stranglehold on human freedom in many areas — race relations, lesbian, gay and bisexual rights, women's rights, freedom of choice, sexual harassment, demilitarization and environmentalism, to name a few. Still, pervasive patriarchy and the exertion of (predominantly Caucasian, heterosexual) male power makes progress seem painfully slow.

Certainly it is painfully slow for those of us who believe that God calls us not to repression, but to freedom. It is easy to lose sight of the fact that the first organization to facilitate dialogue among Christians concerning homosexuality — the Council on Religion and the Homosexual (CRH) — was founded as recently as 1964. In the expanse of church history, that is not long ago. The pioneering consciousness raising done by CRH continues to have a positive effect upon the struggle within Protestant churches.

It was not until the 1970s that a climate began to be created within Protestantism that encouraged lesbians and gay men to emerge from our closets. Recent history attests eloquently to the power of visibility by lesbian and gay people of faith. Over the past several decades, much progress has been made toward openness to, and affirmation of, lesbians and gay men within Protestant churches. Indeed, the progress is remarkable given the church's ignorance, fear and investment in repressing non-procreative sexualities for economic (not biblical nor theological) reasons.

Certainly we who are committed to this struggle are aware that many of our lesbian sisters and gay brothers think us foolish for contending with the church. In the course of my own ministry, I have heard more times than I can count the question, "How can you stay in the church?" For me, there are several answers. I affirm the tenets of the Christian faith. I know that God loves me and affirms me in the fullness of my being as a gay person. I refuse to give in to bigots and allow them to run me out of the Christian community. I know that faithfully contending with injustice — especially injustice perpetrated by the church itself — is fundamental to Christian discipleship. Human activity has created all institutions in our culture, including the church, and I believe that committed human activity, inspired by a vision of freedom and respect for human dignity, will constructively change them. This is not to say change will be easy.

We who are lesbian and gay Protestants face the challenge of being true to our faith despite the mythology in our own community (and in the larger culture) that it is not possible to be both lesbian or gay and Christian. Increasing numbers of lesbian and gay Protestants have found within ourselves a resolute faith that claims for ourselves the freedom proclaimed in the Gospel — the good news that we are loved of God, called to freedom, and empowered by grace. Our lives are living testimonies to our determination to be whole persons who affirm our sexuality and our spirituality.

One of the legacies of the Protestant Tradition is the conviction that each of us has the freedom to evolve spiritually and to nurture our own biblical understanding and theology. Personally, I've long believed that Christian discipleship demands a conscious commitment to active loving and to living with faith, not fear. That belief caused me to come out publicly in 1970 as a gay seminarian and to seek ordination to the Christian ministry.

RELIGIOUS FREEDOM

The teachings of Jesus promote love, inspire trust and demand justice. His was good news that liberates. Throughout the centuries, there have been individuals whose comprehension of the liberating Gospel of the Christ caused them to daringly challenge the church's doctrine and practice. Such daring forced the church to abandon its advocacy of segregation among races and the equality of women. Today the church is increasingly being challenged to confront its Machiavellian role in the perpetuation of injustice against human sexuals.

Such challenge is but one form of expressing our religious freedom. Many of us can remember boring sermons. When I was a teenager attending weekly church services, I found myself often tuning out the preacher. Sunday after Sunday, as the preacher droned on, I reflected on the morning scripture lessons. To this endeavor I brought my limited experience of life; openness, in faith, to hearing God's word for *my* life; willingness to intellectually struggle with understanding the ancient texts; and expectation that the Spirit that is Holy could, and *would*, interact with me in an illuminating way. I knew one thing for certain: if my faith was to be real, viscerally mine, I needed to sort out, for myself, what it meant to be a Christian on a pilgrimage of faith. I now know that in those teenage years, I was exercising my religious freedom, which was, and is, not only my right as a U.S. citizen, but also, as Luther would affirm, my human right as a mortal/spiritual person. I continue to exercise that freedom of religious thought and practice to this day.

THE ANTISEXUAL TRADITION

As Protestant lesbian and gay Christians, it is important for us to understand the view of human sexuality in general and homosexuality in particular that developed in the Judeo-Christian Tradition. In his enormously helpful book, *Embodiment*, Christian ethicist James B. Nelson offers a comprehensive examination of the antibody, anti-sexual development of the tradition.[1] Addressing the fact of sexual

---

[1] Nelson, James B., Embodiment, *Augusburg Publ. Co., St. Paul MN., 1978*

alienation, in both history and the individual, Nelson explores the ways sexist dualism (patriarchal subordination of women and the "feminine") and spiritualistic (body-spirit) dualism have contributed to a sex-negative, sex-for-procreation-only sexual ethic and theology.

Pre-Christian Hebrew culture considered sexuality a good gift of God and spiritualistic dualism was minimal. In Greece, a body/spirit dualism arose after the death of Alexander the Great which held that "the true state of existence was devoid of any physical sexual activity."[2] In Rome, stoicism was the prevailing ethical philosophy. Though they did not devalue sex, the Stoics considered passionlessness the supreme virtue, especially the repression of visceral emotions such as sexual passion. All of these influences demanded asceticism, sexual alienation and denial of the human experience of embodiment.

The Hebrew culture in which Jesus lived was male dominated, men assuming themselves superior in reason and spirit to women, and thus destined to lead both civil and religious communities. In contrast, women were identified with emotionality, physicality and sensuality; their menstrual flow was deemed a sign of religious uncleanness and emotional instability. Women, with their procreative sexuality, were legally the property of men who secured and disposed of them. Fathering male heirs was the objective of sexual relations and because female reproductive processes were not visible, it was assumed the power of life resided with the male. Sexual expression was a male prerogative. Male control over sexuality guaranteed continued male control over the culture; control established in religious, then civil, law and practiced through both religious and civic institutions.

Into such a world culture, Jesus proclaimed the imperative of fundamental equality of women and men and illuminated the primacy of love and forgiveness in sexual and all other matters. He was clearly not an ascetic, being known for his drinking and acquaintance with persons from every strata of society. He openly defied the patriarchal cultural mores and religious laws; a living contradiction of the prevailing dualisms.

Significantly, Jesus, a Hebrew, spoke no word of condemnation against persons engaging in same-sex acts. Such acts were condemned in the culture because of the procreation-only demand; the condemnation being boldly *ascribed* to Yahweh (Jehovah), the one true God of the Hebrews. In the Hebrew mind, nonprocreative sex acts were equated with the "paganism" outside Judea, and within her boundaries as well. This equation, a tenet of religious law, served to maintain male control of the social and religious life of the culture. Males who did not procreate were devalued. Given the general devaluation of women, same gender sex-acts among women were ignored.

None of the Gospel writers, nor the missionary Paul, nor the formulators of the Tradition, possessed the psychological, sociological and sexological knowledge which now inform our theological reflections about human sexuality. They knew

---

[2] *Ibid, p. 48.*

nothing of sexual orientation or of the natural heterosexual-bisexual-homosexual continuum that exists in human life. They did not postulate that persons engaging in same-gender sex acts could have been expressing *their natural sexuality.* They *presumed* that persons engaged in same gender sex acts were heterosexual, *presumed* only one purpose for sexuality (procreation) and *presumed* that anyone engaged in same gender sex acts was consciously choosing perversion of what was assumed to be the natural sexuality (i.e., heterosexuality).

We now know that same gender sex acts have been observed in a multitude of species from sea gulls to porcupines and that homosexuality justifiably can be considered a minority expression, but a natural expression nonetheless, within the created order. We know that there are three natural and normative human sexual orientations — heterosexual, homosexual and bisexual. We know that same-gender oriented persons can experience deep love with one another and can nurture meaningful, long-lasting relationships. Until this century, our knowledge of same gender relationships was limited. Though lesbians and gay men have survived centuries of repression and genocide, our lives remained largely hidden through much of recorded history. Only in the past 30 years have we, as a people, emerged from the shadows into the sunlight of personal affirmation. This has happened for many reasons but most certainly it has happened, in part, because we now have an ever enlarging reservoir of factual information about human sexuality in general and lesbian/gay people in particular. Integrity demands that we acknowledge that the biblical writers, to the limited extent they addressed the subject, condemned same-gender sex acts from ignorance of human sexuality rather than from a comprehensive understanding of the complexities, meanings and natural expressions of the wonderful gift of human sexual response.

The church has applied flexibility and nonliteral interpretation to many of the moral judgments in scripture. In its homophobia, the church has too often abandoned biblical scholarship and held dogmatically to literal interpretations of presumed biblical references to same-gender sex acts. In the early church, the mystery and miracle of embodiment and affirmation of sexual expression were lost in a contradictory body-spirit dualism and the sex-for-procreation-only dogma prevailed. In view of the power struggles within the early church and ecclesiastical commitment to maintaining male prerogatives despite Jesus' egalitarian teachings, this is not surprising.

The Protestant attitude toward lesbian/gay sexual expression has remained largely unchanged over many centuries. From the 13th century, when Thomas Aquinas declared same-gender sex acts "a crime against nature" until the 1950s when Derrick Sherwin Bailey engaged in research that hastened decriminalization of same-gender sex acts in England,[3] the reality of lesbian/gay sexuality and relationships remained seriously unexamined within the Tradition. Amazingly,

---

[3] Bailey, Derrick Sherwin, Homosexuality and the Western Christian Tradition, *Longmans Green, Ltd., London, 1955, Republished: Archon-Shoestring Press, 1976.*

some people still believe the nonsensical view offered by Thomas Aquinas that same-gender sex acts cause earthquakes, droughts, famines and other natural disasters.

We, and all sexual people, are victims of the church's historic sexist and spiritualistic dualisms. We are fortunate to be living in a time when the Judeo-Christian tradition is being challenged with faith and intelligence in its narrow and culturally determined perspectives on human sexuality. We might well be witnessing the evolution of another great reformation within the church, fostered by understanding and abandoning the sexist and spiritualistic dualisms of patriarchal theology. If so, its success will be due in large part to the fact that thousands of lesbian and gay Christians have abandoned the closet — one might say the tomb — of self-negation and affirmed our love and our lives, openly, proudly, with dignity and integrity. We have shown with our lives the bankruptcy of sexist and spiritualistic dualism. Our lives are living contradictions of the lies told about us.

In our visibility, we are also personifying the viability of our Christian faith. Our *lives* give evidence that the "argument from scripture" historically used to condemn homosexuality is a smokescreen for prejudice. It is, in fact, an "argument from homophobia" that justifies itself through an intellectually dishonest abuse of scripture.

INTERPRETING SCRIPTURE

The manner in which scripture is interpreted can be a stumbling block to full affirmation of God's grace in human sexual community. There are, essentially, two ways of interpreting scripture: literally and critically. Either can be employed by persons of faith; the difference between them is qualitative.

The Bible we read today has a complex history, having been translated and edited over centuries. The claim that the words of the Bible are *actually* the "words of God" is a gross, intellectually dishonest oversimplification. Though translators and editors of the Bible may have been inspired to undertake their tedious work, their work was not perfect and none could escape the adulterating cultural and ecclesiastical influences of their particular historical contexts.

Literalists are necessarily selective in quoting passages of scripture to denounce the "sin" of others while turning a blind eye to their own sin of arrogant judgmentalism. More often than not, the "sin" denounced in others are realities the *literalist* finds *personally* repugnant or terrifying. Recognizing that such judges are themselves victims of the homophobic development of the Judeo-Christian Tradition, we may empathize with their ignorance and fear, but we cannot ignore the fact that their selective use of scripture out of context betrays personal prejudice. They worship an authoritarian, not a liberating God.

To be sure, Protestantism is not without its literalists, though historically the Protestant Tradition has adhered to a critical approach to the scriptures (literary and textual scholarship) informed by faith in God's grace, the continuing revelatory activity of the Spirit that is Holy, and contemporary knowledge, through which God's intention for humanity also is made known.

United Methodist theologian Robert Treese has suggested five guidelines for Biblical criticism necessary for the appropriation of the scriptures for our time:

(1) The Bible is not the word of God, but the words of humans, in which and through which we believe the living, active, constantly contemporary Word of God comes to men and women.

(2) A Bible passage is to be interpreted in terms of the experiences, life setting and problems of the specific writer and with respect to the purposes for which it was written.

(3) A passage is to be further explicated in the light of our contemporary experience and knowledge. We must try to see it in relation to our social-psychological-historical-philosophical understanding as well as to our existential knowledge. There may not be agreement, for sometimes — in fact, often — the Bible stands in judgement of our contemporary life, but the task is to discern, as nearly as possible, the meaning for us today.

(4) Although the Bible writers faced the same basic existential questions we face, many of their answers are time-caught, as ours are, and valid only for them. But the values they affirmed by their answers are of significance to us.

(5) The whole Bible is to be seen in light of the Gospel of Jesus Christ and the experience of the early Church.[4]

Believing, as I do, that the scriptures nurture the soul in faith in God's grace and impart to human understanding those things necessary for freedom, I do not advocate a retreat from the scriptures. I do believe the proof-texting used by literalists to justify *their* prejudice against gay people (and, historically, against other peoples) betrays an incomplete understanding of the meaning of the life of the Christ. We who are lesbian and gay Protestant Christians have a special responsibility not to be diverted by the widespread use of scripture to undermine our essential humanity imbued with grace and the capacity to love. Our task is to explore the scriptures with a keen commitment to understanding the central message of the Bible with regard to human sexuality: Sexuality is a good gift of God that is not a mysterious and alien force of nature but is integral to an understanding of what it means to be human in the fullest sense of embodiment of spirit. Its deepest meanings are made known in the honoring of ourselves and others in loving. It is not to be abused in exploitative or manipulative relationships but celebrated in ourselves and in others as the most intimate experience of physical and spiritual communion. In affirming our sexuality, whatever our affectional and sexual orien-

---

[4] *Robert Treese quoted in Fearhart, Sally and Johnson, William R.,* Loving Women/Loving Men: Gay Liberation and the Church, *New Glide Publ., San Francisco, 1974, p. 28.*

tation, we affirm God's grace to us and to all humanity. In affirming our physicality, inclusive of our sexuality, we move towards deeper understandings of the incarnation of God in Jesus Christ.

FAITHFUL VISIBILITY

The rigid sexuality of the Judeo-Christian Tradition in its sex-for-procreation-only emphasis has caused many of us to isolate our sexuality from other integral parts of our personhood. This compartmentalization is encouraged by the entire culture which rewards sexual conformity and invisibility and causes many persons — of every sexual orientation — to feel sexuality must be kept in a closet of secrecy.

Our intrapersonal struggle is one of reintegrating our sexuality into a meaningful understanding of ourselves as persons in an affirming way. For those of us who are lesbian and gay this means affirming our physical, emotional, psychological, social, spiritual and erotic responsiveness to persons of our own gender as integral to our personhood. The challenge of human experience is to integrate these components of personhood into a meaningful whole and to love ourselves as fully as we are able, as we are. God calls us not to fragmentization but to integrity. The quest for integrity is the ongoing process of integrating the components of self into a congruent, meaningful whole. Affirming our same-gender orientation, and its expression in social and erotic relationships, rather than accepting negative cultural or ecclesiastical definitions of our identity, is essential to the process of integration. As human sexuals we have a God-given right to responsibly express, not deny or repress, our natural sexuality.

The church has created human suffering and violated the spirit of the Gospel by using guilt to maintain ecclesiastical control over sexual people and the expression of sexuality. Yet, in Christ, there is no condemnation. We are free. Each of us must define for ourselves the degree to which we will live with faith, not fear, personifying love in that exquisite freedom. Certainly the church has given us a standard of value for personal integration and social intercourse but has failed to foster an affirming understanding of human sexuality. We can appreciate the limitations of its knowledge in centuries past, but in light of contemporary knowledge, we have a responsibility to reject the continuation of its oppressive non-theology of sexuality.

Contemporary psychological, sociological, sexological knowledge as well as biblical and theological scholarship supports the justice we seek as lesbian and gay Christians. The debate concerning human sexuality in general and homosexuality in particular within the whole church, especially within the Protestant Tradition, is raging. It will be enriched by the full participation of lesbian, gay and bisexual Christians who, with faith in the grace of God, are becoming increasingly visible and are articulating within the church the truth of our lives.

Many lesbian and gay Christians are today engaged in the process of growing toward a new understanding of ourselves as spiritual persons. For most of us, the Acquired Immune Deficiency Syndrome (AIDS) pandemic has presented challenges to our spiritual selves that have demanded deeper explorations of that part of our being just so we could endure what we needed to endure. In many ways, we have been blessed by this unwelcomed, day to day encounter with the sacredness of life and the realities of suffering and death. Of necessity, many of us have opened ourselves to touching one another center to center, soul to soul.

Historically, the church has understood itself to be an agent of healing and care. Yet, the pandemic thought to be caused by Human Immunodeficiency Virus (HIV) was well underway before religious communities became significantly involved. Lesbians and gay men were the first wave of caregivers, educators and advocates in this global pandemic. Not only did we do it, we did it well, bringing solace and quality care to many who had been abandoned by the church. In doing so, lesbians and gay men unintentionally shamed the church. We found, among one another, a true community of nonjudgmental, loving people for whom compassion had become a way of life.

Ironically, for many the HIV/AIDS pandemic illuminates the spiritual concerns which have always been part of lesbian and gay lives — though often unacknowledged personally or in community. Gay and lesbian people who left the church took their spirits with them. Their spiritual lives did not end. Indeed, for some, spirituality became more vital than ever once de-institutionalized.

Today, many lesbian and gay people struggle with whether or not to become involved once more in the institutional church, or to become involved for the first time. Some lesbian and gay Christians find they can celebrate and express their Christian faith apart from the institutional church and its accoutrements, ritual and (usually) nuclear-family-oriented congregational life. In personal relationships with others who affirm their dignity and share their faith, they experience the caring community Christ sought to foster apart from the church.

Others of us identify with the Protestant church for personal and social reasons known to each of us. We may be drawn by its justice commitments, by its liturgical life, or the opportunities for service it offers. Many of us feel called to be involved in confronting the church with its homophobia, challenging the Tradition and broadening its narrow view of human sexuality. We remain because we are not without hope that the liberating spirit of Christ will make itself known through our insistence upon sharing fully in the life of the church as lesbian and gay Christians. We also stay because of the vital experiences of community with other lesbian, gay, bisexual and affirming Christians — community made possible by our mutual willingness to become visible to, and vulnerable with, one another.

Lesbians and gay men have been organizing within religious structures since 1968 when the Reverend Troy Perry organized the Metropolitan Community Church of Los Angeles to be a church with a special ministry with lesbian/gay persons. Today, congregations of the Universal Fellowship of Metropolitan Community

Churches provide a spiritual home for lesbians and gay men all over the world. In addition to MCC churches, a number of independent lesbian/gay congregations exist around the country. There are also at least five lesbian/gay United Church of Christ (UCC) congregations in the United States.

Within mainline Protestant faith traditions, lesbian and gay persons have engaged in extensive organizing as well. There are lesbian/gay coalitional ministries in most denominations. Locally, many congregations — in the United Church of Christ, United Methodist, Presbyterian, Disciples of Christ, Lutheran, Episcopalian, Unitarian and American Baptist faith traditions — have publicly declared themselves open to, and welcoming and affirming of lesbian and gay people. Our coalitional ministries have organized programs to encourage local churches to make such public declarations.

Many heterosexual and bisexual persons who honor our dignity and who support our struggle for full human and civil rights within society and the church have joined our organizing efforts. Together, we are addressing a wide variety of concerns through our coalitional ministries: social policy, theology, education, counseling, mutual support, liturgical expression, placement of clergy, new church development, civil rights advocacy, HIV/AIDS ministry, and more.

Ordination of openly gay and lesbian persons is an issue for many denominations. Only the United Church of Christ (UCC), the Unitarian Universalist Association (UUA), the Episcopal Church, the Christian Church (Disciples of Christ), and the Universal Fellowship of Metropolitan Community Churches (UFMCC), as denominations, place no official barriers on lesbian/gay ordination. Only the UUA has an active denominational program for recruitment and placement of lesbian/gay clergy. Numerous lesbian and gay candidates have been ordained in all of these denominations. It should be noted that ordination processes are complex and that because there are not official barriers, each ordination requires confronting the socialized homophobia of church leaders and laypersons before approval is given. Challenged ordinations of lesbians and gay men have taken place in the Presbyterian Church USA, the Evangelical Lutheran Church in America and the Southern Baptist Convention.

Of course, there are thousands of gay persons, clergy and laity, in the professional leadership of the church. Given the prejudice that exists, and the threat of loss of employment, it is understandable that many church professionals who are lesbian or gay have not openly affirmed their identity. It is to the credit of some that they are involved in lesbian/gay coalitional ministries and are furthering the education/advocacy process through their positions within the structures. Conversely, many church leaders, consumed by their internalized homophobia, abuse their power to maintain the status quo and further oppress their sisters and brothers.

Our coalitional ministries provide pastoral care for lesbian, gay and bisexual persons, our families and friends within the respective denominations. Within these organizations, we have created dynamic communities built upon relationships of trust, caring and spiritual vitality. Our ministries facilitate education and offer understanding, support and opportunities for ongoing involvement in the lesbian/gay religious movement. Lesbian/gay Christians who are open and self-affirming, as well as for those who, for whatever reasons, feel they cannot yet be open are equally welcomed into these communities. Together we are alleviating much of the isolation and alienation experienced by lesbian/gay persons who seek to express their faith.

For a complete listing of lesbian/gay coalitional ministries in your area, consult your local lesbian/gay newspaper. Another reliable source is the listing of religious organizations in the *Gayellow Pages*, available from local lesbian/gay bookstores or from Renaissance House, Box 292, Village Station, New York, NY 10014 (212) 929-7720. Most denominational offices, local, regional or national, will assist interested persons in making contact with the coalitional ministry in their respective faith tradition.

As lesbian/gay Christians we are called to fully accept ourselves and our sexuality as persons loved of God. We know our Christian faith is the foundation of our values in human relationships and of our commitment to social justice. It inspires our vulnerability in loving. We recognize that our Christian faith is a vital part of the physical/spiritual pilgrimage that is our life.

Our ability, not disability, to relate to persons of our own gender is a blessing. The truth of God's love for us, and in us, has been distorted by the Judeo-Christian Tradition. Let us be gentle with ourselves and not fear our spiritual power. Let us celebrate our faith and the ways in which we are able to give expression to it in our daily lives. No less than others, we stand within the circle of God's love and grace.

We are called by Christ as the persons we are to love one another. When we do so, we are being faithful to God and the revelation of the Christ, who personified the new humanity.

Suggested Reading

The Church and the Homosexual, by John J. McNeill; Kansas City: Sheed Andrews and McMeel, 1976.

Is the Homosexual My Neighbor?, by Letha Scanzoni and Virginia Ramey Mollenkott; San Francisco: Harper & Row, 1978.

Christianity, Social Tolerance, and Homosexuality, by John Bowell; Chicago: University of Chicago Press, 1980.

The New Testament and Homosexuality, by Robin Scroggs; Philadelphia: Fortress Press, 1983.

Embracing the Exile, by John Fortunato; New York: Seabury Press, 1983.

Our Passion for Justice: Images of Power, Sexuality, and Liberation, by Carter Heyward; New York: Pilgrim Press, 1984.

Gay/Lesbian Liberation: A Biblical Perspective, by George R. Edwards; New York: The Pilgrim Press, 1984.

Uncommon Calling: A Gay Man's Struggle to Serve the Church, by Chris Glaser; San Francisco: Harper & Row, 1988.

Harper's Bible Commentary, James L. Mays, Gen. Ed.; San Francisco: Harper & Row, 1988.

Taking a Chance on God, by John J. McNeill; Boston: Beacon Press, 1988.

Touching Our Strength: The Erotic as Power and the Love of God, by Carter Heyward; San Francisco: Harper & Row, 1989.

Come Home!, by Chris Glaser; San Francisco: Harper & Row, 1990.

Resources

GAY/LESBIAN RELIGIOUS CAUCUS LISTING (current as of 1992)

Affirmation/Mormons
Box 46022, Los Angeles, CA 90046; 213/255-7251

Affirmation/United Methodists
Box 1021, Evanston, IL 60204; 708/475-0499

American Baptists Concerned
872 Eric Street, Oakland, CA 94610; 415/465-8652

Axios — Eastern & Orthodox Christian Gay Men & Women
328 West 17th Street, #4-F, New York, NY 10011; 212-989-6211

Brethren/Mennonite Council for Lesbian & Gay Concerns (BMC)
Box 65724, Washington, DC 20035-5724; 202/462-2595 (Brethren *and* Mennonites)

Buddhist Association of the Gay & Lesbian Community
c/o Box 1974, Bloomfield, NJ 07003

Conference for Catholic Lesbians
Box 436, Planetarium Station, New York, NY 10024; 718/921/0463

Dignity, Inc. (Roman Catholic Church)
1500 Massachusetts Avenue NW, Suite 11, Washington, DC 20005;
202/861-0017; FAX: 202/429-9808

Emergence International (Christian Scientists supporting Lesbian/Gay People)
Box 581, Kentfield, CA 94914-0581; 415/485-1881

Evangelicals Concerned 212/517-3171
c/o Dr. Ralph Blair, 311 East 72nd Street, Suite 1-G, New York, NY 10021;
(212) 517-3171

Friends for Lesbian/Gay Concerns (Quakers)
Box 222, Sumnaytown, PA 18084; 215/234-8424

Gay, Lesbian, and Affirming Disciples (GLAD) Alliance
(clergy/laity/friends of Christian Church [Disciples of Christ] in the U.S. and Canada)
P.O. Box 19223, Indianapolis, IN 46219-0223; 319/324-6231

Honesty (Southern Baptist Convention)
c/o David Tribble, 603 Quail's Run Road, #C-1, Louisville, KY 40207

154 Protestantism and Gay and Lesbian Freedom

Integrity, Inc. (Episcopal Church)
Box 19561, Washington, DC 20036-0561; 201/868-2485 (New Jersey)

Lifeline Baptists (all Baptists)
Rev. James T. Williams, Sr., M.D.
8150 Lakecrest Drive, P.O. Box 619, Greenbelt, MD 20770-0619

Lutherans Concerned
Box 10461, Dearborn Station, Chicago, IL 60610-0461

National Gay Pentecostal Alliance
Box 1391, Schenectady, NY 12301-1391; 518/372-6001

Nichiren Association (Buddhist)
Box 1935, Los Angeles, CA 90078

Presbyterians for Lesbian/Gay Concerns
James D. Anderson, Communications Secretary
Box 38, New Brunswick, NJ 08903-0038; work: 908/932-7501; home: 908/846-1510

Reformed Church in America Gay Caucus
Box 8174, Philadelphia, PA 19101-8174

Seventh-day Adventist Kinship International
Box 3840, Los Angeles, CA 90078-3840; West: 213/876-2076; East: 617/436-5950

Sovereignty (Jehovah's Witnesses)
Box 27242, Santa Ana, CA 92799

Unitarian Universalist Office for Lesbian/Gay Concerns (denominational hdq.)
25 Beacon Street, Boston, MA 02108; 617/742-2100

Unitarian Universalists for Lesbian & Gay Concerns (caucus)
25 Beacon Street, Boston, MA 02108; 617/742-2100
(same address, but they forward to current chair/officers since they change regularly)

United Church Coalition for Lesbian/Gay Concerns (United Church of Christ)
18 N. College Street, Athens, OH 45701; 614/593-7301

United Lesbian and Gay Christian Scientists
Box 2171, Beverly Hills, CA 90213-2171; 213/850-8258

Unity Fellowship (denominational hdq.)
5149 W. Jefferson Blvd., Los Angeles, CA 90016; 213/936-4949

Universal Fellowship of Metropolitan Community Churches (denominational hdq.)
Attn: Field Director, Ecumenical Witness & Ministry
5300 Santa Monica Blvd., Suite #304, Los Angeles, CA 90029; 213/464-5100

World Congress of Gay & Lesbian Jewish Organizations
Box 18961, Washington, DC 20036

OTHER GROUPS CONCERNED/WORKING ON CIVIL RIGHTS:

AIDS National Interfaith Network (ANIN)
300 "I" Street, NE, Suite 400, Wash, DC 20002; 202/546-0807; 800/288-9619;
Fax: 202/546-5103

Catholic Coalition for Gay Civil Rights
Box 1985, New York, NY 10159; 718/629-2927

Christian Lesbians Out Together (CLOUT)
Box 758, Jamaica Plain, MA 02130

Common Bond (former Jehovah's Witnesses and Mormons Support Group)
Box 405, Ellwood, PA 16117

The Evangelical Network (TEN)
Box 32441, Phoenix, AZ 85064

Evangelicals Together (regional group) 213/656-8570
7985 Santa Monica Blvd., Suite 109, Box 16, Los Angeles, CA 90046

Methodist Federation for Social Action
76 Clinton Avenue, Staten Island, NY 10301; 718/273-4941

National Council of Churches, AIDS Task Force
475 Riverside Drive, Room 572, New York, NY 10115; 212/870-2421

National Council of Churches, Human Sexuality Office
475 Riverside Drive, Room 850, New York, NY 10115; 212/870-2151

National Council of Churches, Washington Office
110 Maryland Avenue, NE, Washington, DC 20002; 202/544-2350

New Ways Ministry (Roman Catholic educational ministry)
4012 29th Street, Mt. Rainier, MD 20712; 301/277-5674

Reach Out (former Jehovah's Witnesses and Mormon Support Group)
Box 1173, Clackamas, OR 97015

Catholicism: On the Compatibility of Sexuality and Faith

Father Robert Nugent

In March, 1989, I spoke to a fledgling and embattled gay and lesbian student organization at the Catholic University of America in Washington, D.C. My talk, "How to be Gay or Lesbian and Catholic," described three choices which almost all gay Catholics have to face sooner or later in their lives.

They could hold on to the practice of the Catholic religion and deny their homosexuality; they could live gay and lesbian lifestyles and give up their religion; or they could try to combine both.

Until recently most gay and lesbian Catholics had only two real choices. They either abandoned Catholicism and "left the Church" in order to be fully gay or lesbian. Or they tried to live according to the teaching of the Church that genital sexual union is morally permissible only in the context of marriage.[1]

For many gay and lesbian people raised in the Catholic faith the first choice meant a painful separation from the community and an ongoing feeling of anger against the Church and its representatives. Catholicism provided them with meaning for some of life's most fundamental questions and issues; with forgiveness in times of sin and failure; with comfort in times of pain; with nourishment in ritual, symbols and stories of a hopeful vision of the future; with a challenge to build a world of justice and love; and with an appreciation for the basic goodness in people and the world around them.

---

[1] *A complete and contemporary exposition of Catholic teaching on sexuality can be found in* Human Sexuality: A Catholic Perspective for Education and Lifelong Learning, *United States Catholic Conference, Washington, D.C., 1991.*

The second choice for total sexual abstinence was more likely — though not always — made by those women and men who felt called to priesthood and religious vows. They had built in support systems and a public status in the Church as part of their practice of celibacy. For those lay Catholics without such helps, the second choice frequently meant an unsuccessful and dangerous attempt to deny or repress the sexual part of themselves and to feel guilty and anxious about any physical expressions of their sexuality. For many this resulted in a short circuiting of the sexual energies that fuel human lives and draw people into creative friendship and intimacy with one another. For some, this choice sometimes led to severe emotional problems and dysfunctional patterns of living. This choice could stunt their human and spiritual growth, and filled their lives with long periods of anguish and suffering from guilt, compulsions, and isolation all in the name of religion.[2]

The stories of lesbian and gay Catholics who have made either or both of these choices, at different times in their lives, are only recently being heard in the Church.[3] All share a common experience of tension between themselves and the Church with whom many continue in a love/hate relationship. Many of them make a third decision which leaves them in a more peaceful and mature relationship with the Church, though not one without its own built in tensions. Their stories echo common themes found in the individual struggles that lesbian and gay Catholics experience in trying to make mature and healthy decisions about religion and sexuality. Their goal is to integrate both sexuality and religion into their lives in a way that respects the authentic values and unique formative influences of each reality.

Some gay and lesbian Catholics have made all three choices at some point or other in their personal journeys. Lesbian and gay Catholics are increasingly finding printed resources and supportive groups to help them to understand that they need not necessarily reject one or the other, their sexual identity, or their Catholic identity. The Catholic Church is often perceived by outsiders as a controlling, monolithic institution that allows no freedom of thought or action whatsoever. Those who experience life inside the Church and those who are aware of contemporary developments in reform and renewal, however, know that this is not an accurate portrayal.

It is this personal and realistic experience of Church life combined with some knowledge of Church history that motivates, energizes and sustains many Catho-

---

[2] *A healthy and positive Catholic understanding of human sexual development can be found in* Your Sexual Self: Pathway to Authentic Intimacy, *Fran Ferder and John Heagle, Ave Maria Press, Notre Dame, 1992.*

[3] *A recent collection is* Listen to the Stories: Gay and Lesbian Catholics Talk About Their Lives and the Church, *Raymond C. Holtz, Garland Publishing Inc., New York, 1991.*

lics in the task of reforming the Church in its understanding of and teachings about homosexuality.[4]

The teachings of any religious body, especially one as ancient and honored as the Catholic Church, have the potential to shape societal values and structures and, historically, have done so in both constructive and destructive ways. In some cultures the Catholic Church has a strong impact on societal norms. Much of the anger and hostility directed at the Catholic Church from activists groups such as Queer Nation and ACT-UP comes not because of what the Church teaches its own believers, but what these groups feel is the "imposition" of those teachings or their harmful consequences, on society at large.

Few would deny the right and responsibility of religious groups to help shape morals and values in a society. Many even welcome the Catholic contribution when it has to do with teaching on economic justice, racism, capital punishment, human rights, and labor relations. Catholic teachings on sexual issues, however, are generally not as enthusiastically received in the larger society. As current polls indicate, many Catholics seriously question these teachings.

The Dilemma

Lesbian and gay Catholics often find themselves caught between two forces which seem to militate against a resolution of the conflict between homosexuality and the Catholic Church. On the one side is the Church which seems to be saying that a Catholic cannot be gay or lesbian. In 1986 the Vatican said that the "homosexual inclination" is an objective "disorder." This judgment reinforced a sense of alienation from the Church in some Catholic gay men and lesbians.

On the other side are those elements of lesbian and gay communities who are critical and judgmental toward those who believe it is worth attempting to reconcile religious beliefs and homosexuality. The shocking Vatican statements excusing the irrational reactions of society against gay and lesbian people when they struggle for civil rights and ignoring the contributions of the gay community in the HIV-AIDS crisis fed the anger of these people against a Church which they view as the major oppressor of gay and lesbian people. Why, they ask, would anyone want to belong to that kind of church? The individual Catholic who is trying to reconcile homosexuality with a Catholic commitment can come to feel there is little support from either the Catholic church or the gay community. Fortunately, this is only part of the story.

---

[4]*A document from the Catholic bishops of the state of Washington acknowledges that "rethinking and development in this and all other areas of the Church's tradition" is necessary and that the Church should foster ongoing theological research with regard to its own theological tradition on homosexuality, "none of which is infallibly taught."* "The Prejudice Against Homosexuals and the Ministry of the Church," *Washington State Catholic Conference, April 28, 1983.*

In the United States over the past ten years there has been a gradual but steady effort on several levels of Catholic life to understand the reality of homosexuality, and how it affects individuals, society and religion. These efforts include trying to respond more honestly and realistically to the needs, questions and challenges of gay and lesbian Catholics within the parameters of Catholic tradition.[5]

One result of these attempts is that more and more gay Catholics are opting for the third choice of being faithful both to their sexuality, which they view as part of their giftedness as a human being, and to their Catholic identity which is also experienced as gift. This is a choice for life in the Church as an involved and active Catholic. It is also a choice for a gay or lesbian identity which means that gay Catholics experience and value their sexuality as an important part of their being Catholic.

What does this choice to positively affirm both one's homosexuality and one's Catholicism require of gay and lesbian individuals? What are the risks necessarily involved in making such a choice? And what are the rewards of a choice to live out one's adult Catholic faith and one's sexuality responsibly?

REQUIREMENTS FOR CHOOSING

Gay Catholics growing up in the post-Vatican II Church of the 1960's have inherited a new way of being Catholic, and new ways of living out that awareness. A fundamental principle of contemporary Catholic renewal is that the Church is basically a community of equals in which the life and truth of each and every member is important. There *are* distinctions and offices (teachers, bishops, theologians, Pope, etc.) in the Church which are meant to serve a hierarchically ordered community. But a more fundamental truth is that every baptized member of the community shares in the same faith, lives by the same communion and celebrates the same signs of God's presence and action in Jesus, which we call sacraments.

The Church *does* teach certain truths about God and salvation and holds up certain ideals about morality, including human sexuality. The Church is always faced with new questions or new applications of old principles about moral issues including homosexuality. When this happens, the members of the Church have a contribution to make in helping the Church make effective responses. This is especially crucial when the topic under discussion is one which people are living out and experiencing in their own lives.

When the Church reflects on homosexuality and its relationship to Catholic life and values, lesbian and gay Catholics have a crucial role to play in speaking from

---

[5]*For an overview of these attempts see* Building Bridges: Gay and Lesbian Reality and the Catholic Church *edited by Robert Nugent and Jeannine Gramick, Twenty-Third Publications, Mystic, CT, 1992.*

their own experiences. The more committed to their faith lesbian and gay Catholics are, and the more they understand what they can bring to the larger Catholic community by sharing their own affirmation of their sexuality, the more effective their witness will be. When the gifts and graces of these individuals manifest the work of the Spirit among us, the whole church is enriched.

Being involved in the Catholic Church through active participation in a parish, a Dignity chapter, a campus ministry organization, an intentional community or Religious Order, helps lesbian and gay Catholics become aware of some of the positive and encouraging developments in the Church on the topic of homosexuality. During the fifteen years there has been more and more "good news" about homosexuality from various Catholic sources in the United States. It is especially important for those who are trying to make a positive choice for both their faith and their sexuality to be aware of these efforts. It will probably comes as a surprise to many readers to learn that official Catholic teachings on homosexuality have asserted that:

• homosexual orientation is not truncated sexual development;

• many homosexual persons realize that God loves them as they are and that this moment of grace cannot be ignored or discounted;

• the Church does not condemn homosexual orientation and gay and lesbian people are not to be blamed for not changing their orientation;

• homosexuality can be a building block in the search for harmony;

• lesbian and gay people should be helped to respect their own individual inner "secret core";

• homosexual orientation is the starting point of one's response to Christ's call;

• many gay and lesbian people possess important attributes that are often lacking in their straight counterparts;

• Church teaching is positive with regard to homosexual people considered in their totality;

• prejudice against lesbian and gay people is a greater infringement of the norm of Christian morality than is homosexual activity;

• Catholics should confront their own fears about homosexuality and curb the humor and discrimination that offend homosexual persons.

Gay Catholics attempting to combine their faith with their sexuality should also be aware of the many gay-positive support groups and organizations, both official and grassroots, which have emerged in the past twenty years. Many Catholic dioceses in the U.S. have official ministries that include worship services, retreats, counseling, spiritual direction, parish education, parental support and other services. In some places Catholic parishes have welcomed gay and lesbian communal participation and have offered meeting spaces for their own specialized gatherings and programs. Many mainline progressive Catholic organizations are sensitive to the issues of gay and lesbian Catholics and have publicly endorsed their struggle for civil rights. Many knowledgeable and affirming Catholics including lay people, nuns, Brothers and priests have developed quiet but effective ministries of friendship and support, often in conjunction with their positions in the Church as spiritual directors, educators, personnel directors, social justice advocates, administrators, etc.

National Catholic organizations exist to provide direct services to meet the needs of gay and lesbian Catholics who want to affirm both their faith and their sexuality. Dignity, the oldest and largest of these groups with chapters in many cities, is on a rebound in both membership and effectiveness after experiencing some decline in 1986, in the wake of the Vatican letter on the pastoral care of homosexual persons mentioned above.

Other national Catholic groups are New Ways Ministry working for justice and reconciliation in the Church for gay and lesbian Catholics through educational resources and programs; Communications Ministry Inc., a support network offering a newsletter and retreats for priests and Brothers; the Conference of Catholic Lesbians with regional groups and annual meetings; and the Christian Community Association, a support group for gay celibates.

Yet still other Catholic ministries, both official and independent, hold that a homosexual orientation manifests a psychological developmental problem. These groups do not believe that growth in self-esteem and self-worth relate positively to one's homosexuality, which is seen by them as a burden rather than as something that requires a positive or affirming response. Some of these groups encourage an attempt to change one's homosexuality or reorient oneself to heterosexuality. It is an important caution to be aware of the underlying theological and psychological beliefs of any group offering "help" to gay Catholics.[6]

RISKS OF CHOOSING

What are some of the risks and challenges for gay and lesbian Catholics who attempt to integrate their Catholic identity and their homosexuality? Positive developments in the understanding of homosexuality and education designed to eliminate ignorance, fear and prejudices do not always move on an even path and are almost never without conflict and misunderstandings.

For some gay Catholics the modest changes that have taken place in the past few years are considered inadequate and not very helpful to them in maintaining a Catholic loyalty. Those who demand, or even expect, immediate and far reaching changes in Catholic beliefs and teachings about human sexuality will have the most difficulty maintaining their sense of belonging. Many who look for major changes in the attitudes and convictions of the general membership of the Church about

---

[6]*An organization called "Courage," for example, employs the A.A. Twelve Step program and considers homosexual orientation a psychological developmental problem. It also suggests that change in orientation is possible for certain individuals and embraces some of the causation theories popular in the "ex-gay" movement.*

human sexuality will be risking disappointment or frustration, if they see no immediate results of their attempts at dialogue and education among Church leaders. In such situations, there is also the risk of anger born of frustration which can lead to an emotional decision to withdraw from the task simply by withdrawing from the Catholic community. For some individuals this can be a healthy and good decision for personal spiritual growth. It can even lead to healing and re-incorporation later on.

The challenge to gay Catholics who face these feelings is to use available resources to deepen their own sense and experience of being a part of the Church. They need to learn how to forgive the Church at times, to bring the gift of their patient presence to their relationship with the Church, and a courageous voice which can help heal the Church in this area.

Personal faith renewal and psychological growth combined with a kind of "peer ministry" of others who are making the same journey as gay and Catholic, are both strong antidotes to the risk of alienation and isolation from one's religious family.

A second risk for gay Catholics is one that faces all lesbian and gay people, the decision to "come out" and affirm their sexuality in a public way. This also impacts on the life of the Catholic community. For people involved with organized religions and committed to active membership in various church structures, it means a public, personal, and positive affirmation of homosexuality in the midst of Church life.

Ideally, Catholic parishes and other Church-related groups ought to be the safest and most favorable for such a venture if they are living up to their professed values of compassion, justice and respect for human dignity. The most important place where ministry to lesbian and gay Catholics should occur is the parish. It is at the parish level where "homosexual men and women will feel welcome" and where "they will see themselves as genuinely an important part of the Church."[7]

We have all heard the painful stories of gay and lesbian Catholics who have experienced rejection, condemnation and even expulsion from parishes, prayer groups and organizations. These actions violate fundamental Catholic beliefs and contradict Jesus's gospel message of love of neighbor. And they stand as compelling evidence of the persistence of homophobia in the Catholic community.

Every gay or lesbian person — whether "out" or not — knows how damaging, even in subtle ways, homophobia can be. This is especially true when one's own internalized homophobia prevents a gay or lesbian person from affirming homo-sexuality in church groups or religious circles. There are growing number of gay Catholics who refuse to abandon either their sexuality or their Church. They have become secure and free enough to be able to claim that double identity, gay and

---

[7]*A pastoral plan for ministry in San Francisco says that the Church should be a place where gay and lesbian people "may responsibly and sensitively understand the interplay between their religious faith and their human sexuality, and to live the sacramental life of the Church in all of its rich meanings."* Ministry and Homo-sexuality in the Archdiocese of San Francisco, *May, 1983.*

Catholic, in a unified way. Their next step is to be able to share that two-fold identity in responsible ways with others in the Church. Until they can offer that gift to the community as a part of who they really are, the Church will be deprived of a valuable resource in its own task of proclaiming good news to everybody about sexuality.

There is a temptation for gay Catholics who have made a positive life choice for both their sexuality and faith to keep the light of that choice "hidden" under the proverbial bushel basket. But it has to be acknowledged that there are potential problems associated with the coming out process in religious or church circles. This is especially true for clergypersons. Each individual has to make a wise and balanced decision about coming out in the Church. What impact will it have, positive and negative, on life in the parish, university, seminary, Religious Order and on one's own life.

The decision to publicly acknowledge one's gayness or lesbianism, in harmony with rather than in opposition to one's practice of the Catholic faith, is a decision that needs to be taken after reflection, counsel and personal prayer. A decision not to come out to the larger Catholic community beyond specialized support groups means living a gay Catholic ghetto existence. A positive decision to come out to the larger Catholic community requires sufficient spiritual and emotional strength to respond to the language of "sin," "scandal" and "disorder" that will be the reaction in some Catholic settings to the revelation that one is both a "practicing Catholic" and "gay and proud."

Christianity has a two-thousand year old tradition which affirms heterosexuality as the Creator's plan for human sexuality.[8] The Catholic Church is also a community which believes that God gifts it with a guarantee of truth through the continuing presence of the Spirit. It is Catholic belief that this Spirit is present in a special, though not exclusive, way in the official teaching office (magisterium) of bishops and pope in the community. The role of the Spirit is to guarantee that the Church teaches truth to assist the whole community in its continued growth in understanding truth about those things which have to do with salvation. This means even truth about the mystery of human sexuality.

Gay Catholics often find themselves experiencing a different "truth" about their own sexuality and its expression from that proposed by the teachers in the Church. They have also frequently experienced a deepened sense of being Church, a growing involvement in its communal life, a use of the many contemporary Catholic resources about sexuality and homosexuality and a shared journey with other like-minded people. Yet they may still feel ambivalent, conflicted or even guilty over decisions about embodying love for another physically. Sometimes such feelings result from bad decisions about sexuality influenced by other psychological factors.

---

[8]*This teaching is articulated in A Letter to the Bishops of the Catholic Church on the Pastoral Care of Homosexual Persons from the Vatican in 1986. The letter and critical responses are found in* The Vatican and Homosexuality *edited by Jeannine* Gramick *and Robert Nugent, Crossroad Publishing, Co., New York, 1986.*

The position of Dignity that gay Catholics can express their love "in a physically unitive way" stands in opposition to the discernment of the Christian tradition on sexuality. For these gay and lesbian Catholics homosexuality is experienced as part of God's will or call for them in their lives.[9] These tensions and struggles are neither new nor unique to gay Catholics. They have always been part of gay Catholic life. Other Catholics share similar feelings about other complex moral decisions in the Church.

Still, there is always the personal dilemma: "I could be wrong." How do I know that this decision is really a good one? How can I be sure that this course of action, this relationship, this lifestyle is really the best one for me?

Those who articulate traditional Catholic doctrine, say that in making a moral decision each person is bound to live with and stand by his or her own perception of God's will. And, if the content of that experience of making choices and decisions is in harmony with the gospel and tradition, and results in "a rekindling of faith, strengthening of hope, and fostering of love, then it probably is an experience of God."[10]

When you listen carefully to the stories of many gay Catholics in both official and unofficial Church ministries, you hear expressed deep feelings of new faith, a sense of hope in themselves and others and an experience of love in their choices about their sexuality. Many have also felt "a greater sense of integrity, peace and joy or renewed call to a personal conversion of heart"[11] in small and worship communities, in support groups, in parish involvements, and in peer ministries. These are what the bishops call "validating qualities" of a conscious decision. Could they not also be legitimate criteria for determining the validity of a choice to affirm and integrate both a gay/lesbian identity and a commitment to an active role in the Catholic community?

The Bishops also say that each person must ultimately discern his or her own moral decisions and wider vocational calling drawing on all the resources available. Still, with all these helps, after all the discernment, study, reflection and prayer:

... one must still face the future based on decisions made before God in the recesses of one's own heart. As the bishops at Vatican II phrase it, "Conscience is the most secret core and sanctuary of a person." There one is alone with God, whose voice echoes in the depths.[12]

Rewards of Choosing

One of the rewards of making the choice to be Catholic and gay is the continuing association with other Catholics. To withdraw from the community because of

---

[9]*The Dignity Statement of Position and Purpose says that "We believe that we can express our sexuality physically in a unitive manner that is loving, life giving and life affirming. We believe that all sexuality should be exercised in an ethically responsible and unselfish way."*
[10]Human Sexuality, p. 26.
[11]*Ibid.*
[12]*Ibid.*

tensions and conflicts over sexual issues is to cut oneself off from a potential source of strength and nourishment. To leave the faith community is to deprive oneself of the possibility of transforming worship and the opportunity to discuss, learn and minister to other lesbian and gay Catholics.

Every minority group looks for role models within the group, people whose lives demonstrate the ability to rise above the particular social deprivation, institutional marginalization and self-excommunication that an "outsider" status invariably entails. The gay Catholic who has come to terms with both a healthy, self-acceptance of sexual identity and also a personal commitment to the fundamental Catholic belief and value system, can serve as a guide or mentor for others who face the same challenge.

Pre-Vatican II gay and lesbian Catholics tell their individual stories of growing up in a strong Catholic environment which molded them according to traditional Catholic beliefs and customs. The roots of some of their present attitudes and feelings towards the Church — both positive and negative — can be found in Catholic teachings or experiences with Catholic authority figures including their own parents and family, teaching nuns, Brothers and parish priests. When these memories and stories of past events focus on matters of sex, there are often additional implicit and nonverbal clues and messages about sexuality and homosexuality which they have carried to adulthood.

A gay or lesbian Catholic who has made the personal journey from alienation and anger, or from crippling conflict and unhealthy guilt about sexuality, can be a healer for others on the same pilgrimage. They can provide guidance and support for the other since they share similar histories, images and symbols arising out of a Catholic view of life and reality.

There is a final reward for those who decide to live as fully gay/lesbian, and as fully Catholic, to risk the challenges that this venture entails and be a Good Samaritan for others along the road. It is the realization that their lives are contributing to shaping the quality of life in the Church for the next century. Working for change and renewal in any institution, especially in such a deeply personal and involved way of witnessing to sexuality and faith which are so profoundly a part of human life, can be energizing and spiritually uplifting.

Historically, the Catholic Church had witnessed a gradual but steady enrichment of its understanding of human sexuality and marriage. This process has invariably involved people and groups who were courageous and responsible, yet respectful enough to ask honest questions, debate unsettled issues and challenge views that were pastorally harmful in the lives of people. Many of these were theologians, Popes, scholars, teachers and clergy. At times they also included more educated members of the laity such as rulers, university scholars, academicians and other professionals.

In his monumental history of Catholic teaching on contraception Judge John Noonan notes two major differences between the development of Church doctrine on contraception and that on usury. First, there was a lack of *institutional* investment in the movement for change in the contraception teaching. Although there was a great deal of ferment for modification of the teaching against contraception, celibate Church leaders had no identity of practical interests with the married laity. Questions about sex and marriage did not affect the personal concerns of celibates.

Secondly, there was no organization to represent the laity or spearhead a movement for change; women, whom contraception affected most of all, were silent. If women did speak or write about how contraception affected their lives and what they believed or even practiced, they did not do so to the bishop. And so development in Church teaching on this issue came slowly.

By contrast, the Church and its various organizations were very much involved in the use of credit. They knew from personal experience the difficulties encountered with Church teaching on usury. There were also identifiable bankers who were willing to argue for a revision in the teaching on usury. As a result of institutional interests and organized spokespersons, the doctrine on usury did develop and change eventually.

Many of the leaders, teachers and public figures in the Catholic community today are not unaffected in their own lives by gayness or lesbianism — either personally or through their relationships with family, friends or people in ministry. There are also Catholic organizations speaking for the validity of different theological and pastoral understandings of homosexuality. Some of these groups are composed of gay and lesbian Catholics who are willing to openly witness by their lives to the compatibility of faith and sexuality. They are ready to speak and write about this journey to others who feel that the Church needs to hear their testimony for the good of the whole community.

The reward for those who assume this task is the awareness that they are making a valuable contribution to Catholicism in an area that touches the lives of millions of people. It is also the call to be an instrument of the Spirit in moving the whole Church to assure its gay and lesbian members of their active role in the Catholic community. These rewards are not always palpable to those engaged in the process. But the words of Jesus to those who refused to bury their talents or hide their gifts surely apply: "Well done, good and faithful servants."

Suggested Reading

Gramick, Jeannine. *Homosexuality and the Catholic Church*. Chicago: Thomas More Press, 1983.

Gramick, Jeannine and Nugent, Robert (Eds.) *The Vatican and Homosexuality.* New York: Crossroad, 1988.

Holtz, Raymond. *Listen to the Stories: Gay and Lesbian Catholics Talk About Their Lives and the Church.* N.Y.: Garland Publishing Inc., 1991.

McNeill, John. *The Church and the Homosexual.* Boston: Beacon Press, 1988.

McNeill, John. *Taking a Chance on God.* Boston: Beacon Press, 1988.

McNaught, Brian. *On Being Gay.* New York: St. Martin's Press, 1988.

Nugent, Robert and Gramick, Jeannine. *Building Bridges: Gay and Lesbian Reality and the Catholic Church.* Mystic, CT: Twenty Third Publications, 1992.

Nugent, Robert. *A Challenge to Love: Gay and Lesbian Catholics in the Church.* New York: Crossroad, 1983.

Woods, Richard. *Another Kind of Love.* Ft. Wayne, IN: Noll Publishing Co., Inc. 1988.

Zanotti, Barbara. *A Faith of Our Own: Explorations by Catholic Lesbians.* Trumansburg, N.Y.: The Crossing Press, 1986.

Resources

Official Church ministries for gay and lesbian Catholics are operative in the following Archdioceses and dioceses: Seattle, Chicago, Baltimore, Milwaukee, Erie, San Francisco, Camden, Buffalo, Richmond, Kansas City, MO, Dallas, Washington, D.C., Oakland, Los Angeles, San Jose and Charlotte.

Catholic Pastoral Committee on Sexual Minorities
Box 10891
Minneapolis, MN 55458

Christian Community Association
Box 28
North East, PA 16428

Communication Ministry, Inc.
Box 60125
Chicago, IL 60660

Conference for Catholic Lesbians
Box 436
Planetarium Station
New York, NY 10024

Dignity, Inc.
1500 Massachusetts Ave., N.W.
Suite 11
Washington, D.C. 20005

New Ways Ministry
4012 29th St.
Mt. Rainier, MD 20712

THE PRACTICAL ASPECTS: TAKING CONTROL OF YOUR LIFE

Job Security in the Workplace: Legal Protections for Lesbians and Gay Men

David Link and Thomas F. Coleman

Approximately two years before the first edition of *Positively Gay* was published in 1979, a federal court held that an employee who was "openly and publicly flaunting his homosexual way of life and indicating further continuance of such activities" could legally be fired for those activities alone.[1] The activities the employer found objectionable included the employee kissing his lover in the elevator of the building where he worked, giving an interview to a newspaper in which he shockingly disclosed both his name and his opinions on "closet queens," and stating that he intended to continue living his life as a gay man. According to the court, the employee had nothing to complain about when he was fired.

In the years since, the law has changed considerably, although not sufficiently. Several states have now passed laws prohibiting employment discrimination based on sexual orientation. In some contexts, such as public employment, court decisions have held that the Constitution protects gays and lesbians against such irrational discrimination. Fortunately, the list of municipalities passing ordinances against sexual orientation discrimination grows longer each year.

Although much has changed, much has remained the same. Despite the emergence of a larger number of openly gay workers on the job, many employees still fear they will be victims of discrimination if their sexual orientation becomes known. Far too many jurisdictions do not provide any protection against discrimination based on sexual orientation. The primary purpose of this article is to give

---

[1] *Singer v. United States Civil Service Commission (9th Cir. 1976) 530 F.2d 247.*

some guidance to job applicants or employees who suspect they are experiencing discrimination — denial of a job, demotion or loss of promotion, harassment, or being shortchanged on benefits — so they can take appropriate action to correct the unfairness. Keep in mind, though, that not all unfair treatment is prohibited by law and that the law varies from place to place.

1. Victims Should Develop Proof and Then Complain

If you experience discrimination, keep a few principles in mind. One of the first things to remember is that not all employment decisions taken against lesbian or gay employees will constitute illegal discrimination. An employee wishing to contest the employer's action must have some evidence that the employer took the adverse action *because of* the employee's sexual orientation. In most such actions, and particularly in those which result in a lawsuit being filed, the burden is on the employee to show that the employer took its action based on irrelevant factors such as sexual orientation, rather than legitimate employment criteria, such as work history, attendance, productivity, etc.

In some situations it will not be difficult to prove that the employer's action was founded on homophobia. The employer may say something like "We don't hire faggots," there may be graffiti scrawled on the employee's locker, or something equally blatant that will show that sexual orientation was the motivating factor for the discrimination. However, the gay community has become increasingly open in recent years, and many employers who are uncomfortable with openly homosexual employees may fire, refuse to hire or deny benefits to lesbian or gay employees, but create a smokescreen by referring to seemingly legitimate reasons which make no reference to homosexuality.

Therefore, there are two initial things to keep in mind when you suspect you are being treated unfairly on the job because of your sexual orientation. First, be clear about the reasons why you think the discrimination is based on your sexual orientation. Keep notes, take pictures, save offensive "gifts" that have been left, talk to other workers (or perhaps customers or clients) who may have been witnesses. These will all be useful to back up your claim, should it become necessary.

On the other side of this coin, you will also want evidence of your good employment record. If you can present evidence of promotions, commendations, awards, pay raises, or, especially, a long and productive work history, it is far more likely that a court or agency will shift the burden to the employer to prove that something other than homophobia prompted the employer's actions.

In addition to keeping good records, you should also make sure you have exhausted whatever remedies the employer may have made available. Are there internal grievance procedures, or formal or informal chains of command in the workplace? This consideration applies primarily to larger corporations or public employers. Even some smaller companies, though, may have some kind of procedure that is normally utilized to resolve internal disputes, even if it is an informal one. If such a procedure exists and has been used in the past, the employee may be required to use it to make her or his grievance known.

There are two reasons for an employee with a grievance to complain internally before filing a civil rights complaint or lawsuit. First, exhausting internal remedies may be a requirement for taking legal action against the employer. If your employer has provided a mechanism to resolve workplace problems that you have not taken advantage of, this may, in some cases, weaken or defeat any lawsuit or administrative action you might later take against the employer.

But even when compliance with internal remedies is not required, the use of internal procedures may serve to educate the company and resolve many problems that upper levels of management were unaware of. This will be especially true when the problem is not termination, but the creation of intolerable working conditions for lesbian or gay workers, either by fellow employees, or by certain management personnel. The overt homophobia of a few employees may not reflect company policy, or may expose the fact that the company does not have an explicit equal employment opportunity or so-called "EEO" policy on sexual orientation discrimination. When such renegades go unreported, management may have no reason to suspect that anyone objects. It is an irrefutable fact that most managers are heterosexual, and do not ordinarily consider the problems faced by lesbian or gay employees. Until someone points out that homophobia is becoming a problem, they may not even know there is a problem. Using grievance procedures to make it clear that certain employees or lower-level managers are making your job far more difficult will give your employer the opportunity to deal with the people who are causing the problem. Giving the employer notice of a problem gives the employer an opportunity to fix it, if that is possible or desired.[2]

The third fundamental principle to keep in mind when there are problems at work due to your sexual orientation is probably the most important, and the most overlooked. Make sure that the real difficulty is always kept in focus. It is not homosexuality that is the problem. It is homophobia.

While this is usually obvious to lesbians and gay men, it may not be so obvious to the employer, and it is important to clarify this distinction. Curing the problem of homophobia in the workplace will nearly always work to the company's benefit. The sexual orientation of good and productive workers is irrelevant to the job they do. After all, how is heterosexual sexual orientation a job-related criterion? If

---

[2]*It should also be pointed out that this requirement of using existing company procedures works both ways. If there are established procedures for demoting or firing an employee, the employer must abide by them, too. For example, public employers are required to comply with the Due Process clause of the Constitution, and give employees notice and an opportunity to be heard on any employment actions taken against them. Adverse employment actions taken without providing adequate notice to the employee may be violations of this rule. Any time such a procedure exists, employees also may have a right to use it to make her or his own case before being subject to demotion, termination, or other action.*

heterosexuality is irrelevant, why would it be relevant that an employee's sexual orientation is homosexual or bisexual?

The only difference in the workplace between homosexuality and heterosexuality is the continued existence of homophobia. But the homophobia of a fearful and vindictive worker can, and often will, work against an employer's best interests by adversely affecting employee morale, or by forcing lesbian and gay employees to leave, taking their skills, training and talents elsewhere. Most employers want to keep good employees, especially those who are well-trained, creative, or have been with the company for a long time.

The question, then, is how much homophobia will the employer tolerate before the adverse effect of the homophobia starts to affect the company's productivity and bottom line. It is now much harder for a homophobic person to argue that homosexual employees will go away if enough people in the workplace make it clear that lesbians and gay men are not wanted there. As the number of ordinary, productive and open lesbians and gay men increases, it is probable that the people they work with on the job will realize that they have nothing to fear from their gay and lesbian coworkers. Ultimately, employers will learn that bias against gays and lesbians in the workplace is not only unfair, it is against the company's best interests.

It is, though, not always easy to frame the issue in that light when those who run the company either want to ignore the issue of sexual orientation discrimination or are themselves homophobic. It is those types of companies and managers which have created the need for this discussion.

2. The Law is Complicated and Evolving

The law is clear that there is no general right to have a job. In the absence of some contractual, constitutional or statutory provisions, employers may hire and fire almost anyone.[3] Different rules apply to employers of different kinds. For legal purposes, it is most convenient to discuss two broad kinds of employers: public employers and private employers.

A. Government Employees Have Many Legal Problems

The provisions of the United States Constitution have been held to give some form of job protection to most government employees. Employees who work for the federal government, for administrative agencies, the courts, police or sheriff's departments, public school districts, or hundreds of other government bureaucracies come into this category. In many cases, though, such as privately owned companies providing public utility service, this distinction is not so clear. In some cases, however, such utilities have been found to be "quasi-public," a status which subjects them to constitutional requirements.[4]

---

[3]United Electric Radio & Machinists Workers v. General Electric Co. *(D.D.C. 1954) 127 F.Supp. 934, cert. denied 352 U.S. 872 (1956).*
[4]Gay Law Students v. Pacific Telephone and Telegraph Co. *(1979) 24 Cal.3d 458 [156 Cal.Rptr. 145, 595 P.2d 592].*

Constitutional protections are often phrased in broad language, guaranteeing the "equal protection of the laws," "due process," and "freedom of speech." Under the due process provision, the courts have long held that civil service employees may not be discharged unless the employer makes a rational determination that the discharge will promote the efficiency of the civil service.[5] The due process clause has often protected lesbian and gay civil servants from discharge or other discriminatory actions. In some cases, courts have held that sexual orientation discrimination against government employees violates the equal protection clause of the Constitution.[6]

The law in this area is still developing, and various legal precedents sometimes appear to be in conflict. In the context of military service, at least, some courts have ruled that the military must show that its discrimination has a rational basis. A federal appeals court has specifically ordered federal judges to conduct hearings to determine whether it is rational for the military to exclude lesbians and gay men.[7] Other courts, though, have held that discrimination by the Department of Defense against lesbians and gay men is rational, based on the most minimal evidence that the KGB sometimes "targets" homosexual Department of Defense employees.[8] An important point to remember is that federal courts usually defer to decisions by the military, whereas in other areas of public employment the courts would be more likely to declare discrimination to be unconstitutional.

The constitutional protections of free speech and freedom of association have provided mixed results in various forums.[9] Nevertheless, freedom of speech is one area where even the current U.S. Supreme Court has been fairly consistent. An employee who was fired merely for giving an interview, or otherwise publicly discussing homosexuality might be able to claim this protection.[10] The California Supreme Court has used a state statute to do the work of these constitutional protections.[11]

---

[5]Norton v. Macy *(D.C. Cir. 1969) 417 F.2d 1161*
[6]Gay Law Students v. Pacific Telephone and Telegraph Co. *(1979) 24 Cal.3d 458 [156 Cal.Rptr. 14, 595 P.2d 592]*
[7]Pruitt v. Cheney *(9th Cir. 1991) 943 F.2d 989*
[8]High Tech Gays v. Defense Industry Security Clearance Office *(9th Cir. 1990) 895 F.2d 563*
[9]*Compare* Childers v. Dallas Police Dept. *(N.D. Tex. 1981) 513 F.Supp. 134 with* Van Ooreghem v. Gray *(5th Cir. 1980) 628 F.2d 488.*
[10]*Even in the military context, any discussion of the issue of homosexuality would be protected speech. There, however, due to military regulations, when the subject of the speech includes identification of the speaker as homosexual, discharge from the service does not violate the first amendment.* Pruitt v. Cheney *(9th Cir. 1991) 943 F.2d 989, 992.*
[11]Gay Law Students v. Pacific Telephone and Telegraph Co. *(1979) 24 Cal.3d 458 [156 Cal.Rptr. 14, 595 P.2d 592]*

Many government employees are also protected by "merit system" laws and regulations. These laws prohibit personnel actions that are not based on the employee's merit. Employment decisions based on sexual orientation have been considered a violation of the merit system. For example, the federal Office of Personnel Management has concluded that sexual orientation discrimination violates the "merit" system.[12] The California Personnel board has taken a similar position with respect to state employees.[13]

In addition to legislative and judicial protections, government employees also may be protected by executive orders. The first executive order prohibiting state employees from sexual orientation discrimination was issued by Governor Milton Shapp of Pennsylvania in 1975. California soon followed when Governor Edmund G. Brown Jr. issued a similar order in 1979. Today, government workers in several states are protected by executive mandates.[14]

B. Private-Sector Employees Are Gaining More Protections

When the government or one of its agencies is not the employer, then the employer is generally considered to be private. While the federal Constitution does not apply to them, some state constitutional provisions might. State's courts are free to interpret state constitutional provisions to give more protection than similar provisions in the federal Constitution. For example, state courts may interpret a state constitutional provision as applying to all employers, rather than just governmental employers.[15]

Federal civil rights statutes also cover most private employers, as well as public ones. While at present these laws only provide protection based on factors such as race, nationality, gender or handicap, attempts are constantly before the Congress to add sexual orientation to the list. The Americans With Disabilities Act of 1990[16] protects against employment discrimination on the basis of disability, which would include AIDS. It also prevents discrimination against those who are in fact not disabled, but who are perceived as being disabled by coworkers or supervisors, and may be found to be discrimination based on sexual orientation, at least when the

---

[12]*Based on the Civil Service Reform Act of 1978, the federal Office of Personnel Management issued a memorandum to all departments stating that the law specifically covered "social affiliations" and "sexual orientation."*
[13]*In a letter to the chair of the Michigan House Civil Rights Committee, dated February 18, 1981, the chair of the Michigan Civil Service Commission adopted a similar interpretation of "merit principle number two" of the Elliot-Larsen Civil Rights Act.*
[14]*Executive orders are in place in seven other states, including Louisiana, Minnesota, New Mexico, New York, Ohio, Rhode Island, and Washington. An order signed by the Governor of Oregon was repealed by the voters in a statewide referendum a few years ago.*
[15]*See* Sands v. Morongo Unified School Dist. *(1991) 53 Cal.3d 863, 882-83 [281 Cal.Rptr. 34, 809 P.2d 809]*
[16]*101 Pub. L. 336 (1990 S. 933, 104 Stat. 327)*

discrimination, in the mind of the employer, is based on a misconception about the connection between HIV and homosexual orientation.

In some states, statutes now explicitly protect against discrimination based on sexual orientation. The list currently includes Wisconsin, Hawaii, Connecticut, New Jersey and Massachusetts.[17] This is an important and growing new dimension of legal protection to lesbian and gay employees. Even when efforts to amend the Federal Civil Rights law eventually succeed, that law does not cover all private employers, and state laws can fill the gaps, or in some cases provide additional remedies.

Another source of protection may be found in local laws. A growing number of cities, counties and other local governmental entities are passing laws prohibiting discrimination based on sexual orientation. Some of these prevent discrimination against all employers directly, while others prevent discrimination against certain kinds of employers, for example, employers who contract with the city, or who receive city funding. It is now becoming an enormous task to keep the list of these local ordinances updated.[18] Local attorneys will be aware of the laws in your area, and local lesbian and gay community organizations will also be important resources, since in many, if not most cases, they will have been instrumental in getting such laws enacted in their own communities.

Finally, employees should look to their own contracts of employment. More and more employers are making it an explicit policy that they will not tolerate discrimination, and this may well include sexual orientation. Sometimes, statements of this kind will actually be in a document the employee has signed. Usually, however, a statement of nondiscrimination, or a statement that the employer makes decisions based on merit and performance will be found in policy manuals, employee handbooks or other memos.

Many unions have successfully negotiated job protection for gay and lesbian employees. Pursuant to collective bargaining, many employers have added "sexual orientation" to existing nondiscrimination policies. The clauses, however, have generally been limited to employment practices such as hiring, firing, job transfer, promotion, and the like, but not to employee benefits. Eliminating discrimination from employee benefits programs generally requires more explicit language.

Documentary evidence such as an employee manual or union contract is not always necessary to prove that your employer has a policy of nondiscrimination

---

[17]*It appears that California is also on this list for openly gay employees and, at least temporarily for those who have not disclosed their sexual orientation to supervisors or coworkers. The state's Supreme Court has held that it is illegal for an employer to discriminate against an employee who comes out on the job.* Gay Law Students v. Pacific Telephone and Telegraph Co. *(1979) 24 Cal.3d 458 [156 Cal.Rptr. 14, 595 P.2d 592]. In 1991, the state Labor Commissioner ruled that all sexual orientation discrimination is illegal, for openly gay and closeted employees and job applicants alike.*
[18]*More than 75 municipalities in 25 states and the District of Columbia have ordinances prohibiting sexual orientation discrimination in employment, however, in some of these cities, the protection extends only to local government workers.*

which might include sexual orientation. A verbal assurance by a manager that you are a valuable employee, and that you won't be fired for a non-job-related factor such as sexual orientation may be sufficient to show that sexual orientation nondiscrimination is a genuine, although unwritten, term of your particular employment contract. The manager might not even have to refer explicitly to sexual orientation: a promise that you won't be fired as long as you're doing a good job might also be sufficient. In addition, the employer's past course of conduct may be considered. If it can be shown from the way the employer has acted in the past that employees are retained because of merit, and are not fired for reasons unrelated to their job performance, this, too, may be relevant evidence that the employer has a policy of nondiscrimination which may be enforceable.

3. Discrimination May Surface in a Variety of Ways

Discrimination may occur in the hiring process, possibly in the form of intrusive questions or selective recruitment.[19] You may intuitively suspect discrimination when someone less qualified is hired. Only a handful of the most ignorant companies will admit outright that they don't hire homosexuals. In most states and municipalities that have sexual orientation nondiscrimination laws, applicants as well as existing employees are protected.

When discrimination occurs against already-working employees, it often surfaces in the form of harassment in the workplace or wrongful termination.

Harassment can arise in any number of forms, limited only by the imagination and resources of those who fear homosexuality so much that they are driven to act. Reports range from veiled verbal taunts, to pornographic or demeaning photographs left on a homosexual employee's desk or in their locker, to outright insults, to actual, violent and physical confrontations.

There are no reported appellate cases, yet, of such harassment by itself constituting a cause of action in the way that sexual harassment of women in the work place is.[20] Therefore, internal grievance procedures may be the best remedy for lesbian or gay employees who do not succumb to the wishes of the harassers and quit their jobs.

When the harassment becomes so bad that the employee is forced to quit, though, the harassment may be a prominent factor in a subsequent charge of

---

[19]*Some courts have considered questions on employment applications regarding sexual orientation or other personal factors as invasions of privacy which cannot be tolerated. Soroka v. Dayton Hudson Corp. (1991) 1 Cal.Rptr. 2d 77 (rev. granted, 4 Cal.Rptr. 2d 180 (1992))*
[20]*There is an unpublished decision in California, however, in which the state Fair Employment and Housing Commission ruled that same-sex harassment of an employee violates the prohibition against sexual harassment.* Department of Fair Employment and Housing v. Vernon O. Ring, *Case No. FEP82-83, filed November 15, 1985.*

wrongful termination. Even though the employee has not technically been fired in such a situation, the harassers have created a situation at work which any reasonable person would find intolerable. As a general rule, when that happens, the employee has been "constructively terminated," a legal term meaning that, for all intents and purposes, the law will view the employee's decision to leave as a kind of forced termination sanctioned by the employer. Again it should be stressed that there may be a requirement that the employer had notice of the harassment, had an opportunity to cure it, and decided not to, before the employee can show she or he was constructively terminated.

When the employee can prove a constructive termination, the ordinary law of wrongful termination comes into play and, depending on the law in your jurisdiction, you may be able to successfully sue the employer. An attorney specializing in employment discrimination law or a gay civil rights organization will be able to determine what laws are applicable to a particular set of facts, and make an assessment of whether it would be worthwhile to pursue your case in court. Most lesbian and gay community services facilities can provide the names of attorneys who will understand the issue. In larger cities, lesbian and/or gay telephone directories will certainly include advertisements for such lawyers and organizations.

4. Discrimination in Benefits is the New Battleground

The most recent battlefront against discrimination is in the area of employee benefits. Nearly all employers provide certain benefits to their employees, and "eligible family dependents," as part of their overall compensation package. Certain benefits, such as sick leave, bereavement leave, health insurance, dental care benefits, credit union membership, and other privileges or discounts are also offered to the employee's family members. Whether gay and lesbian employees are single or have a domestic partner, they are often being undercompensated, even though they are performing the same job as coworkers with spouses or children. To a growing number of gay and lesbian employees, the rallying cry is "equal pay for equal work."

The problem faced by lesbian and gay employees is twofold. The single worker without legal dependents is shortchanged because most benefits packages pay more to workers with spouses or minor children. Gay and lesbian employees with domestic partners also are cheated because benefits plans define "family" to include only a limited type of relationship based on blood, marriage, or adoption. Same-sex couples don't qualify under these restrictive definitions, no matter how long the employee has been with the company or how long the employee and his or her lifemate have been together.

It is not necessary, however, for employers to use such a restrictive definition. First, employers can, and some do, eliminate marital status discrimination from benefits plans by adopting a "cafeteria style" plan that lets each worker choose the benefits he or she needs or to take cash instead. Also, for those employers that insist on paying workers with family dependents more than single employees without legal dependents, they can define "family" in a more expansive way.

Every employer is legally permitted to use an inclusive definition of family for purposes of benefits eligibility. In fact, an increasing number of employers are redefining "family" in ways that include unmarried couples, whether opposite-sex or same-sex partners, and their children, who view themselves as one another's family members.[21] In addition, a number of lawsuits have been filed challenging the inequity of employment policies that give unmarried employees with domestic partners less compensation than married employees with legally recognized spouses.[22]

5. Activism Promises to Bring a Better Future

Due to the activism of gay rights organizations and prodding from gay and lesbian employees, many companies have adopted, and more are on the verge of adopting, sexual orientation nondiscrimination policies. Others are giving serious consideration to domestic partnership benefits. Because of outside political and economic pressure as well as inside agitation, a growing number of companies are beginning to take these issues much more seriously.

A heightened level of corporate interest in issues of marital status and sexual orientation discrimination is evidenced by the agendas of two large conferences held recently. On April 2, 1992, the Risk and Insurance Management Society of America, an organization comprised of 9,600 private and governmental employers held a West Coast conference that included two separate workshops on employee benefits entitled "Recognizing Non-Traditional Families: The Future is Now." And

---

[21]*Many public employers have expanded the definition of "family" to extend benefits to employees with domestic partners. They include several cities in California. Berkeley, San Francisco, Santa Cruz, Laguna Beach, and West Hollywood provide sick and bereavement leave as well as health and dental benefits. The City of Los Angeles provides only sick and bereavement leave to employees represented by two large unions. Many cities outside of California have done the same. The largest is Seattle which provides sick and bereavement leaves, and health and dental benefits. Madison, Denver, District of Columbia, Tacoma Park, and New York City also provide various domestic partner benefits. Private-sector employers are beginning to jump on the benefits bandwagon. The largest employers to do so are Levi Strauss and Lotus Development Corporation. Many others currently have the issue under study.*
[22]*Regrettably, the only reported appellate case of this kind so far holds that an employer does not violate sexual orientation discrimination laws by limiting health and dental benefits to the spouses and children of married employees.* Hinman v. Department of Personnel Administration (1985) 167 Cal.App.3d 516 [213 Cal.Rptr. 410]. *This opinion is a model of misunderstanding by an uninformed judiciary. Despite this temporary setback, lawsuits for benefits discrimination are pending in several states against public and private employers.*

on September 20, 1991, the Human Rights Campaign Fund, together with the Lesbian and Gay Community Services Center of New York sponsored an East Coast forum called "Invisible Diversity: A Gay and Lesbian Corporate Agenda." This conference was attended by 80 of the Fortune 500 companies.

The future is promising *if* — and this is a big IF — gay and lesbian employees continue to speak up. Things will change if employees actively and visibly participate in workplace reform, enlist the support of unions and straight coworkers, insist that EEO policy statements include sexual orientation and marital status, demand equal benefits for their lifemates and children, encourage employers to seek outside help from consultants with expertise in these areas, and, when all else fails, complain about discrimination to appropriate government agencies and file lawsuits when necessary. Ultimately stronger legislation may be necessary if voluntary action by employers or lawsuits fail.

In any event, lesbians and gay men in the workplace should remember, if you're not part of the solution, you're part of the problem. Whether you are the owner of a company, part of the management team, a union representative, or a rank-and-file worker, don't sit on the sidelines or be an automatic defender of the *status quo*. Choose to be a champion of fairness and equality.

Resources

GAY AND LESBIAN LEGAL ORGANIZATIONS

The following organizations may be able to give you legal advice, refer you to a private attorney, or provide direct legal representation if you experience discrimination as an applicant or employee, including situations involving denial of a job, unfair termination, harassment of the job, or unfair denial of employee benefits.

American Civil Liberties Union
Gay and Lesbian Rights Project
132 W. 43rd Street
New York, NY 10036
(212) 944-9800

Lambda Legal Defense and Education Fund
666 Broadway
New York, NY 10012
(212) 995-8585

Gay and Lesbian Advocates and Defenders
P.O. Box 218
Boston, MA 02112
(617) 426-3594

National Center for Lesbian Rights
1370 Mission St.
San Francisco, CA 94103
(415) 621-0674

Texas Human Rights Foundation
2201 N. Lamar, Suite 203
Austin, TX 78705
(512) 479-8473

GAY AND LESBIAN PUBLICATIONS

The following publications regularly feature current developments on legal, economic, and political issues involving employment discrimination based on marital status and sexual orientation as well as updates in the area of domestic partnership benefits.

Lesbian/Gay Law Notes
Prof. Art Leonard, Editor
New York Law School
57 Worth St.
New York, NY 10013
(212) 302-5100
$25/yr. (issued monthly)

Partners Magazine for Lesbian and Gay Couples
P.O. Box 9685
Seattle, WA 98109
(206) 784-1519
$21/yr. (issued quarterly)

Sexual Orientation and the Law
Achtenberg & Newcombe, Editors
Clark Boardman Co. New York, NY
(Release #3 Published in 1990)

NON-PROFIT RESEARCH AND EDUCATION

The following organization does public policy research and issues publications on domestic partnership rights in the workplace.

Family Diversity Project
Spectrum Institute
P.O. Box 65756
Los Angeles, CA 90065
(213) 258-8955, ext. 707

Financial Planning: Making the Best Use of Your Money

Ronald J. Jacobson and Jonathan A. Wright

Financial planning for gays and lesbians — whether you are single or whether you have a lover — is a matter of emphasis. If you are single, planning your finances is not unlike it would be if you were straight. If you are in a relationship with a domestic partner, you have an advantage over your straight counterpart who is married: you can, as we will explore, take advantage of the law to allow yourselves many of the benefits of a legally sanctioned marriage or you can tailor your financial relationship with your lover to suit you on a level that is not as committed as a marriage.

This chapter will deal briefly with federal income tax, principles of property ownership, retirement planning and estate planning. Each is an important area, requiring special planning for gay people, and of course, each applies to you whether or not you are currently in a domestic partnership relationship. Some of these areas can be very complicated, so it is best to seek professional guidance for the legal issues involved.

FEDERAL INCOME TAX

Federal income tax is so complicated that if you want to be creative you almost have to consult with an accountant or attorney. Short of that, however, the Internal Revenue Service publishes many helpful pamphlets that summarize various aspects of the tax laws. A list of these pamphlets is available at any Internal Revenue Service office.

Any of these pamphlets could be useful, but several might be of special interest to gay/lesbian people because they contain information suited to many typical gay/lesbian situations. Publications include such topics as Tax Information on Business Expenses; Child Care and Disabled Dependent Care; Information for Divorced or Separated Individuals; A Guide to Federal Estate and Gift Taxation; Your Exemptions and Exemptions for Dependents; Business Use of Your Home; Tax Information on Partnership Income and Losses; Record Keeping for a Small Business; Information on Self-Employment Tax; and Travel, Entertainment and Gift Expenses.

Among the areas that you should explore are deductions for dependents, home mortgages and business deductions. Briefly, if one person qualifies as a dependent of the other (which in most instances means a child or parent), the dependent is worth a deduction from the other person's taxable income. For the most part, this deduction does not apply to a person's domestic partner, as such, unless one has legally adopted the other. There are also numerous other technical requirements that you must meet.

Home mortgages bear particular emphasis for gay/lesbian couples because there is no requirement for any legal relationship between the parties in order to take advantage of the special tax benefits attributable to home ownership, so long as both parties are liable on the loan. If you do own property together, be sure to understand the various types of joint ownership, as we discuss below.

Another way for a gay/lesbian couple to lower their combined income tax is to form a business corporation or partnership. For example, you might consider holding title to a second vacation home, which you rent out, in a legal partnership with your domestic partner. This business, as a separate legal entity, then becomes eligible for various tax and other financial benefits. Be sure to consult an attorney.

PRINCIPLES OF PROPERTY OWNERSHIP

If you are a gay/lesbian couple, you may want to have control over each other's bank accounts and safe deposit boxes. This can be done very easily. You can open a bank account in "joint tenancy." This requires one or two signatures (at your preference) for withdrawal or to write checks. Legally, a joint tenancy means that during your joint lifetimes you each have equal control, and upon the death of one, the survivor would automatically own the accounts — without the need for a will or probate. This is discussed in greater detail further on.

The principles of joint tenancy apply to other forms of property, such as real estate or a new grand piano. In addition to equal control of the property, though, you both may want to receive the tax advantages from owning certain types of property (for example, deducting from your taxable income the interest payments on the condominium). This can be done by holding the property as joint tenants or by forming a business partnership and holding the property in the name of the business. You should probably consult an attorney or an accountant about a partnership, but you can arrange a joint tenancy on your own. Simply request that the title papers or receipts or whatever other evidences of ownership you receive say "A and B as joint tenants." Note that the tax benefits to each of you will be in proportion to the payment each makes on the property. In other words, A cannot get half of the deductions if B makes all of the mortgage payments.

If you both want access to a bank safe deposit box, rent the box as "co-renters." There is no joint tenancy for safe deposit boxes because the property inside the box is owned separately from the safe deposit box itself. The most you can accomplish with a safe deposit box is to be sure that each of you has equal access to the contents of the box.

An alternate way of having control over each other's property (that is, if it remains in one person's name) is to give each other "power of attorney." Power of attorney is the right that A gives to B to legally sign A's name in place of A. Most stationery stores have general power of attorney forms, which are fine for most situations. Some banks have their own forms, though, and do not like to accept general powers of attorney. So, for bank transactions, use the bank's forms. A power of attorney is no longer legally valid when the person giving it dies or is legally incompetent, unless it is a "durable power." A durable power, unlike a general power, survives death and illness, but you must be careful to complete the proper form for a durable power; this form of power of attorney is also usually available at a stationery store.

If you wish to keep your property separate, you should take title as "tenants in common." Each of you will then have a one-half interest which will *not* go to the other automatically when you die. Instead, it will be a part of your estate. (See Principles of Estate Planning below.)

If one of you has been involved in a heterosexual marriage and is still legally married, watch out. In states in which there are community property laws (such as California, Texas, Washington and Louisiana, among others) the husband and wife each own half of the property and the money earned during the marriage — even if only one works. These rules continue until there is a legal separation. It is, therefore, important to be sure that you are legally separated. Consult an attorney.

While professional couple counselors would emphasize the importance of trust and commitment in building a lasting relationship, as lawyers we would be remiss if we did not address the matter of practical issues involved in separation. Some couples feel more secure knowing that there is an arrangement agreed upon beforehand about who owns what: property, furnishings, cars, pets, *etc.* This extends to purchases made during the relationship. In the event of separation it is at least clear that the cocker spaniel was bought by Partner A for Partner B and therefore goes where Partner B goes. Having such agreements does not necessarily mean that a couple is planning the end of their relationship. It simply establishes an understanding and a basis for negotiation should the need arise to divide things up.

Other couples favor pooling their financial resources and owning everything jointly as an act of faith in the permanence of their partnership. The decision to choose either option should be made carefully since there are advantages and disadvantages either way.

PRINCIPLES OF RETIREMENT PLANNING

Contemporary culture is truly youth oriented. Everything from fashions to food seems to cater to those with young, healthy bodies and an unlimited future. As a result, younger people, gay and non-gay, lack awareness of the need to plan today for retirement tomorrow. There is such a need, however, since the average person retiring now at age 65 can expect to live another 15 years. This figure will undoubtedly increase with better medical care. It certainly is a substantially long and an important part of your life. Remember, there are a number of things that can be done now no matter what your age.

First of all, retirement systems in the United States deserve a few words. Traditionally, workers have based their retirement on Social Security payments, private pension plan benefits and personal savings. Retirement planning is especially important for all gay and lesbian people, since Social Security, private retirement plans and government retirement plans, as a rule, do not grant the same survivorship rights to domestic partners as are granted to legally married couples.

Social Security
Social Security taxes are paid equally by you as a worker covered by Social Security and by your employer. The taxes are withheld from wages, matched by your employer and credited to your Social Security account.

In order to qualify for Social Security benefits, you must accumulate the minimum work-time credit, measured in number of calendar quarters of covered employment. Normally ten years are required (40 quarters). In addition, you must be at least 62 years old, or 60 if you are a widow or widower.

In order to figure out your benefits under the current law, consult the brochure Estimating Your Social Security Checks, obtainable free from any Social Security office. It is a good idea to check with the Social Security Administration in Baltimore, Maryland 21235, every three years to make sure that its records of your earnings agree with yours. (Check your W-2 forms or tax returns.) You only have three years, three months and 15 days to correct an error or it will become permanent.

Remember that Social Security was not designed to provide you with enough money to live comfortably. It is strictly to supplement your income from other sources.

Private Pension Plans
Many employers maintain one or more pension or profit-sharing plans that can be an important source of retirement income for you. Be sure to inquire about such

plans where you work and whenever you get a new job with a different employer.

Congress in 1974 passed the Employee Retirement Income Security Act (ERISA), or as it is sometimes called, "The Pension Reform Act." This complicated law is your Bill of Rights as an employee with regard to your company's employee benefit plans. ERISA requires your employer to furnish you with a statement of your benefits and a summary description of each employee benefit plan in which you participate. Study these provisions carefully because subtle differences between plans may have a great impact on your job decisions. You may, for example, decide to quit after working nine years. If your plan requires ten years' service, you won't receive a pension when you retire. Had you realized this at the time, you might have decided to work another year.

There are many types of employee benefit plans. A popular one is the *pension plan* under which you receive certain benefits when you retire, usually a certain percentage of your salary at retirement. Normally the percentage increases the longer you work for the company. Most pension plans require you to work for a set number of years before your benefits become "vested." *Vesting* is the continuing process of accumulating permanent rights to pension benefits. Once vested, a benefit may not be taken away even if you are fired or quit. Pension plans vary as to vesting periods, but generally you must be fully vested after five years of credited services. Once you are a participant, your prior years of service will normally be counted for vesting purposes.

ERISA established the Pension Benefit Guarantee Corporation (PBGC), a federally supported insurance company to provide insurance coverage for benefits from certain types of pension plans in case they terminate or are improperly funded.

Another type of employee benefit plan is profit-sharing. These plans differ from pension plans in that they do not promise a defined benefit but are geared to the company's profits or to performance of the company stock. They are designed to act as an incentive to work harder for the company. The company contributes a certain percentage of its profits to the plan and, typically, your share is allocated to an account in your name. These funds may be invested in the common stock of your employer or in some other investment medium. The value of your account will vary depending on investment performance and company profits. In most profit sharing plans you receive the balance of your account when you retire or terminate employment. The 401(k) plan is a popular variation of the profit-sharing plan where you can make before-tax contributions and your employer can match all or part of your contributions. These plans help to build funds for retirement **and** reduce current income taxes. Profit sharing plans and 401(k) plans are not covered by PBGC insurance and the rules for participation and vesting are the same as for pension plans. Most of these plans also allow you to designate a beneficiary (who doesn't have to be a legal spouse). Consult your plan documents and benefit statements for information.

Another broad category of employee benefit plans are known as "employee welfare plans." These are not retirement-oriented plans but are very important to gays and lesbians because of the health, disability and life insurance benefits that are often a part of these plans. Some progressive companies now offer domestic partners the same "spousal" benefits as are offered to legally married couples. Before taking on a new job, be sure to ask about medical plans, disability plans (including sick leave policies), vacation plans, prepaid legal services plans or any number of related fringe benefits. Chances are that part of your compensation is going to pay for them and it's to your benefit to know about them and to take advantage of them. Some medical plans, for example, may specifically disallow claims related to AIDS, exclude preexisting conditions or place low caps on maximum benefits that can be paid. Also, plans sometimes allow retired employees to participate even though they no longer work at the company — a great opportunity because health insurance is difficult to get after retirement or leaving a company due to disability.

If you work for a federal, state or local government, you will be a participant of the governmental employee's pension plan (no government earns a "profit," so there are no profit-sharing plans). Congress exempted these plans from the strict rules of ERISA, so the requirements for participation and vesting may be different. Consult your benefit statements and plan documents for information.

Individual Retirement Accounts
Even if you are not covered by a government pension plan or a private tax-qualified employee benefit plan, you may be eligible to start your own retirement plan, by setting aside up to $2,000 (as of 1992) a year from your earnings in an individual retirement savings arrangement. Depending on your income and whether you are covered by a qualified plan, you may get an income tax deduction for the amount you contribute and the earnings on the contributions will not be taxed until you withdraw at retirement. There are several types of these plans: The Individual Retirement Account (IRA) offered by many banks and savings and loan associations, brokerage houses, mutual fund companies and other entities; individual retirement bonds and individual retirement annuities from some insurance companies. There are complicated rules for setting up these plans, so be sure to check them out before you plunge in. There also are substantial tax penalties if you contribute too much, not withdraw enough when you should or withdraw too much when you shouldn't. The Pension Reform Act requires each institution offering one of these services to give you a complete disclosure statement in plain English. If you still have questions, ask.

Self-Employed Retirement Plans
If you own your own business as a sole proprietor or partner, you may want to set up a plan for the business under the rules established by the IRS for so-called "Keogh Plans." Ask your broker, bank or savings and loan for information.

Investment and Savings
As a final backup for your retirement years, plan early to save as much as you can so that you'll have extra money to do the things you want to do to enjoy a satisfying

gay lifestyle. This sounds old-fashioned, but it's good advice. If you manage to accumulate more than you need to live on, then, plan how to invest the funds, even if you have only a modest amount.

Savings Accounts
The most basic investment is an insured savings account. These accounts are normally considered the foundation for other types of investment, because they do not require large sums of capital and they are safe. Also, they can be owned in joint tenancy by gay and lesbian partners.

Passbook Savings Accounts and Certificates of Deposit
Unlike stocks or bonds or mutual funds, passbook savings accounts and certificates of deposit are types of savings that are insured by the federal government (FDIC). (Review the principles set forth above under **Principles of Property Ownership.**) A certificate of deposit is a form of savings account which will pay a higher rate of return than a standard bank passbook savings account. Essentially, the difference is that you can withdraw your money from a passbook account at any time, whereas there are restrictions placed on the period of time which you must keep your money in a certificate of deposit before being able to withdraw from it. The longer the restriction, the higher will be the rate of return.

Even if you do nothing more than save, you should plan your savings programs carefully. There is a confusing variety of interest rates, term deposits, maturities and the like. Study them carefully before deciding what is best for your financial situation. In addition, every financial institution computes interest differently and some may be more to your advantage than others. Be sure to check out savings arrangements with your credit union if you are eligible. Also, be sure to check out the FDIC insurance limits and avoid unsound financial institutions.

Securities
You may be interested in diversifying your investments by buying one or more types of securities, even if only a few U.S. Government Series E Savings Bonds. Although space does not permit a more detailed discussion of all the different types of securities, here are two basic types.

Common Stocks
Stocks are shares of ownership in a corporation. When you buy stock you become an owner of a part of a business. If the business is profitable, it will normally pay dividends to you. Stocks vary in value, of course, and may result in gains or losses when you sell them.

Bonds
Technically a bond is evidence of a "loan" you have made to a government or company. They provide income because interest is paid on the amount of money loaned and they "mature" at a certain date when the "loan" becomes due. Bonds are called *fixed-rate investments* because their rate of return is determined at the time

they're issued. They tend to be more stable than stocks, but because they are less risky they won't offer the dramatic increases in value that stocks can. Some government bonds provide tax-exempt income.

Mutual Funds
Mutual funds are a means of collectively investing in a pool of stocks or bonds, and each mutual fund typically has a specific investment objective. For example, you can invest in a mutual fund specializing in municipal bonds or one specializing in high risk growth stocks. Also, be aware that there are two potential streams of income from a mutual fund: both the value of your piece of the fund, itself, and the interest or dividend payments emanating from the bonds or stocks which the mutual fund holds on your behalf. Money market funds are a form of mutual fund that usually have a stable unit value and a slightly higher rate of return than a savings account. However, they are not insured by the FDIC.

With all of these securities, joint ownership by partners is another way of sharing assets.

Life Insurance
Many gay and lesbian people discount the need for life insurance. Not only is it an important part of estate planning, as we will discuss later, but it can also be helpful in providing money after retirement. "Whole life" policies, for example, can be converted into an annuity to pay you a certain sum of money regularly.

Real Estate
A very popular investment at the moment is real estate. For gay and lesbian people, owning your own home can be an effective means of beating inflation while providing tax advantages. You may want to buy a second home for vacations where you may want to live after retirement. If you sell your home, be sure to check out the rules for deferring taxes on the gain by purchasing a new home within the required period. If you wait until age 65 to sell, there may be certain tax advantages. Consult IRS publication #523 — Tax Information on Selling Your Home.

CHECKLIST FOR RETIREMENT

Since the system doesn't give us a lot of built-in safeguards, it is important to take every advantage. In summary, here are the practical steps you can take:

To Prepare for Retirement
1. File for a statement of your Social Security account once every three years. Forms are available from the Post Office, your local Social Security office or the Social Security Administration, Baltimore, Maryland 21235.
2. Study your pension and other employee benefit plans carefully. Take them into consideration when making job-related decisions.

3. If eligible, consider establishing your own Individual Retirement Account savings program or Keogh Plan.

4. Analyze your assets. Consider the liquidity and income generating capacity of each one, especially as you near retirement.

5. Review your liabilities, debts, mortgages, *etc.* Make sure you'll have enough income to pay them; perhaps pay some off while you are still working.

At Age 62

1. Determine whether you're eligible for a property tax rebate on your home. (In California file an application with the local office of the State Franchise Tax Board.)

2. Check for other benefits, like free banking services.

3. If you are considering early retirement do as follows:

One year before retirement, check to see if you can extend your coverage under your employer's group health insurance plan. If not, begin to look for another plan. Be sure the plan you choose covers extended illness and convalescent care. If you are a member of a trade or professional organization, ask about a group health insurance plan, since it will almost always carry the lowest rates.

Three to six months before retirement, check with the personnel department where you work to begin filling out all the necessary forms for pension benefits and continued health insurance coverage.

File for Social Security benefits two to three months before you retire. You must file for benefits in person at a local Social Security office and bring the following: (a) your Social Security card; (b) a copy of your last W-2 form or previous year's income tax return; (c) certified copy of your birth certificate or baptismal record. (There are documents you can substitute if you don't have either of these. Ask at the Social Security office.)

If you collect Social Security, you'll get Medicare automatically. If not, you'll have to apply for it independently, no earlier than three months before your 65th birthday and no later than three months after it. Check out the Medicare option that covers additional services for a small monthly fee; it may be worth it.

Check with your life insurance agent to decide when or whether to convert your policy's cash value into annuities.

PRINCIPLES OF ESTATE PLANNING

As you near retirement you will undoubtedly begin to think about what you would like to happen to your property after you die. This process, called estate planning, is something that should be started even earlier than retirement planning, since death could occur at any age.

Prior to AIDS, it was a common misconception that gay and lesbian people had no need for estate planning. Generally, the theory went, they had few if any dependents, did not have lasting relationships and could not take advantage of many of the tax-savings arrangements available to married couples. This, however, is not accurate now, if it ever was. You undoubtedly have some property that you wish to leave to your lover or to others. You might want to have some of it go to one or more charities. To accomplish either of these ends, you need to think about estate planning.

Definitions

In order to discuss the planning of your estate and some of the basic concepts associated with it, you should know the meanings of a few simple terms. The first term is *estate*. Basically, your estate consists of all the assets you hold at your death, including life insurance proceeds, trusts (unless irrevocable) and others. Your estate is probably bigger than you think.

The second term is *probate*. Probate is the legal process by which the property in your estate is placed under the jurisdiction of a probate court, your debts and taxes are paid, and your property is disbursed to the beneficiaries you have either named in your will or who are identified under the particular laws of your state. Probate can be complicated and time consuming, but it will result in your property being transferred to the beneficiaries you choose.

The third term you should be familiar with is *will*. A will is a legal document which must be signed by you in accordance with the particular law of your state and witnessed by the appropriate number of witnesses, also determined by the law of your state. Your will should name a person to handle your estate (executor) and should name those people or charities who will receive your property (beneficiaries). If you die without a will your property will pass to your heirs-at-law under the laws of intestacy (without a will) of your particular state. If you are not legally married, in most cases your children, if any, or your parents would receive the bulk of the estate. Obviously, if you are a couple, your lover would not normally be named under the laws of intestacy. If you want to leave your property to each other, both of you definitely need wills. The wills should be drafted by an attorney, because your family may want to get your property and contest the will. The gay or lesbian person who is concerned about leaving an estate (total or in part) to a lover should never use a preprinted will form. They're just too dangerous!

Another important term is a *trust*. Unlike a will, which only goes into effect when you die, a trust becomes effective when you sign the trust agreement and transfer property to the person or bank you name as *trustee*. You are called the *trustor* (or *settlor*) because you have established (or *settled*) the trust. Many people call these arrangements *living trusts* because they are set up during life. The trust agreement names one or more persons as beneficiaries. A living trust avoids probate for the trust assets and is totally private. Many gay and lesbian people have found them to be the best solution to their estate planning needs. A further benefit is that the trustee can provide funds for the trustor (or a beneficiary) if he or she becomes ill, thus avoiding the need for a conservatorship or guardianship.

Taxes

The federal government assesses a federal estate and gift tax on the property you own at death. Some states also assess an estate or inheritance tax; this should also be considered. Normally, you would not have to pay any federal estate tax if your estate does not exceed approximately $600,000 (as of 1992).

There are a few tax-saving techniques that can be used to minimize the amount of federal estate tax and state inheritance (if any) which your estate will have to pay. Since the marital deduction is not available for gay or lesbian couples, charitable deduction is the primary tax-saving technique for you. Basically, if you leave a portion of your property to charity then no estate tax will be assessed on that gift. Thus, by lowering your taxable estate by the amount of the charitable deductions, you reduce the overall level of estate tax that will have to be paid.

Avoiding Probate

There are other ways, of course, to leave your property to your lover or to friends. Some of these have been discussed above, but the most common is joint tenancy. By placing your assets in joint tenancy during life you will insure that the surviving joint tenant (your lover) will receive them at your death. Holding assets in joint tenancy provides for little or no tax planning, but if you have only a modest amount of property this might be the best solution.

Placing your assets in joint tenancy results in giving your lover, as joint tenant, some control over your property. If you are not quite sure about doing this, consider the alternative of leaving part of your property in a "payable on death" bank account through a will. And, of course, placing your assets in joint tenancy does not provide for the contingent beneficiary who will receive the property if your lover does not survive you or if you both die in a common accident. You might also name your lover in an "informal trust" bank account (*i.e.*, "Mary Jones, Trustee for Virginia Johnson"). This has the same effect as joint tenancy at death, but it does not allow the lover to have any control over the account during your lifetime. You, as trustee, may withdraw the proceeds held in the account at any time. The arrangement has the same disadvantages as a joint tenancy, however.

Another way to provide for your lover or other beneficiaries is through life insurance, discussed above under **Retirement Planning**. Life insurance can provide not only a method of saving for retirement but also a vehicle for leaving cash to your beneficiaries to pay the debts and expenses remaining at your death, including federal and state death taxes. If you have a sizeable portion of your estate in real estate or other assets difficult to sell, you should definitely consider purchasing life insurance while you are young enough to do so, so that your lover will not have a difficult time selling the properties to raise cash for these expenses. Life insurance proceeds are included in your estate for tax purposes, but they do not pass through probate. If your lover or other beneficiaries die before you, however, you have the same problems as with informal trust accounts and joint tenancy arrangements.

But You Still Need a Will

It is important for you to have a will even if all of your property is held in joint tenancy with your lover. You can have an attorney draft a will for a modest price. Unless you have minor children to provide for in a trust or other complicated provisions, your total estate plan should not amount to much more than a minimum figure.

You may be motivated to plan your estate because you want to leave your property to your lover, friends or charities. Even if this is not the case you should realize that without a will or other arrangement, your property will either go to your heirs-at-law under the laws of intestacy or it may be forfeited to the state. And your heirs-at-law, of course, may not necessarily be those whom you would put in your will. Certainly, forfeiture to the state is not an attractive alternative either. Even if you don't have close friends or family to whom you wish to leave your property, you should consider having a simple will drafted to provide for a gift to your favorite gay or lesbian charity rather than allow your estate to be confiscated by the state as unclaimed property.

The above discussion of gay and lesbian issues in financial planning is meant as a checklist of areas to explore as you plan for your own protection and that of your loved ones.

Take Back the Day: Opening the Corporate Closet

Brian McNaught

Throughout the country, from high tech corporate offices to restaurant kitchens, gay, lesbian and bisexual employees are coming out and coming forward to insist upon equal rights, equal consideration and equal benefits. Where a decade or so before, the gay battlegrounds had names of counties and cities like Dade and Seattle, the new rallying cries have been over names like the Cracker Barrel Restaurant chain and the U.S. Army. Our feelings of pride have come from successes at Lotus, AT&T, Disney World, Stanford University and Levi Strauss, to name only a few.

Gay issues in the workplace are basic. Will the company guarantee through a nondiscrimination policy that we will not be denied employment because of our sexual orientation? Will the company work hard at creating a productive work environment by eliminating homophobic and AIDSphobic behaviors from the workplace? Will the company pay us in wages and benefits equal to our heterosexual peers, whether we are partnered or single? Will the company evaluate our work and offer the opportunity for advancement without regard to our sexual orientation? Can we participate in all aspects of corporate life? Will the company publicly support us?

Many years ago, such a listing of expectations by lesbian and gay employees might have seemed ludicrous not only to the nation's employers but perhaps also to many gay and lesbian employees. It was enough for some gay people to be hired without being subjected to a lie detector test as was once administered by Coors; to not have termination papers state "moral turpitude"; to be left alone. We gay people often married to "pass" or to be promoted, endured "queer" jokes, quit if we sensed exposure or sought careers which allowed for autonomy. Though that is still true for some today, ever increasing numbers of lesbian, gay and bisexual employees are coming out to their supervisors and/or their peers. We are forming support groups within the corporations to meet our social and political needs. We are lobbying for nondiscrimination policies where none exist; for educational programs; for domestic partner benefits. Some of us are taking our significant others to company social functions; are setting up information tables outside the cafeteria or in the lobby during Diversity Awareness Weeks; are marching under our company's logo in Gay and Lesbian Pride parades and AIDS fundraising walks.

In response to the demands of their employees and to the demands of the market place, an ever expanding and impressive segment of corporate America is taking the lead in addressing the needs of their gay employees. Corporations like Xerox and Walt Disney World publicly state they will not discriminate on the basis of sexual orientation. Sensitivity trainings about homophobia are taking place throughout the country in companies like Bell Communications Research (Bellcore) and U.S. West. Employee support groups have been formed in corporations like AT&T and Digital. At Levi Strauss, Lotus and Ben and Jerry's Ice Cream, the domestic partners of gay and lesbian employees receive the same benefits given the spouses of their heterosexual co-workers. Some companies do it quietly, others with press releases. Nearly all of them have done what they have done because they were asked and because it made good economic sense.

Coming Out vs. The Closet
Being asked is important and much of the change in the last several years is due to the emergence of the gay worker from the closet. When we come out today, gay employees often do so to a management that is already convinced of the need to create a work environment which is conducive to the productivity of *all* employees. Old styles of management and old attitudes toward labor set U.S. companies back in their efforts to compete in the global market. The most successful companies seemed to be those which valued the diversity of their workforce. Such an approach optimized teamwork by honoring individual differences. The ideal workspace has become that in which every employee can grow to his or her full potential and produce at their highest level.

Studies indicate and common sense underscores that gay and lesbian people who are afraid of coming out because of a hostile work environment produce at a lower level than gay and lesbian employees who are not afraid of coming out. If we are in the closet, we tend to spend a lot of time and energy protecting our private lives; energy that does not go into our work. We don't put the picture of the person we care most about on our desk; we may not take personal phone calls in front of our office mate; we shy away from discussions of weekend plans; we stay home, come alone or bring a date of the other sex to office social functions; we may bite our lip in the presence of homophobic comments; we don't take assignments which would make us personally uncomfortable; we don't call attention to ourselves for fear of people asking questions about us; we isolate. We don't want to come into work early or leave late. All of that takes energy. All of that can make us angry, unhappy, dissatisfied. Clearly, this situation is not good for us or for our employers.

Corporations which have come to understand the effect of homophobia on the productivity of their employees are making changes in the workplace. One example of a company that is responding positively to the emergence of its gay, lesbian and bisexual employees is AT&T.

AT&T has a corporate policy that prohibits discrimination based upon sexual orientation. Though the policy is valued differently throughout the company, AT&T does have openly gay managers. It has a gay and lesbian employee support group with chapters throughout the country. In various sites, those support groups have sponsored Gay and Lesbian Awareness Week. Activities during such weeks might include noon-hour speakers, videos, panel discussions, information tables and displays. Members of the group hold annual national conventions, the expenses for which are generally covered by their employer. AT&T offers sensitivity training on "Homophobia in the Workplace," a workshop I developed for Bellcore and which I have given to several thousand employees at both corporations. Though AT&T does not now provide domestic partner benefits, it is in on-going dialogue with its gay employee support group about implementing such benefits. (A well-publicized legal suit by the surviving partner of a lesbian employee seems certain to be influencing such dialogue currently.)

AT&T does not advertise its response to its gay employees, but neither did it back off from its position of support when confronted by a large, well-orchestrated angry letter writing campaign by a conservative "family values" group. Thousands of people wrote and threatened to cancel their service or to destroy their Universal credit card. AT&T responded that they are not endorsing a lifestyle but rather are valuing the contributions of their gay and lesbian employees.

In addition to building loyalty from their gay, lesbian and bisexual employees, such actions as those taken by AT&T also make the company more attractive to the "best and the brightest" gay and lesbian college graduates and those in other companies who seek a more conducive work environment. Likewise, I feel that such actions are generally rewarded by gay and lesbian consumer loyalty. (For example, I, for one, will never eat at a Cracker Barrel restaurant but AT&T will be my long distance telephone service because I want to reward their efforts at creating safe space for their gay employees. I continue to boycott all Kellogg products because of their cavalier attitude toward their offensive "Nut'n Honey" television commercial but I am delighted to buy jeans from Levi Strauss and ice cream from Ben and Jerry's.)

Having been fired from my job in the early 1970s because I came out, it is exciting for me to see today the growing trend in corporate America of affirming the contributions made by gay and lesbian employees. Still, I know, that many gay, lesbian and bisexual people continue to work in environments which make it pretty difficult for them to feel safe and to feel appreciated. For many of us, it is still a real challenge at work to grow to our full potential and produce at our highest level.

In such situations where we feel unprotected, unwanted and unhappy, it seems to me as if we have at least four options. We can endure it. We can look for employment in a company which values its gay employees. We can change professions in order to work more independently. Or, we can choose to stay and change the environment. It is this last option that I wish to address.

Models for Change

Changing the environment at work so that it protects and nurtures the development of its gay and lesbian employees can begin with simply asking the affirmative action officer, the legal department or one's supervisor to amend the company policy so that it will forbid discrimination based upon sexual orientation. Believe it or not, sometimes, though not often, that is all it has taken. If that feels impossible or impractical, my first step would be to establish an employee support group. There are at least two models for this.

At Bellcore, the first corporation with which I worked, a group of employees, many of whom were heterosexual, all of whom had some awareness of gay issues, came together and formed the Sexual Orientation Equity Committee. Bellcore already had a nondiscrimination policy. These employees wanted the company to provide sensitivity training as it did for other issues like racism, sexism and disability. The result of their efforts was the highly successful "Homophobia in the Workplace" workshop. For their pioneering work the group was given an award of appreciation by the company.

In this model, the power to generate interest and action came from a group of people who didn't feel the need to identify their sexual orientation, who came from varying levels of responsibility at work and who set for themselves a clear agenda. Word of mouth and subsequent publicity in the company newsletter helped build the group's membership.

The other model for action with which I am familiar is the employee support group at AT&T known as LEAGUE (Lesbian and Gay United Employees). This group started out in Denver and spread throughout the AT&T network via the electronic mail system which all employees can plug into. One LEAGUE chapter got jump started by placing an ad in a local gay newspaper announcing an offsite meeting of all gay, lesbian and bisexual AT&T employees. Each chapter is autonomous and has its own personality. Some chapters have a primary focus on social support. Recreational events are held offsite. Other chapters have a stronger political focus. They may meet socially, but their primary objectives are education and equal treatment. While the majority of LEAGUE's members are gay, lesbian or bisexual, there are also heterosexual members who see the issue of sexual orientation equity worthy of their time and effort. When I conduct the "Homophobia in the Workplace" workshop at AT&T, a male and female LEAGUE representative speak at the end of the session to the workshop participants about the goals of LEAGUE.

Regardless of the model, employee support or lobbying groups will have the best chance of securing a policy of nondiscrimination. What is being asked here is amending the company's policy to include sexual orientation. Gay people are not asking for special privileges, just equity. Though the 1964 Civil Rights Act does not yet state "sexual orientation," several states do guarantee protections, as well as many counties, cities, towns, companies, colleges and professional organizations.

As was learned through the passage of the 1964 Civil Rights Act, legislation is important but education is essential if attitudes are going to change. Having a company policy that prohibits discrimination will not guarantee a change in atmosphere at work. The environment may still feel hostile to gay, lesbian and bisexual workers. The most effective way of improving the climate is through education.

Companies like Bellcore and AT&T expect their employees to attend at least one workshop a year that addresses minority concerns. Employees can pick from a menu of options, like sessions on race, gender or age issues. Attendance at these workshops is noted in the employee's record and taken into consideration during performance review. Given the precedent, it was not difficult to add a workshop on "Homophobia in the Workplace." Initially, there was some concern regarding the content and some protest by Bible Study employee support groups or individuals, but pilot workshops alleviated the concern of managers and word of mouth on the workshop was good. Pre- and post-workshop evaluations underscored not only the popularity of the session but also its effectiveness in raising consciousness about the issues gay, lesbian and bisexual employees face on a daily basis.

Sensitivity Training
Building a case for employee sensitivity training when there is no precedent presents a major obstacle. Under these circumstances it is not uncommon to hear, "Gay employees want special privileges. Why should we do for them what we don't do for others?"

Faced with that scenario, I suggest approaching both the Affirmative Action or Diversity Management Office and the most sympathetic persons in management and ask if time could be set aside to make a presentation to them on gay issues in the workplace. Raising their consciousness and making allies of these key people is essential. In addition to conducting a training session for them, I would keep them updated on developments in other corporations, particularly the competition, on what is being done around this issue. News clippings about the issue, such as those reporting the move by Levi Strauss and Lotus to provide domestic partner benefits or a copy of the December 16, 1991 *Fortune* cover story on "Gay in Corporate America," can help build the case for why the company should be taking steps to create a more conducive work environment.

Homophobia sensitivity trainings should have clear objectives. The format is flexible, depending upon available resources and the amount of time allowed. The premises for my work are that: approximately 10 percent of the work force is gay; homophobia, defined as the fear and hatred of gay people, exists in the workplace (give concrete examples); homophobia takes a toll on people's ability to produce (give concrete examples); unfamiliarity with the issue, not people, is the enemy; we can educate about unacceptable behaviors in the workplace without endorsing a lifestyle, i.e., people are free to believe what they want to believe but not do what they want to do in the workplace.

The objectives I state in my workshop are that employees will: understand the corporate policy toward nondiscrimination (if there is one); explore and articulate their feelings about homosexuality and homophobia; replace myths with accurate information; understand the effects of homophobia on all employees; strategize means of eliminating destructive behaviors toward gay men and lesbians from the workplace.

The advantage of having an outside consultant do sensitivity training on this issue is her or his familiarity with all of the arguments that are used against and all of the questions that arise from such a discussion. Experience working with an uncomfortable audience and success at communicating essential information in a non-threatening way are important assets here. If having an outside consultant is beyond the budget, employee groups can put together very effective programs. The two key issues are information and personal role modeling.

Strategies for Progress

I find audiences want and need factual information about sexual orientation. Myths about homosexuality are rampant and destructive. They prompt unthinking and insensitive jokes and comments in the workplace. Accurate information can be made available through presentation, use of videos and handouts. The role modeling by openly gay people and by supportive nongay people is also essential and highly effective. If there are openly gay people in the workplace who are able and willing to answer questions, it allows for potential allies to hear firsthand what it is like to be gay at work. Most of the heterosexual people in the audience have never had the opportunity to ask a gay man or woman a personal question.

Providing workshop participants with a means of recording their feelings and with a means of showing support are other important steps in creating a safe work environment. Workshops should be followed with evaluations. Pre-workshop and post-workshop questionnaires allow one to measure change in attitudes. Likewise, giving supportive co-workers ideas of how to participate in the creation of a safe work environment is also helpful. There are reactive and proactive things they can do. Not laughing at "fag" or AIDS jokes is a reactive measure. Putting something on their office wall or bookshelf which indicates they are an ally is a proactive measure. The AT&T support group, for instance, came up with a magnet which features the pink triangle surrounded by a green circle. These they offer at workshops with the request that they be displayed in offices which are "gay friendly."

Other steps which can be taken include:

Form coalitions with other employee support groups. The issues of the African American, Latino, Asian American, women's, older workers' and gay groups are very similar. Forming alliances strengthens all of the groups and may help ensure that the gay group is more sensitive to the needs of their minority members and that the other employee groups are better prepared to address the needs of their gay and lesbian members;

Network with other Gay Employee Support Groups. A listing of these can be secured through the Human Rights Campaign Fund or the Wall Street Project (see below). It may be possible to tie into a computer network. The obvious advantages of such an effort are having the benefit of other's efforts, mutual support and encouragement;

Build a resource library in the Affirmative Action or Diversity Management Office. If in-house workshops are going to be created, presenters will need access to videos, books, news clippings, brochures, etc. Also, the corporation's legal department and public relations department will need access to current information on gay and lesbian workplace issues;

Encourage the participation of the company's Affirmative Action Officer in national conferences which address the issue of gay people in the workplace.

For the last several years, men and women have marched in various cities throughout the country demanding safer streets for their citizens during the evening hours. They do so under the banner: "Take Back the Night."

This makes me think that our gay efforts to create a conducive work environment could appear under a similar banner: "Take Back the Day." We seek to "take back the day" with a work environment free of homophobic and AIDSphobic behaviors, in which we will be paid equally in wages and benefits to our heterosexual co-workers, in which we can participate fully as gay workers in every aspect of corporate life, and where we feel encouraged and able to grow to our full potential and to produce at our highest level.

Resources

Information, Model Policies, Strategies:

Wall Street Project
c/o Community Lesbian and
   Gay Rights Institute
208 W. 13th Street
New York, NY 10011

Human Rights Campaign Fund
1012 14th Street, NW
Washington, DC 20005
(202) 628-4160

Interfaith Center on Corporate
   Responsibility
475 Riverside Drive
Room 566
New York, NY 10115
(212) 870-2296

Legal:
Lambda Legal Defense and
   Education Fund
666 Broadway
12th Floor
New York, NY 10012
(212) 995-8585

Gay and Lesbian Advocates and
   Defenders
P.O. Box 218
Boston, MA 02112
(617) 426-1350

Audio Visual:
"Gay People in the Workplace"
TRB Productions
P.O. Box 2362
Boston, MA 02107
(617) 236-7800

Using Your Gay and Lesbian Voting Power

R. Adam DeBaugh

THE LESBIAN/GAY CONSTITUENCY

The initial task facing the Lesbian and Gay community in organizing for political influence is to identify it as a constituency. Who is the Lesbian/Gay community? How do we reach them? Crucial questions for constituency education and especially important for the Lesbian/Gay political effort, since this constituency is not readily visible.

By *Lesbian/Gay constituency* I mean all people who have something to gain by the passage of Lesbian/Gay civil rights legislation, the repeal of sodomy laws, changing discriminatory immigration laws, funding for AIDS research and education, and other sexually related legislation. I believe very strongly that Lesbian and Gay people have an important stake in women's issues, in marriage laws and in any law that attempts to limit personal freedom of sexual, relational and affectional lifestyles. Thus, the Lesbian/Gay constituency I refer to includes all men and women who identify themselves either publicly or in their own minds as Gay, Lesbian, homosexual or bisexual. It also includes people who may be heterosexually married or otherwise publicly identified or assumed to be heterosexual, but who engage occasionally in sexual behavior of a homosexual nature which is prohibited by law. It also includes most heterosexuals as well, although they may not understand this, since many states that still have sexual conduct laws also prohibit all but the most "traditional" forms of sexual contact. And it includes all other people who share the hope for the end of discrimination and who ask that the government neither continue nor permit the unwarranted persecution of people based on their sexual orientation or practices.

As the Lesbian/Gay community has become better organized, our potential political power has grown as well. Most minority groups that have organized for their liberation have quickly begun to develop not only political awareness, but also a knowledge of how to use the political system for their ultimate benefit. The Lesbian/Gay community is no exception.

The first big step any group needs to take when organizing for political influence is to educate and organize its constituency. For the Lesbian/Gay community, this poses unique problems.

Most minority groups are easily identified. African-Americans, Native-Americans, Latino-Americans, Asian-Americans, women and other groups are highly visible in our society. But homosexuality cuts across these and all other groups. Gay and Lesbian people are, in essence, an invisible minority, and this fact makes our oppression unique. The weapons needed to fight our oppression are also unique.

Some Gay men and Lesbians feel the best way to fight Gay oppression is to hide their homosexuality. Yet this head-in-the-sand approach to life is just not realistic. As long as laws exist affecting what people do in the privacy of their bedrooms, we can be prosecuted for our sex acts. Any demagogue who thinks he or she can further an otherwise lackluster political career by cracking down on "perverts" can start the process. Any mayor, sheriff, chief of police, district attorney or city council member can push for enforcement of the law.

The inescapable conclusion is that Gays and Lesbians *must* work in all areas starting with the education of each other. If we are discussing organizing for political power, we should first define politics. Politics is the way Americans select the people who make up their government. It boils down to a fairly simple formula: people + money + communications = power. The *people* component is made up of voters, workers and warm bodies: voters to get out and vote for the candidates they support; workers to campaign for those candidates; and warm bodies to appear at political meetings, rallies, demonstrations and speeches. *Money* is a major tool in political work, especially in campaigns. Lesbian and Gay organizations can back up their efforts to influence legislators and other politicians by contributing financially to the campaigns of people who support Gay rights. *Communication* is very important for organizing a constituency. Gays and Lesbians need to show they can communicate to large numbers of people who will in turn respond by, for instance, contributing money to a campaign, volunteering to work for a candidate, writing letters to a Congressperson or just voting. Communication means alerting the Lesbian and Gay community to the good things our *supporters* do and to the bad things our *opponents* do — it is as simple as that. Gays and Lesbians also need to be able to follow up on promises made by politicians. If that city council-person who promised to support Gay rights gets into office and fails to do anything, we should inform the Gay community so that pressure can be applied. Another aspect of this part of the equation is the media, and the Gay and Lesbian community is getting better at gaining access to mass media to achieve our goal of fair and equal treatment.

About 10% of the American population are Gay and Lesbian. That is at least 25 million Gay men and Lesbians in the United States. A city of one million people would then have 100,000 Gay men and Lesbians. But in most areas, the vast majority of our Gay brothers and Lesbian sisters are invisible. Adding together the members of Lesbian/Gay organizations, the people who patronize Gay bars and other businesses, the subscribers to Lesbian and Gay publications, and the people who attend Lesbian and Gay religious services and functions would never yield anywhere near the number of Lesbian and Gay people a given city is statistically supposed to have.

In order to begin to identify the Lesbian and Gay constituency, you need to start where Gay and Lesbian people are. Begin by making a list of the Gay and Lesbian organizations which are, of course, the first source of active and involved Gay and Lesbian people. Most areas also have Gay and/or Lesbian bars. Many have Gay or women's bookstores and movie houses. More and more cities now also have religious groups serving the Gay and Lesbian community like Metropolitan Community Church, Dignity, Integrity, Affirmation, Gay synagogues, and chapters of Lesbian/Gay caucuses of other religious denominations. There are often medical and health clinics that serve the Lesbian/Gay population, hot lines or switchboards, and doctors and lawyers who have a large Lesbian or Gay clientele. Especially since the AIDS crisis, the number of health-related services to the community has grown, as has the number of organizations committed to political action of various kinds. Specialized social clubs are ideal places to contact Gay and Lesbian people. Finally, every Gay man and Lesbian involved in even the smallest way with Gay life knows others, many of whom are not involved in any way. We mustn't forget to include as constituents the people who are not involved in any organizations, who never go to bars or other Gay businesses, and who never come in contact with Gay and Lesbian publications or speakers.

Now that we have lists of Lesbian and Gay organizations, businesses, political organizations, religious groups, clubs, discussion groups, bridge clubs, coffee klatches and parties, what are we going to do with them?

ORGANIZING FOR POLITICAL INFLUENCE

While many Lesbians and Gays have become politically savvy in the past fifteen years there is still much work to be done by people who have not yet entered the arena of participative politics. Therefore, the following suggestions are offered in the hope that even larger numbers of Lesbians and Gays become active in our community's struggle for equality.

Constituency education implies that there is an organization working to develop the political presence of the Lesbian and Gay community. This organization should develop a program of action. We will discuss some suggested areas of action later in this chapter. After a relatively simple statement of general purpose is drawn up, and after requirements and cost (if any) of membership are decided upon and regular (or the next) meeting dates are planned, and once the organization has something in the way of real programs to offer, then a brochure should be produced for distribution at all places where Gay and Lesbian people are likely to obtain a copy. This means leafletting the bars, bookstores, and movie houses. It means making sure every member of every other organization gets a copy. It means, perhaps, posting signs on bulletin boards around town. It certainly means news releases and stories in Lesbian- and Gay-oriented newspapers, magazines and newsletters in your area. It may mean advertisements in campus or regular newspapers and magazines in locales that have few other Gay and Lesbian information outlets. It also means getting the word out to all of your friends and acquaintances. This process doesn't stop after one big effort; it should be continual if you want your organization to grow and if you want to inform more and more people.

What kinds of programs are appropriate and important for an organization devoted to organizing for political influence? Let's consider six types of programs: voter registration and voting, public education, polling candidates, endorsing candidates, fund raising, and lobbying.

REGISTER AND VOTE

If we are truly to organize for political influence, the only place to start is with voter registration. Unless our supporters are registered and voting on election day we will never have the political base necessary for real political power.

Registering and voting are two of our most important civic responsibilities. Our system of representative government only works if the people take these responsibilities seriously. More importantly, we need to register and vote for a selfish reason: political survival. Unless the citizens of this country care enough about good and truly representative government, we won't have a good and representative government. It begins with us, the voters.

The first step, then, for any Gay and Lesbian political organization is to make sure all of its members are registered to vote. The second step is more involved: making sure as many people as possible are registered to vote — Gay men, Lesbians, bisexuals, and others who support the quest for basic human rights. This can be done in a number of ways, depending on what kind of voter registration system your community has.

Some areas have postcard registration. Organizations can obtain voter registration postcards from the registrar of voters and go out and register voters. Many groups have had great success in doing this in Gay and Lesbian bars and other Gay businesses. Once filled out, the forms are taken to the registrar's office. This serves two purposes. First, it assures that the forms *will* be filed rather than stuck in someone's pocket and forgotten. Second, a Gay and Lesbian political organization bringing large numbers of voter registrations to the registrar will make an impact on local politics as word gets around that Gay and Lesbian people and their friends are registering. That means *power*.

In cities that don't have postcard registration, the registrar of voters will explain the registration process to any caller. Your group might want to organize a Voter Registration Day when you gather a lot of people together and go, en masse, to the registrar's office. Some cities have even had success in getting a Gay/Lesbian establishment (for instance, an MCC church, a Gay/Lesbian community center, a bar) designated as a voter registration location by the local registrar. Mobile registrars will often agree to set up registration facilities at your building on a given day. Advance notice can bring a lot of people to register at this kind of event.

During the registration process it may be possible for your organization to develop a mailing list. As people register, ask if they want to be on your mailing list in order to keep informed about issues of common concern. Be sure, however, to protect the anonymity of the people on your list and assure people that their names will not be made public. This mailing list can be the core of an effective political organizing network.

I think it is important to keep our goals relatively small. I remember visiting a small city in the Midwest one year and the local MCC pastor had gone to the registrar of voters and gotten himself authorized as a deputy registrar. He announced to his congregation that they were going to register *500 new voters!* The 25 people there were a little overwhelmed. I suggested to him that it was probably a good idea to keep his goals small and manageable. If we announce a goal of, say, 50 new voters, we can probably meet that goal relatively easily. Then two things happen. First, we have a record of success — we met our first goal, we have a track record of accomplishment, we have begun to build momentum. If the goal is so high that it will take a very long time to reach — if ever — there is no sense of achievement, no victory, no success, just the seemingly never-ending work of struggling toward the goal. The second thing that happens is that we have an opportunity to celebrate and thank our volunteer workers. If a group, no matter how important and weighty its goals and mission, doesn't have some fun together, it will have a hard time attracting new members. The celebration of our victories is energizing. Our people are inspired to set and meet new goals.

Once people are registered, it is important to make sure that they vote. Letters and posters urging people to vote can be followed up by phone calls on election day. Your organization could organize car pools to help people get to the polls. It will be especially important to get out the vote if the race pits an opponent of Gay/Lesbian rights against one of our friends. The more voters we generate, the more political clout we develop.

PUBLIC EDUCATION

Public education is central to any Lesbian and Gay political organization's work. We can break this area down into a number of different tasks.

Know your representatives. It is important to be able to tell people who their elected representatives are. Many good and responsible Americans are ignorant about the people they elect to serve them. Keep up-to-date lists of the names, political party, office addresses, and phone numbers of all your elected representatives: city government, that is mayor and city council; county government; state government, members of the state assembly and senate, and governor; and federal government, members of the U.S. House of Representatives and Senate. Urge your people to write and visit these representatives.

Know where your representatives stand. Spread the word about your elected representatives' positions on Gay and Lesbian rights, AIDS, and other issues of interest and concern to your community. (We will discuss later in this chapter some techniques for finding out where politicians stand.) It is important to let our constituency know who our friends are, as well as our enemies.

Educate your representatives. Not only should we educate our constituency about our representatives, but we should make a real effort to educate our representatives about us. Communicate with city, state and national elected officials. Provide them with information about the Gay and Lesbian community. One of the biggest obstacles we face is the massive ignorance about Gay, Lesbian and bisexual people that prevails in the non-Gay community. We have a major responsibility to provide accurate information about the Lesbian/Gay community to those who govern us.

Educate the media. The same educational priority is needed for members of the media. The electronic and print media need information about the Gay/Lesbian community if they are to report accurately about it. It is important to develop a good working relationship with members of the press and to provide them with information that will help them do their job well.

Educate non-Gays. The process of public education must expand to reach all people. Ignorance about Gay and Lesbian people is a prime cause of our oppression. If people understood who we really are, rather than the stereotypes they have been fed, then homophobic attitudes would begin to change. Public education is a crucial role for the Lesbian/Gay rights organization.

Some suggested public education possibilities include a speakers' bureau; bus and/or subway ads; newspaper ads; and such events as National Coming Out Day; Lesbian/Gay Pride marches, rallies, and demonstrations. Other options for education of the public are positive newspaper/magazine articles; Lesbians and Gays assisting in the training of police, fire department, hospital workers, and teachers; a visible Gay and Lesbian presence in non-Gay organizations; Gay and Lesbian speakers at local churches and synagogues. There are many other ideas — spend some time brainstorming ideas that are possible in your community.

POLLING CANDIDATES

We talked earlier about letting our constituents know the stands candidates have taken on our issues. Many Lesbian/Gay organizations have had remarkable success in polling political candidates on their views. The first step is to put together a list of questions to ask each candidate. Make them specific; it isn't enough to ask a candidate if he or she supports Gay and Lesbian rights. Ask whether a congressional candidate, for instance, will co-sponsor a national Lesbian/Gay civil rights bill. Ask whether a city council candidate will support a civil rights bill in your city. Ask if a candidate for the state legislature will support the repeal of sodomy laws (if they still exist in your state) and if they will support Gay and Lesbian civil rights legislation on the state level. Ask candidates if they will support public financing for health clinics, Gay/Lesbian help lines and other services to our community. Ask all candidates where they stand on public education on AIDS, funding for AIDS treatment and research, and the distribution of condoms.

After the list of questions has been drawn up, get the names and addresses of all candidates who have announced for the election (obtainable from your elections board). Then send the questionnaire with a cover letter to *all* the candidates. Explain that their responses will be published widely in the Lesbian and Gay community and supportive non-Gay community. Let them know that you represent a large block of votes.

A week or so after the questionnaires go out, *call* candidates to urge them to respond. Within a few days of the deadline call those who have not responded and urge them to. You may not hear from some candidates, but it is important to give them every chance to answer your questions. When all the responses are in, publish them. Make sure you list all candidates, even those who refused to answer your questions. This protects you from charges of bias. "No Answer" *is* an answer, after all, and hostile answers are clear demonstrations of the way the candidate feels.

Then be sure the word reaches as many people as possible. If there is a Gay and Lesbian publication in town, make sure the results of the poll get published, well enough in advance of the election so that as many people as possible see it. Distribute the poll results in the bars, bookstores, religious groups, social groups, wherever Gay and Lesbian people gather. Ask local Gay and Lesbian organizations to include a copy in their mailings. Have members of your organization give copies to friends and neighbors. Gathering this kind of information is useless unless large numbers of Gays and Lesbians and supportive non-Gays find out the results. Dissemination of the information is as important as gathering it.

Nonprofit, tax-exempt organizations can educate the public about political candidates, so long as they do not endorse specific candidates. If the organization (and this includes religious organizations) simply reports to the people the positions of *all* the candidates, they are well within their rights under the Internal Revenue Code. Refrain from endorsing candidates. You can and should urge people to vote in the election, but if you are a nonprofit organization, you shouldn't tell people whom to vote for.

In addition to the formal poll of candidates, raise relevant Gay and Lesbian issues at candidates' public appearances. Everywhere a politician appears, he or she should be confronted with valid questions about Gay/Lesbian rights from concerned voters. Question them at public meetings as well as in private. The more they hear about Gay and Lesbian concerns from a wide variety of people, the more they will be inclined to support us.

Your organization may want to invite political candidates to speak before your group. Such candidate forums have been used effectively by a number of Gay and Lesbian groups. Get as many people as possible at such forums to hear the candidates; candidates are going to be impressed by large numbers of voters. Individual candidates and politicians may always be invited to speak at special events of your group, in addition to having all candidates for a specific office speak at a candidates' forum.

In addition to polling candidates at election time, it is important to keep track of incumbent politicians' actual voting records on issues of importance to our community. What public statements have they made? What promises did they make in their campaigns and are those promises being kept?

ENDORSE CANDIDATES

If your group is specifically a political organization, you may endorse candidates running for public office. Once again, no religious organization or other nonprofit, tax-exempt organization may endorse political candidates. But if your group is a Lesbian/Gay Democratic or Republican club or another kind of Gay and Lesbian political organization, you can and should endorse candidates.

Endorsement should be based on the candidates' responses to questionnaires, on personal interviews, on their past records, and perhaps on speeches made before your group. Don't be afraid *not* to endorse someone in a specific race. Don't fall into the trap of thinking that any candidate who supports Gay and Lesbian rights is the best person for the job. Gay and Lesbian rights are important but should not be the only issue on which to judge a candidate. By the same token, a person is not necessarily the best one for a political office simply because he or she is Gay or Lesbian. Sexual orientation alone is not reason enough to support a person for public office.

Endorsing a candidate, if it is to have maximum impact, should involve three components: votes, money, and people. First, spread the word. Let as many Gay and Lesbian people and supportive non-Gays know about the endorsement as possible. News of the endorsement should reach every Gay, Lesbian and bisexual person in your community, one way or another. That means that leaflets should be made up with your organization's list of endorsements and circulated in all the places Gay and Lesbian people congregate. Newspapers, both Gay and Lesbian and nonGay, should get the word. As many people as possible should find out about the endorsement.

Second, a campaign runs on money. A political organization that endorses a candidate and doesn't give a monetary contribution is missing the boat. It doesn't have to be a large contribution (be careful to stay within the election contribution laws of your state). A discussion about fund raising comes later in this chapter.

The last aspect of political endorsement is providing volunteers for the campaign. Envelope lickers and stuffers, canvassers, telephone bank staffers, and other campaign workers are usually desperately needed by candidates. Supplying the candidate you endorse with volunteer campaign workers shows the candidate your commitment to materially help in the campaign, and also gives you a chance to reach the community. On election day, volunteers are always needed to drive people to the polls, to staff telephone banks and to act as poll workers.

With this kind of assistance to candidates, our impact on their performance in public office will be measurably increased. If you are successful at getting out the Gay and Lesbian vote and raising money and providing volunteers, candidates will come to you for your endorsement.

FUND RAISING

Raising money is an important function for any organization. A political group that expects to endorse candidates needs money for a campaign chest, that is, money to give to candidates, as well as funds for printing, advertising and other expenses.

There are a lot of ways to raise money and it would be impossible to present an exhaustive list here. Your people should get together to brainstorm and find ways to raise funds that involve a minimum of staff time for the maximum amount to be raised. Fund raising activities should also be fun.

Cities with an active theatre should explore the possibility of theatre parties. All that is needed is the money to buy a block of tickets to a play, concert, show or other event that you are sure a lot of people want to see. This initial capital can be borrowed. Then add a few dollars to the per-ticket cost and sell the tickets to the community. Gay and Lesbian organizations should be encouraged to assist in the sale of tickets. After the initial outlay is met, all additional income is profit.

Anything that people do together can be turned into a fund raiser — boat rides, tours, picnics, dances, games, movie parties, dinners, speeches, and so on. Individuals who are reluctant to get involved publicly may agree to have small fund raising parties at their homes for an invited list of friends. Any party can be a fund raising event; simply ask for a contribution at the door.

LOBBYING

Ideally, elected officials represent the concerns of their constituents. If we are not in communication with our representatives about our concerns, however, they cannot be expected to know what positions to take on issues that are important to us.

In my work as director of the Washington Field Office of the Universal Fellowship of Metropolitan Community Churches from 1975 through 1981, and as the first full-time, paid lobbyist for Gay and Lesbian civil rights in the United States Congress, I had a lot of contact with members of Congress. Unfortunately, many members of Congress have never gotten a personal letter or a call or a visit from someone who told them that they are Gay or Lesbian or that they wanted the representative to support Gay and Lesbian rights legislation. If we are not telling our politicians about what we want them to do for us, we have failed in our responsibility as citizens. Writing letters is a major way of letting our elected representatives know how we feel about the issues confronting them once they reach political office. Organize letter writing campaigns. Let people know the names and addresses of their representatives. Provide model letters for people to use. Have letter writing parties, where you provide the paper, envelopes, stamps, addresses and ideas and get people to write a letter to their Congressperson, state representative or city councilperson.

Letters to your elected officials *are* effective. President John F. Kennedy told a group of editors in 1963, "I think letters have an effect on Members of Congress. Everybody's vote counts in America, but those who sit down and write letters make their votes count more times."

I remember three Members of Congress who changed their decision not to co-sponsor the Gay and Lesbian civil rights bill after as few as six letters from constituents.

Lobbying is very simply defined: attempting to influence legislation. Every time we write a letter to a representative, we are lobbying. But there are other ways to lobby as well. Telegrams and mailgrams are useful when there is a matter of urgency, for instance, when a vote is imminent. Telephone calls are often helpful as well and if the staff knows you are calling long distance and your representative is in the office, it is sometimes possible to get to talk to the representative directly. Talking to staff is a close second. The staff is there as adjuncts of the representative and they should be lobbied as such by constituents.

A very effective lobbying technique is the personal visit. This doesn't always mean a trip to Washington, D.C., or to your state capital. Each member of Congress and each state representative has district offices, often very close to where you are. Since the district offices are customarily staffed year round and the representative usually has regular office hours there, it is not difficult to see your representative right at home.

Remember that letters, calls and visits to elected representatives are not the sole responsibility of community leaders. Anyone can participate in this basic political act. And lobbying should be the responsibility of everyone who cares about their future. A brochure on writing to Congress is available from Chi Rho Press, P.O. Box 7864, Gaithersburg, MD 20898, USA, for $1.

Our community now has a number of Washington, D.C.-based organizations that lobby Congress regularly on our issues, such as the National Gay and Lesbian Task Force, the Human Rights Campaign Fund, and the AIDS Action Council. They are all deserving of our support. However, there is still a great deal that you as individuals can accomplish.

Finally, I wish to point out that constituency education for the purpose of building political power is really nothing more than people *getting together* to help each other attain common goals. In that getting together we must remember to agree to disagree with love and tolerance for each other. We are going to disagree about tactics, plans and programs from time to time, but we have to recognize our common goal. Disagree, by all means, but if you allow disagreement to become significantly divisive, you have given up your power to your enemies.

We are a very diverse community. We come from all conceivable backgrounds — economic, religious, political, educational, racial, ethnic and cultural. Our diversity is our strength. As we develop awareness that our role in the political arena is a part of our struggle for equality, we are engaging in constituency education. It all begins right where we are, with ourselves.

AIDS: ITS IMPACT ON ALL OUR LIVES

Gay Male Sexuality: Exploring Intimacy in the Age of AIDS

Michael Shernoff

Nothing has had more of an impact upon gay men's sexuality and upon our relationships with friends and lovers than AIDS. Living in the midst of this plague has caused many of us to reassess what is really important in life. AIDS has been the impetus for many in our community to examine themselves in terms of their needs for intimacy and love. Many men have begun to question their assumptions about what constitutes a gay male lifestyle as they never have before.

In the early 1970s I was a college student, just beginning to embrace my identity as a gay man. Luckily for me, this included a large dose of gay activism that centered around two organizations, the newly formed gay student group at State University of New York at Binghamton and (when I was not at school), the Gay Activists Alliance (GAA), in Manhattan..

The periodicals *Gay Sunshine*, *Body Politic* and *Fag Rag* provided a constant supply of interesting and provocative articles to read, many of them equating various sex acts practiced by gay men with acts of revolution. Articles such as these often became the focus in consciousness raising and discussion groups that I participated in with other gay men both at the university and at the GAA Firehouse located in lower Manhattan. In those early years of the gay liberation movement many of us talked about such topics as "Was Monogamy just an internalization of heterosexual norms?" "The politics of being exclusively a top or a bottom," "group

---

I dedicate this article to Lee Chastain, who is continuously helping me discover new and wonderful things about sharing life, friendship, love and intimacy

sex," "leather sex," "drag," etc. It was exhilarating and frequently a turn-on to be discussing the hows and whys of particular sexual behaviors with other men, many of whom were intoxicatingly attractive. I now realize that at least part of my motivation for attending gay activist events was the hope of meeting and making sexual contact with some of the other activists.

For all of us it was tremendously important and unbelievably validating to be talking with other gay men about sex, not to mention actually getting to have sexual experiences with an amazing variety of people. Positive connections to the gay men's community were bound up with both our activism and our sexual adventures. We placed a lot of emphasis on our right to do whatever we wanted with our bodies; we gave ourselves permission to experiment. This sexually charged time was for many of us the beginning of a positive gay self-image.

COMPARTMENTALIZING SEX

In hindsight I see that something important was missing from all of these discussions. There was little if any exploration of the fact that any of us might have feelings as a result of what we were learning to do sexually with other men. Thus, the separation of sex from feelings, and of sex from love was almost institutionalized for certain segments of the emerging gay men's community. Sexual freedom became synonymous with gay liberation, and a steady supply of "fast food sex" was taken as a right of passage for liberated urban gay men.

Of course there was a lot more than just sex going on in those days. People were coming out, making friends, forging a community with political agendas, having affairs and sometimes even beginning long term lover relationships that might or might not be sexually exclusive. Yet there was no denying the fact that erotic energy was one important fuel for much of what happened in those years.

When I told lesbian friends what my life was like, or what we were talking about in the various groups, they expressed surprise and concern that there was so much emphasis on sex for sex's sake. In contrast, they were exploring the meaning of love between two women, power in a lesbian relationship, and of course questions about sexual desire and sexuality. Being women, much more of their focus was on their feelings, while as men, many of us were unaware that there was a lot more to intimacy than just having hot sex. Looking back, I now understand that the lack of emphasis on the connections between feelings and sex, or sex and intimacy was a result of our having been socialized as men. Even as gay men many of us were not really able to integrate the feeling component of our lives with our sexual exploration.

Of course, very often there were powerful and intense feelings that accompanied a sexual liaison, and I for one almost always wanted to see the man with whom I had had great sex again. In those days I thought that sexual compatibility was the basis for beginning the relationship I so desperately wanted. Being in my twenties I didn't know that I felt desperate. Nor did I know the first thing about figuring out who might be an appropriate man for me to become involved with.

By 1974 I thought of myself as a liberated gay man. I was completely out about my sexual orientation in all areas of my life. I had met a man at a Gay Academic Union meeting with whom I became lovers for the next ten years. We had an active sex life, that included mutually agreed upon permission to be sexual with other people also. Yet I rarely was completely happy or satisfied. Often I felt lonely, even when I was with my lover. No matter how enjoyable sex had been either with my lover or with someone else, I was *always* looking for someone else to have sex with.

In hindsight, and after years of therapy I began to realize that there was an intangible quality missing from my life. If my sexual drive was the need that I was attempting to satisfy, how come even really great sex never left me feeling like I had had enough? Something was unclear and very confusing. It certainly was fun to have lots of sex with different men; often I became friends with the men I "tricked" with. Many gay men were unaware that we had needs for intimacy which no amount of sex could ever satisfy, but which friendship seemed to fulfill.

This was the climate that formed so much of the contemporary gay male value system around sex. A generation of men learned how to perform various forms of sexual acrobatics with a variety of partners. This same generation of post-Stonewall gay men became adept at saying hello sexually with a stranger as casually as they might shake hands with a new acquaintance. Cruising and the search for sex seemed to take on a life of its own. The search for sex often had no connection to "horniness" and frequently became an attempt to squelch loneliness, meet people, ward off boredom, bolster self-esteem or look for a lover.

I am not trying to devalue the importance of the free wheeling nature of sexual exploration in those years before AIDS. I do not have any regrets about anything I did. It was a crucial part of the evolution and growth of myself and thousands of other gay men to have had the opportunity to discover our sexuality and the erotic bonding that was a hallmark of that period. I am simply trying to look back honestly at what it was like for many of us.

THE 1990s

So here we are in the 1990s — in the midst of the second decade of a sexually transmitted plague that has been decimating our community. There is a lot more emphasis on coupling within the gay men's community. I have written and conducted workshops for gay men on sex, dating and intimacy. These workshops regularly attract up to a hundred men, no matter what part of the country they are conducted in. I hear from friends, my psychotherapy patients and colleagues that concerns about intimacy, dating and how to find and sustain a relationship are very much on gay men's minds these days. One comment I hear very often is that prior to the onset of AIDS, for many men a date meant that they were going to have sex. Now a date doesn't necessarily mean that, even if both men find themselves attracted.

Of course there are men who are still not interested in having on ongoing, monogamous relationship and who are satisfied with having a series of partners. It's important that these men not be judged for this choice of lifestyle, and that the gay men's community doesn't create a norm where coupling is the only state to aspire towards. We are a community that must continue to encourage, be tolerant of and celebrate diversity of lifestyles. With that said, I'm going to focus the rest of this chapter on suggestions for sustaining intimacy and sexuality within a relationship.

WHERE TO LOOK FOR A MATE

Bars and clubs are about the worst places to meet a potential mate. Most people who are in a bar or club are there either to dance and hang out with their friends or to try and pick someone up. In addition many people hanging out in a bar have probably had something to drink or are high on some kind of "recreational chemical." People drink or take drugs because it makes them feel more relaxed. Yet meeting a potential spouse while one or both of you are under the influence can certainly diminish your ability to make good choices.

It's a lot easier to meet potential partners when you're engaged in an activity that you enjoy. Thus the gym, gay athletic events, gay trips or community organizations provide you with the opportunity to meet someone with whom you share at least some interests. For instance if you like scuba diving, hiking, playing volleyball, writing poetry, politics, or two-step dancing, many cities have organizations for lesbians and gay men that are built around these specific interests. Doing volunteer work at any lesbian or gay community social service organization is another good way to meet potential dates. Caring people who are willing to give of themselves by providing community service are much better prospects as potential partners than people who are only consumed with themselves and their own interests.

If you are HIV positive or have AIDS, good places to meet people also include organizations like Body Positive, Positive Action or The People With AIDS Coalition in New York City, or Being Alive in Los Angeles. Each of these organizations sponsors socials and other activities so that people living with HIV and AIDS can meet each other for friendship, mutual support and dating. Volunteering at a local AIDS service organization is another place where you are liable to meet people who will be able to deal with your health status.

Increasingly, people living with HIV are placing classified advertisements that state up front what their health status is. One friend put an ad in *The Body Positive* stating "I've got a song in my heart and a catheter in my chest" in order to be completely honest about his physical condition.

FIRST IMPRESSIONS

If you are hoping to meet someone who will be a companion, or friend, as well as a lover, you will need to base the relationship on a lot more than the fact that the two of you put each other's hormones into an uproar. Therefore it's necessary to spend a lot of time talking early on. Does he encourage you to talk about yourself, or is every word out of his mouth "me-me-me"? Do you feel comfortable opening up to him, and becoming increasingly vulnerable? This is not just an intuitive process, but happens because he responds with sensitivity and empathy to concerns you share with him. These concerns may be your awkwardness about dating, health fears, body image or any other personal information. At the same time, does he talk about personal issues in a way that results in your beginning to care about him? Getting to know another person and feeling safe with him is how genuine intimacy begins to develop; intimacy is linked to trust. Trust takes time, and this doesn't happen overnight. Trust and intimacy have to be earned.

Learning certain basic things about a person (like where does he live, where is he from, what kind of work he does, and what kind of things he enjoys recreationally) can immediately provide clues as to whether this is someone you want to know better. Many men have met someone in a sexual situation, gone home together without having done much talking, and had good sex. Afterwards they discovered that "Mr. Hot Sex" is someone with whom they have nothing in common, someone whom they are happy to be rid of after breakfast (or before).

TAKING IT SLOWLY

Making love with someone you don't know can seem like a very intimate thing to do, but in reality it may just provide you with the illusion of intimacy. Often people use sex to ameliorate feelings of loneliness or aloneness. I remember very clearly how lonely I'd feel waking up with someone I had just met after a night of breathless sex in the morning after, he would be distant and not very interested in me.

By not going home with someone you just met you have the opportunity to find out if he responds to you in nonsexual ways. Does he initiate phone calls or dates with you? Does he return your calls promptly? It's never fun or easy having someone we like not be interested in us. Having sex with someone you don't know has the potential for putting you out on a limb emotionally. If a man you like a lot doesn't feel the same way and wants to stop seeing you, this is going to be a lot more painful if you have already had sex. On the other hand when you have sex with someone who has a similar intensity of feeling for you as you have for him, the sex becomes a way of bonding and expressing a growing sense of closeness. This is sex as an expression of intimacy and in fact, can be the most exciting and satisfying kind of sex.

AIDS AND DATING

AIDS has provided new reasons for not having sex with someone you don't really know. If you are HIV positive or have AIDS, or are a widower who is only recently re-entering the dating arena, it is completely understandable that you might hesitate before sharing all this with someone you have just met. On the other hand, if you don't share your health status, have safer sex, and begin to date someone, it only gets more difficult to tell him any of these things as the relationship progresses. In addition, he may feel hurt, betrayed or distrustful of you if he learns about your health status after he has become emotionally and sexually involved with you.

My experience has been that men preferred to learn my HIV status *before* going to bed with me. Some men chose not to continue going out with me upon learning that I was HIV positive. As painful as that was at the time, I was glad that I hadn't slept with them and had the additional feelings that sex would have brought up since they were obviously not the kind of person I wanted to get seriously involved with.

DATING AND HEALTH STATUS

AIDS has definitely influenced the process of coupling for gay men. Some men won't date an HIV-infected person, because they don't want to fall in love with someone who will get sick, die and leave them. "I just don't want to go through the process of opening up, getting close and having it end soon," one of my sero-negative psychotherapy patients explained to me regarding his decision to only date sero-negative men. Some of the men who are in this category are widowers who have already lost a lover to AIDS. There is rancor in some sectors of the community about the political incorrectness of this kind of "AIDS apartheid." As a sero-positive man this doesn't make me angry; I can understand those feelings and respect them. This is an issue about people's feelings and limits, not about political correctness.

There are many in the community who don't see HIV antibody status as a barrier to forming new relationships. Thus, there are men who are beginning relationships where: (1) one man is negative and one is positive; (2) neither knows his antibody status; (3) both are positive; (4) both are negative; (5) one has AIDS; or (6) both have AIDS.

Being sero-positive or even having AIDS doesn't have to mean that anyone's chances for beginning a relationship are over. Obviously HIV can complicate things and make the process of meeting people and dating more difficult. In conversations with my single psychotherapy patients and friends who have HIV I've heard many different opinions expressed regarding the kind of person being sought as a lover. There are the men who only want to go out with other men who are also HIV sero-positive, feeling that this will make things less complicated. Others only want to meet someone who is sero-negative so that in case they get sick their partner will be able to take care of them.

A NEW RELATIONSHIP

By 1985 the relationship with the man with whom I had been lovers for ten years had evolved from being lovers to being roommates, good friends and definitely "family." That began a seven year period of my being single, dating and wanting to begin a new love affair.

I met my current lover at the gym one afternoon after we had been seeing each other around the neighborhood and gym for several weeks. We were both on the stair master so the initial conversation was punctuated by a lot of huffing and puffing. Early in our conversation he mentioned that his lover had died five months earlier on Gay Pride Day, so I rashly (and correctly) assumed he was still single.

Physically he was in great shape so I also assumed that he must be negative, and wouldn't want to date someone who was sero-positive since he had just gone through the trauma of having his lover, Vinnie, become ill and die within three months. Having been single for several years I felt vulnerable about my HIV status. Though asymptomatic, and in the best physical shape I've ever been in, with many years of my own good therapy under my belt, I still felt like damaged goods in the dating arena because of my HIV status. Having just met him, I decided not to bring up antibody status at this point. We exchanged phone numbers, and wound up going out to lunch that afternoon. The conversation was fun as well as intimate. I knew that I was beginning to have a crush on Lee, and felt pretty certain that he felt the same.

I asked him to come to a party at my house where we once again had a good time. When he was getting ready to leave I asked him if I could kiss him good night. He agreed and we had a hot, but chaste closed mouthed kiss. Having gotten very aroused by this I asked him if he wanted to stay the night and just cuddle. After some hesitation he agreed. To summarize, it turns out that his hesitation was because he too is HIV positive. Since then we have fallen in love and are in the midst of the most satisfying love affair I have ever had.

When I told my own therapist about asking Lee to spend the night at the end of the party she asked me what was the rush? So not for the first time we talked about the urgency I feel in regard to time, and there not being enough of it since I have this life-threatening condition. Lee and I have often spoken about how strange it is to have found someone who feels like a life-mate and instead of being able to think in terms of decades spent together we will have to go month by month, and hopefully year by year. This definitely increases how precious I feel each moment of the relationship is. It has also contributed to our moving closer more quickly than we might have if we both were negative.

In the first four months of our relationship we had been to a large AIDS remembrance service held by Gay Men's Health Crisis, in New York City, buried one joint friend, and dealt with Lee's platelets dropping drastically. Sharing these experiences, and confiding in one another the feelings that each of these situations elicited made us closer. At the end of the first month of dating, Lee became very sad one night. When I asked him what was the matter he told me that he was beginning to feel very strongly for me and he worried about how he would handle it if he were to get sick and I wouldn't be there for him during the illness. I reassured him that if the feelings we were sharing continued to grow and he got sick, we would go through whatever would happen together. He began to cry and we had a very close and special evening.

On the morning that would have been his and Vinnie's second anniversary he again became very sad. I asked him if he wanted to talk about what he was feeling. He began to talk about Vinnie and how sad it was that they had only had one and a half years together, and that this wonderful man had died so young. I told him that I couldn't do anything other than listen to him, hold him, and care about what he was feeling. He assured me that that was more than sufficient.

During each of these discussions the vulnerability caused me to feel very close to Lee and excited by the bonds that were being forged between us. One of my physical reactions to these feelings was to have an erection. In none of these situations was the erection connected to an immediate desire to make love. I believe it was, more than anything, an expression of the passion I felt for this man opening his heart to me with such trust.

I share these anecdotes to serve as one example of how a relationship can begin and flourish in the midst of the plague. Perhaps hearing this story will give hope to other men living with HIV or AIDS about their own prospects of finding a loving relationship.

One issue of growing importance for an increasing number of male couples is how to deal with one or both partners' lover who has died. Lee still keeps photographs of Vinnie displayed in the apartment. We have spent a lot of time talking about their relationship, what it was like for Lee while Vinnie was sick, and about Vinnie's death and funeral. Lee once asked me if I minded that we spoke about Vinnie. I told him not at all. I was glad that he was comfortable enough to talk with me about Vinnie. I don't feel as if I am being compared to Vinnie nor that the two relationships are in competition. This is an important part of Lee's history, and I respect the fact that he still thinks of Vinnie and values this former relationship enough to want to discuss it at times. It feels to us both that talking about this has brought us closer and increased the intimacy we share.

KEEPING IT INTIMATE AND HOT

AIDS has certainly cast a dark shadow over the sexual play of gay men. Concerns about possibly spreading HIV have appropriately inhibited some forms of sexual play, and reduced spontaneity as condoms need to be put on and taken off.

Some people may choose to become celibate out of fear of contracting AIDS or as a result of an HIV diagnosis. When this happens sometimes it has more to do with a person feeling guilty about his homosexuality or past sexual behaviors, than about actual concerns about getting or transmitting AIDS. As someone becomes increasingly symptomatic it's not uncommon for his interest in having sex to decrease. And yet this does not happen to all people with HIV illness. Many couples where one or both partners has AIDS remain sexually active with each other throughout the course of the illness.

For people in a relationship where sex has been a valued aspect, one partner's loss of sexual desire can cause problems. For couples who may be experiencing stress as a result of this problem, it is crucial for both people to discuss their needs and be honest about their feelings regarding this change in their relationship. There are numerous ways of dealing with this. Just because one person isn't feeling sexual doesn't mean that he doesn't crave close physical contact with his partner.

The partner who still has a desire to be sexual has several options for having his needs met. This is certainly an opportunity for creative problem solving that can address both partner's needs. Perhaps the man who doesn't have any sexual desire is amenable to participating in certain sexual acts where he isn't expected to have an erection, be penetrated or reach an orgasm, but is willing to help his lover achieve sexual satisfaction. Some couples agree that at this point in their relationship it's acceptable for the partner who desires sex to have sexual contacts outside of the relationship. Other couples find this to be too threatening to even consider. What is important is that both parties communicate honestly about their feelings.

Since a large part of sex has to do with body image, as people lose weight, have skin problems, develop K.S. lesions or have a Hickman catheter installed they may no longer like the way their body looks or feels. Thus when they no longer feel attractive or desirable, some people with AIDS avoid sex because they don't believe that anyone could find them attractive. Often when a PWA expresses this during couples therapy, the partner acknowledges the changes in his lover's appearance but usually shares that for him, at this point in their life together, sexual attraction is no longer primarily based upon looks even if it had once been.

Some men have completely shut down sexually as a direct result of fears related to AIDS being sexually transmitted. This can obviously cause a strain on the best of relationships. If talking about this with your lover and discussing the options for being sexual in safe ways doesn't result in these fears being reduced, then it would be a good idea to consult a therapist who has experience both in the areas of working with male couples and with concerns about AIDS. Simply because AIDS is sexually transmitted doesn't mean that we have to stop celebrating being sexual beings. What is necessary is that each of us recognize the abundance and complexity of our feelings about being sexual in the age of AIDS.

There are certain common reactions I have heard from thousands of men around the country who have attended my workshops. AIDS has resulted in losing certain sexual possibilities, and like all losses these need to be mourned. Many men have described feeling very angry and sad that they can no longer engage in certain sexual practices. Other men feel angry, or sad that they never had the opportunity to experience the "sexual Camelot" of pre-AIDS gay male sexuality. The challenge to maintaining a healthy and rich sex life in the age of AIDS is to discover the enormous variety of sexual options that still exist that do not transmit HIV.

Part of creating a personal climate that is filled with sexual possibility and adventure has to do with acknowledging how you feel, what you want and communicating these thoughts and feelings to your partner. It is understandable that the thought of engaging in certain sexual acts might result in your feeling uncomfortable or frightened. It is very important to be able to give yourself permission to accept your feelings and not judge yourself for feeling afraid, hesitant, anxious, clumsy or whatever.

Talking about sex with your partner is necessary and may cause you to feel anxious. Yet this is a crucial way for two people to learn how to improve the quality of their love making. Talking about what you like or desire sexually can result in your feeling very vulnerable. If your partner responds in an encouraging way and is sympathetic to what you are saying you will most likely feel more trusting of him and closer to him, thus increasing the intimacy between you. If you like something that your lover does by all means tell him this. Similarly if you want him to do something specific it will be necessary for you to either guide him or tell him directly. If you are having difficulty saying what you want to your lover, or if he does not respond gently or kindly, than it may be a good idea to seek some professional help.

CONCLUSION

The nature of intimacy has a lot to do with caring enough both about yourself and another person to be open. By opening up and sharing our thoughts and feelings, and encouraging someone else to do the same we have the opportunity to become close. For many people this is a very scary process, especially if they have been hurt before, or abused as a child. Genuine intimacy also requires that at times we put another person's feelings or best interests ahead of our own. Sex can either be a way to make two people feel closer to each other or feel more alone and disconnected.

In *Borrowed Time*, Paul Monette says: "This burning away of the superfluous, the sheer pleasure of an ordinary afternoon — does anybody ever get taught these things by anything other than tragedy?" The tragedy of AIDS affects and colors all of our lives in different ways no matter what our health or antibody status is. It has taught us new dimensions about our needs for intimacy from our lovers and friends, as well as how to live with our fears. For many gay men the AIDS crisis has given us no choice but to accept uncertainty and being afraid. The vulnerability that fear creates makes us more accessible to those who care about us. Their love can fuel and strengthen us, not only in the enormous crisis times of AIDS, but in the best of times as well.

Reunification: Changing Relationships Between Gay Men and Lesbians Coping With AIDS

Terry Wolverton

My friend Linda keeps a vigil, waiting for a young man to die. Six months ago he was a business colleague, someone she knew professionally and at a distance. Now she spoons soup into his mouth, cleans his kitchen, holds his mother's hand. She's a part of the circle of men and women who gather at this bedside, urging him to let go.

"I don't know how to do this," she tells me. Her voice on the other end of the phone is clotted with unshed tears. This is her first AIDS death.

"There's no way to do it perfectly," I assure her. "Just show up and do the best you can."

***

My friend Julia runs a program for HIV education. She plans and directs a campaign to get the word out to gay men, the young ones who think it won't happen to them, the frightened ones who still hide their sexuality, the ones who don't speak English, the ones in denial about the disease.

For a decade she's watched healthy men get sick, and sick men die. She's lost clients, staff members, friends.

When an article in a lesbian newspaper attacks her for working with men, she defends herself fiercely.

Most of the time, she tells me, she just feels numb.

***

My friend Robin edits a newsletter for an organization that provides hospice care to AIDS patients who have nowhere else to go. Although it takes her away from the creative writing she longs to do, she brings to the work an exacting standard, a determination to give her best.

It's the kind of organization where everyone does everything, so she also spends her time strategizing about fundraising, building alliances with other community groups, and putting pressure on elected officials to do more. But because she cares so much, and because AIDS has taken from her people that she couldn't bear to lose, she doesn't stop there. She's also in the streets, marching to combat the bigotry and official indifference that has allowed HIV to reach epidemic proportions.

***

My friend Mary-Linn teaches an art workshop for people with AIDS, and when her students are too ill to come to class, she bundles her art supplies and her enthusiasm and comes to them, sitting beside hospital beds teaching men hooked to I.V.'s to make artists' books. One of these students mentioned that he'd always wanted to make a video tape, and she offered to borrow a camera so he could do it.

"Not yet," he told her, "I'll let you know when it's time."

Day after day she'd visit the hospital, working with him to shoot photographic self-portraits, assembling pages for his book project. One day he announced, "I'm ready to make that video now. It's time."

As she held the camera he talked about his life, the people that he loved, what he was going to miss. Five days later, he died, leaving behind this remembrance, lovingly recorded, for his grateful family.

***

In my Tuesday morning creative writing workshop, I listen as one of my students reads a piece describing the progressive nerve disorder that makes it difficult for him to hold onto a plate or a glass or a pen. He is a handsome man, impeccably dressed, with a gracious easy charm. His words disclose his terror of the day when he will no longer have control over the simplest gestures.

He is moved by what he has written, relieved at having finally shared this terrible secret fear, and we, the other students and myself, are deeply touched that he has entrusted us with this story. I make a space in the workshop for the silence and tears that follow, but also a time for response, so he'll be certain we have heard him.

***

Ten years ago, I couldn't have told you these stories. I am of the generation of lesbians whose coming out took place post-Stonewall, in the early seventies. Too late for butch-femme, right on time for the coming feminist revolution. I never lived through a bar raid or worried about losing my job; I never had to think about whether I was clothed in a sufficient number of women's garments to avoid arrest.

The impact of my leap from straight girl to radical dyke was cushioned by the women's movement, in which context lesbianism was not only considered normal but preferable, the exemplary choice. Straight women were suspect for "giving comfort to the enemy," while lesbians were seen as the natural vanguard in the struggle against male supremacy. Women and men were believed to occupy two different and hostile worlds, with lesbians and gay men standing at the polar extremes of each.

An earlier generation of lesbians had formed alliances with gay men out of isolation and a common oppression, often sharing the same bars and other social networks. The liberation movements of women and gays sprung many of us apart, sending us deep into the encampments of our respective genders, making us adversaries in the war between the sexes.

Lesbian poet and essayist Bia Lowe describes that time in an essay, "Wild Ride,"[1] about her friend Clark, who died of AIDS:

> ... Where the sixties had joined us as siblings, the seventies segregated us into distinct species, ghettoized by our sexualities. Occasionally we'd get together but I found him petty. An hysteric. I think he probably felt my politics had made me twisted and humorless. If you had asked me in the seventies how Clark would die, I probably would have sneered, "Too much sex." ... Now I question a world spun by moral causality.

In 1984 I learned that a childhood friend had died of AIDS. This was the first shadow cast by AIDS across my personal world. Jeffrey had been a gangly boy with a loping run, who was picked on for preferring to play with the girls. I hadn't seen Jeffrey in many years, and the reality of the virus was still distant and remote to me, intent as I was on devoting all my energies to women.

But the world was growing smaller, as the eighties made evident. The conservative shift that characterized the decade posed a threat to feminism, to all progressive movements. Survival meant building new alliances — across race and class, even across gender. Whereas separatism in the seventies had seemed a radical and self-affirming choice for lesbians, in the eighties it appeared short-sighted and self-destructive.

By the mid-eighties I began to see how insulated I had become, sequestered in the world of women. An epidemic was ravaging the gay community, men were dying by the thousands, but *I didn't know them.* My political stance had offered me the privilege of remaining untouched by the catastrophe, and it felt obscene to me, like standing by and passively watching while someone gets beaten to death.

What I'm describing here is my own internal transformation. Whether it is the same for other lesbians or entirely different I cannot say. I once recounted this story

---

[1] *"Wild Ride" by Bia Lowe, published in* Blood Whispers: L.A. Writers on AIDS, *Silverton Books and the Gay and Lesbian Community Services Center, Los Angeles, 1991.*

to a nonlesbian woman, who gaped at me in utter puzzlement. "Why would you feel that way?" she wanted to know. "Why not just be grateful to not have to deal with it?" I could never explain it to her satisfaction; all I could tell her was that it became impossible to continue uninvolved.

In 1988 I established a creative writing workshop for people with HIV. After years of teaching in all-women settings, I found myself the lone female in an otherwise all-male group. This was the beginning of my personal reunification with the gay community.

My initial concern was about whether I was equipped to assist "people facing a life-threatening illness," which was the way I imagined the would-be workshop participants. This was quickly dispelled; from the moment I met my first six students they became three-dimensional to me, no longer defined by their health status, but real people with jobs, boyfriends, histories and life goals. The men who've participated over the four years the class has been meeting also challenged my prejudices about what men were like. Some of them are quite sympathetic to and knowledgeable about feminism, which surprises and delights me; for others, I am the first lesbian to be a significant presence in their lives.

In addition, these men seem to possess an astonishing level of self-awareness, a depth of feeling quite unlike the men I turned my back on a decade earlier. Although I was tempted at first to attribute those qualities to the illness these men are facing, I've also witnessed the same capacities in uninfected men who've nursed friends through sickness and watched lovers die, those who've been touched by the consequences of AIDS. The epidemic has spawned a change within the gay community, and for all the terrible loss, it seems gay men have discovered a courage and a level of compassion previously unexplored.

There've been lessons for me to learn. When I began the workshop I knew only the basics about HIV and AIDS. Little did I imagine the extensive education I would receive: a bewildering array of acronyms, the whole catalogue of opportunistic infections with their insidious destructive capability, and an assortment of treatment options, both sanctioned and underground, each wielding a compendium of side effects. Now I too read the news for any breakthrough, any sign of hope.

I've also had the chance to grow more comfortable with male sexuality, for which, as a radical feminist, I had developed both a theoretical and a visceral distaste. It was amusing to see that the men in the workshop were initially concerned about this as well, the way they would glance at me, almost protectively, whenever something explicit was read. I felt instinctively that sex was an important subject for these students in particular to write about, given the sex-negative messages that surround much of the hysteria about AIDS, and I was careful to give a noncensorious response to that work. After a short time, we all relaxed about it. Through sharing their writing about sex, my students have helped me both to have a better understanding of what men feel, fantasize and fear, and to confront my own inhibitions and taboos and take more risks in my work.

I've had to learn about when to give and when to hold back. From the beginning I've let my students take the lead when it comes to dealing with the topic of AIDS. Some of them come to the workshop eager to address it, to express all the myriad things they feel about it; others attend because they want to write in an atmosphere where their health status isn't an issue. I can't pretend to know what they need, or what's best for them, or what's going to happen. All I can do is offer the tools of creative writing, to coax the words out from the deep place where they reside and be ready with a listening ear, a loving heart. If I had the power to take their illness away I would do it, but I don't. I can never forget that humbling truth.

Of the six initial workshop participants, three have died in the intervening years, and others have come to take their place. I have had to learn to mourn these deaths and to accept them, to love these men and to let them go. And I have loved them, deeply, as a decade ago I would not have thought myself capable. But we have been on a journey together, my brothers and sisters, and discovered strengths and capacities in ourselves and in one another that we could never have imagined.

I have had the opportunity to help seven of the workshop participants to publish their work, and I find I am fiercely committed to getting their writing before an audience. One of my current students has asked me to be his literary executor, insuring that his words survive him, and I was happy to agree. There are, no doubt, lesbians who would criticize me for this, citing the injustices for women that still persist, insisting that we need to do for our own. But I no longer believe in those separate, isolated worlds, in which lesbians' interests are inimical to those of gay men.

Yes, misunderstandings persist, as does inequality. Many gay men remain indifferent to lesbian oppression, and many lesbians still prefer to keep their distance from the gay community. Still, a movement is afoot; a gradual process of reunification has begun.

This is perhaps especially evident among the younger generation of lesbians and gay men, those in their twenties who have come of age in the time of AIDS. They have embraced a new identity, and proudly defined it "Queer," eager to erase the lines of separation forged in an altogether different era.

While not every lesbian is in agreement, women have constituted a large and vital faction in the war against AIDS. We are fundraisers and health care providers; we are activists and administrators; we are journalists and lobbyists and counselors and artists. We run organizations and we are AIDS buddies; we provide leadership and caregiving. The commitment lesbians have demonstrated throughout this crisis is helping to forge the vision of a new community, one in which men and women will regard one another with mutual appreciation and respect.

Resources

Workshops

"Live to Write/Write to Live," a creative writing workshop for people with HIV, and "Healer, Heal Thyself," a creative writing workshop for professionals who work with people with AIDS. Contact the Education Department of the Gay and Lesbian Community Services Center, Los Angeles, CA. (213) 464-7400.

Suggested Reading

Blood Whispers: L.A. Writers on AIDS, edited by Terry Wolverton (Silverton Books and the Gay and Lesbian Community Services Center), 1991.

Indivisible: New Short Fiction by Gay and Lesbian West Coast Writers, edited by Terry Wolverton and Robert Drake (Plume Fiction), 1991.

People in Trouble by Sarah Schulman (NAL/Dutton), 1990.

PEOPLE OF COLOR: THE SPECIAL EXPERIENCES OF MINORITIES WITHIN A MINORITY

African-American Issues: The Soul of It

Ayofemi Folayan

African-American. Black. Colored. Negro. What all these terms have in common is the search for a positive identity, the effort to capture a shred of pride in a reality that often denied my presence, tried to render invisible a continent, a multitude of cultures, a history that reaches so far back it may indeed be the point all humans have in common. I have a legacy, a heritage that is vast and rich, of which I was totally ignorant as a child.

I remember the first time I felt pride specifically as an African-American. It was 1960 and the Summer Olympics were in Rome, Italy. A Black woman from this country named Wilma Rudolph won gold medals in track and field events. I had no idea what she looked like in that era well before satellite television could immediately project her image on my television screen, but the concept of a successful Black female athlete was exhilarating to my young soul. The other heroine of my childhood who shared gender and ethnicity with me was Marian Anderson, the vibrant contralto. My father took me to see her at Symphony Hall when I was about nine years old. My chest still constricts with the pressure of awe that gripped me as I looked through opera glasses from our distant balcony seat. I am sure that feeling dictated my own desire to command attention from stages.

I had never heard the names and achievements of Black women who had preceded me and in whom I could have taken pride: lecturer and women's rights advocate Sojourner Truth, poet and elocutionist Frances Ellen Watkins Harper, sculptor Edmonia Lewis, Underground Railroad conductor Harriet Tubman, Mary McLeod Bethune (founder of Bethune-Cookman College), or Ida B. Wells, who bravely fought against lynching. Black men were equally eclipsed from my consciousness. I did not know of the powerful words of Frederick Douglass, the sensitive poetry of Paul Laurence Dunbar, the inspiring messages of James Weldon Johnson, who wrote the Black Nation anthem "Lift Ev'ry Voice and Sing" or the constellation of artistic luminaries that sparked during the Harlem Renaissance: Langston Hughes, Countee Cullen, Zora Neale Hurston, Claude McKay, and many others.

This is not to say that I was not taught "history." But everything that I learned was full of gaping holes where people of color had been removed from the account, just as later I was to learn that gay people were invisible to historians. I never knew that Benjamin Banneker, a Black man, was responsible for the design of the city of Washington, D.C. or that Alexander Pushkin, the great Russian novelist, was Black.

Nor did I have a sense of geography. I knew nothing of the Great Pyramids at Giza, the teeming markets of Marrakech, the rich ores of South Africa, the game preserves in Kenya. Until I was nearly eighteen years of age, Africa was indeed a "dark Continent," one obscured from my intellectual curiosity by the racism that had so effectively erased any positive images of African contributions to the tapestry of culture and history.

There were other words, words that were slung at me with malevolence and hatred, because of my race and gender, which were both obvious characteristics. Words that created a reality of shame and fear just for being who I was. There was no National Organization for Women, no women's bookstores, no women's music festivals, no place to gather with other kindred spirits.

Queer. Gay and lesbian. Dyke. Other words to define and name that part of me which was not so obvious, which was hidden even from myself. There were no images in the books or films to validate even the possibility of loving women, living with women, passionate sex with women. The few glimpses I had, like *The Well of Loneliness* reinforced my sense that being gay was somehow sick, sinful, perverted.

I grew up in a cultural vacuum. I mean, growing up a lesbian in the specific culture that I come from is like growing up an Eskimo in the middle of the Sahara desert: it's pretty hard to get knowledge about who you are and where you come from when everyone around you is completely ignorant of who you are. I grew up in the Pentecostal Assemblies of the World. That's the church organization that most of my family participated in, nearly seven days a week. My grandmother, my grandfather, my uncles, my cousins all were ordained ministers in the church. They truly believed that the world was divided into those who had been "saved" and those who were consigned forever to the damnation of hell.

Because of the rigid limitations of church doctrine, I had never seen a movie or watched television, I had never listened to any secular music except classical, and I had never thought much about sexuality, except as something terribly sinful to be avoided even in thought. I went to see the movie "Dr. Zhivago" and was captivated by the sweeping romance it celebrated. By that time I was sixteen and seeking to relieve the tremendous tension of sexual energy locked inside me. I never realized there was another possibility besides heterosexuality. I did not see any images that confirmed the passionate pulsing I felt inside when certain women walked close to me. I did not have a frame of reference in which to place my own image, a sense of history or kinship with all kinds of men and women.

I still had not heard the word "lesbian." I didn't see it in any newspapers or in any books. The women that I saw in bars that I thought might be "available" to me were "bull daggers." I knew I wasn't like them; I had heard rumors that they strapped on penises and tried to be like men. I didn't want to be anything but who I was! I didn't want to pretend to be a man, I wanted to love women.

The entire time that I had an affair with another Black woman while I was married, I didn't have a label for who I was or what we were doing. I just thought we were incredibly lucky to have found each other. I was actually pretty positive that we weren't lesbians, because all the descriptions of lesbians that I had heard or read were clearly about white women, just like the words "French" or "Swedish" meant white.

It wasn't until I saw the film, *The Word Is Out*, that I ever dreamed the two ideas could go together. I remember sitting in the back of the now defunct Fox Venice Theatre and watching both showings of that landmark film. There were about twenty characters portrayed from all points within the spectrum of diversity that is our gay and lesbian community. In particular, there was a Black lesbian college instructor named Betty Powell who intrigued me. She was up there on the screen, larger than life, and she looked like me, a woman who called herself a lesbian and wore her hair in an Afro hairstyle, who spoke articulately about her experience.

Until that moment, I had assumed that there would always be a dichotomy inherent in my experience: I could be a closeted lesbian in the African-American community or an invisible African-American in the gay and lesbian community. The pressure of keeping those elements separate was crushing to my already fragile identity, struggling as I was with the same personal and family struggles that we each individually face. The remote possibility that there could be a convergence of that internal schism was almost too frightening to think about.

Around this time I started to hear of Black lesbian authors, like Pat Parker, Anne Allen Shockley, Audre Lorde. The first national Black lesbian conference was held in 1978 in San Francisco. Named *Becoming Visible*, the conference attracted more than two hundred participants from around the country. I remember sitting in a general session and just letting my eyes drift around the room, drinking in the refreshing sensibility of so much dynamic energy. It was a critical turning point in my self-perception and the range of possibilities I was willing to entertain for an African-American gay and lesbian reality. Still, the search seemed isolated and limited. The Nia Gathering, an annual weekend retreat sponsored by a collective of African-American women from the Bay Area originated ten years after *Becoming Visible*, in 1988. In Southern California, United Lesbians of African Heritage (ULOAH) has been developing community events, including participation in the annual Kwanzaa parade as out lesbians and an annual weekend retreat, since 1990. On the East Coast, African-American Women United for Social Change (formerly Salsa Soul Sisters) of New York and Les Femmes Unies have been active in the African-American lesbian community, providing similar functions. In addition, a monthly publication, *Ache*, has been produced by another Bay Area African-American collective. On a national level, *BLK* has been publishing a monthly national newsjournal since 1988. Noted African-American lesbian author Barbara Smith has also been publishing feminist titles under her *Kitchen Table Imprint* since 1976. Several lesbian titles are noteworthy.[1] In 1990 the international conference "I Am Your Sister" was held in Boston to celebrate the life and work of Audre Lorde, drawing nearly two thousand participants. This kind of presence was simply unthinkable when I moved to Southern California in 1973.

The most solid community-based institution within the African-American community is the church. Whatever the denomination (with the exception of clearly homophilic denominations such as the United Federation of Metropolitan Community Churches (UFMCC), they consistently condemn gay men and lesbians for their sexual orientation and condone by their tacit approval the rampant homophobia directed towards Black gay men and lesbians. From subtle coercions by family members to conform and not "make waves" to violent physical attacks by Black youth, still there is a sense of exile, being cast out from the larger communities around us. However, some church and community-based organizations such as the Southern Christian Leadership Conference and the Urban League have begun to work cooperatively with African-American gay and lesbian organizations to address the AIDS crisis.

There is a definite national presence of Black gay and lesbian organizations. The Black Gay and Lesbian Leadership Forum has, since 1988, sponsored an annual National Black Gay and Lesbian Leadership Conference. The conference draws participants from around the country, and has been held in Atlanta, Oakland, and Los Angeles. Another national entity, the National Coalition of Black Lesbians and Gays has local chapters in cities around the country and has been a visible force within the African-American gay and lesbian community since 1976. The National Minority AIDS Council has emerged as a definitive community-resource in response to the health crisis that provides leadership to a variety of local AIDS service

---

[1]*Barbara Smith's* Kitchen Table Imprints, *in Latham, New York, published Audre Lorde and Michelle Cliff in addition to the following titles:*
Clarke, Cheryl. Living as a Lesbian.
Clarke, Cheryl. Narrative: Poems in the Tradition of Black Women.
Smith, Barbara. *Editor.* Homegirls: A Black Feminist Anthology.

agencies specifically targeting African-American gay men and lesbians at risk or already infected.

Two national social organizations that have been key focal points within the gay African-American community are Men of All Colors Together (MACT) and the National Association of Black and White Men Together (BWMT), both organizations with large national memberships and numerous local chapters around the country. In the political arena, openly gay African-Americans have been elected to office in Seattle, WA and Albany, NY and openly gay African-Americans have been appointed in increasing numbers to key political positions in local and state governments around the country.

There are still many areas where the presence of African-American gay men and lesbians is still obscured. While names such as Melvin Dixon and Essex Hemphill and Audre Lorde and Pat Parker are widely known and celebrated within the African-American gay and lesbian community, there are many cultural contributions that are still made without that recognition. *Tongues Untied* and *Young Soul Rebel* by Marlon Riggs and *Paris Is Burning* by Jennie Livingstone are documentaries that celebrate African-American gay men and lesbians and which have been widely distributed in mainstream arenas. That exposure and the ever-increasing contributions of African-American gay men and lesbians to a richer cultural and political identity remind me that we are truly the soul of the soul, the pulsing heart within the larger communities, whose presence is a necessary and vital force.

Latino Issues: Gay and Lesbian Latinos Claiming *La Raza*

Eric-Steven Gutierrez

It was 1933 or '34 that my grandfather remembers playing football with Manuel Acosta and some of the other guys from the barrio in Van Nuys. He was my great-uncle, this Manuel Acosta whom I never knew. There are no pictures of him in any family album. My grandmother recalls his dark, slender form tenderly and although decades have passed, the memory unsettles and stills her voice.

My grandfather and his friends grew mustaches as soon as they were able. If they saw a *mexicano* in the barrio without a hat, they called him *pocho* and accused him of trying to be white. They would never think of wearing pants that weren't either brown or black because that would be effeminate. *Panaderos* (bakers) and Rafaello the milkman, who paid $500 in pennies for a Model T, were teased about being queer because they wore white, a woman's color. Tennis shoes were for fairies, not *machos*.

The afternoon Manuel Acosta played football for the first and last time with other young men from Van Nuys High School it began to storm. The rain came down hard and everyone was laughing as they ran for cover. Until someone noticed that Manuel Acosta's mascara was also running.

Jotin is probably the worst thing a Mexican father can call a son. That is what they called Manuel Acosta, my grandmother's best friend, under her parents' roof. Shortly after that he escaped the Depression, the taunts and the beatings in Van Nuys with Santiago Chago and Johnny Melendez in a stolen car.

Many lesbians and gays are familiar with the conflict of having to leave their families, communities and churches in order to find home. The absurdity and pain of making such a choice is even more complicated for lesbians and gays of color for whom few roles exist other than the extremes of insider or outcast. Even when we are integrated within our own family and community it is usually as an honorary heterosexual rather than as an out and acknowledged queer of color.

Gays and lesbians of color will not necessarily find total acceptance in the urban queer capitols of New York City, San Francisco or West Hollywood either. Contemporary lesbian and gay communities are undergoing the same intercultural growing pains as the rest of American society. Issues of racism, homophobia, exclusion, the progressive "queer" vs. conventional "gay" name identification controversy, discrimination against the HIV-positive, sexism, ageism and the whole damn dysfunctional tamale that you thought you left back in the 'hood are just as alive and oppressive now that you are out, or starting on your way.

Our governments, churches, neighborhoods, gay and lesbian centers, families and friends (both queer and straight) and other institutions of influence and change will continue to see us as a minority within a minority until we stop defining ourselves that way. It does not matter if Latina lesbians on Harleys or queerz in the 'hood or rocker Asian studs become the largest demographic affiliation in the next U.S. census. Our minority status in the places we are born and the places we choose to be reborn is guaranteed as long as we abandon our right to belong to anything larger than our marginality. The only chance we have of overcoming the unique difficulties of being a Latino gay or lesbian is in claiming its unique advantages, integrating the multiple communities we belong to and functioning as the synapse between them.

In the places we grew up we gays and lesbians are known as *jotos, marimachas, putos, maricones*, and freaks. In the gay and lesbian "Community" some of our "brothers and sisters" know us as taco belles, bean boys and cha cha queens. Instead, we must make ourselves known as citizens and parishioners, neighbors and co-workers, sons and daughters. Such integration of our cultural, ethnic, sexual and geographic communities allows us to define our own lives and claim our rights to effective AIDS education and treatment, safety from hate crimes, and the opportunity to pursue a free and open social life.

For too long gay, lesbian and Latino communities have gotten away with narrow definitions of who belonged and who didn't. Gay and lesbian Latinos most definitely did not. We were either unnatural or undesirable. We seemed to exist only to be bashed or prayed over at home and either sexually exoticized or ignored by potential partners addicted to the blond, blue-eyed porn aesthetic. While virtually all marginalized groups have had to pass through a period of separatism, finding strength and clarity apart on the way toward self-acceptance and civil rights, our evolution and role in society now depends on integrating, not abandoning the communities that have formed us. To escape cultural condemnation, sexual racism or exoticism and familial shame we need no longer steal a car and run away from the only places we know and the people we love. We must, instead, stand our ground and make our homes.

The police caught up with Manuel Acosta in the fields of Fresno where he was picking lettuce for $5 a week. That day, at 18 years of age, he began his life as a *maricon* and a stranger to his past.

He wrote to my grandmother from jail, telling her that he left home because he didn't want to give the family a bad name. After trying to escape his life in a stolen car, he simply stayed away. He was bashed frequently and had to have a steel plate inserted to reinforce his skull. He developed a stutter and was arrested several times for sodomy, serving his time in solitary confinement. He began to drink and ended up venting his rage with a bottle. He fell in love and lived with a man in Oxnard and for a time, it seems, he lived quietly and worked hard. When the man announced that he was going to marry, Manuel Acosta got blind drunk, stabbed him and ended up in Folsom.

It isn't easy being out in a Latino family, in a Latino neighborhood. But as you probably know, it's no big kick being invisible either. Once you are out, each of your actions within your neighborhood, your home and your self, resonate where before there was only shame and secrecy. That's power.

It isn't easy to be part of a gay and lesbian culture whose rites and institutions too often consider us to be peripheral or an acquired taste. As an out gay or lesbian Latino you are significantly altering that perception by embracing the realities of our own unique cultural role. That's power.

To an unprecedented extent, queers of color are crossing borders into different political and cultural worlds where we have a legitimate claim. It doesn't matter if you haven't exercised that prerogative before. If you acknowledge and participate in more than one community you are in the vanguard of a growing movement toward diversity and equity *in action*. Whether you like it or not, every out gay and lesbian Latino is a role model for others who have not yet taken the step.

We must assume the responsibility of leadership that is ours as gays, lesbians and Latinos by finding ways to reconcile our competing cultural affinities. For some that may mean political activism through organizations like Gay & Lesbian Latinos Unidos in California or Hispanic United Gays & Lesbians in New York City. For others it could mean the more personal revolution of rejecting the silence and the shame and introducing the *novia* to all the *tias* and *tios*.

The '80s resurgence of activism in gay and lesbian communities was largely in response to AIDS and the homophobia it nurtured even in those communities hardest hit. The shock, grief and rage unleashed by AIDS fueled direct action groups like ACT-UP and Queer Nation, creating a warrior brigade in counterpoint to the older, more institutionalized community centers and political clubs with a more conservative vision of the status and role of the gay and lesbian "community." While most of these organizations are now making strides toward addressing health and social issues important to ethnic communities, activists of color have often felt forced to establish alternative organizations in order to be heard.

These Latino activist groups have put municipal governments and gay and lesbian organizations alike on notice, demanding a response to how AIDS and other issues uniquely affect the Mexican, Puerto Rican, Cuban and various other Latino communities. The result is that organizations targeting gay and lesbian Latinos now exist in most major cities, providing health, legal and counseling services. In large part, these services are available to you at reduced cost and sometimes even free of charge.

The overwhelming majority of us are not political activists but we still must take some action on our own behalf. By addressing your personal concerns at the crossroad of Latino and queer cultures you will be building bridges between them. If you've just recently come out, chances are you're only a few steps into unfamiliar territory. By all means, get a map. Find out what services exist out there for you. Use them. Start with the list at the end of this chapter. Taking care of yourself is power.

No one in the family spoke about Manuel Acosta. Shortly after my grandparents married, they angered the family by allowing him to live in their home while he was on parole. My grandfather got him a job and my grandmother tried to get the rest of the family to visit. They refused. When he got drunk and disorderly he was arrested for violating probation. No one heard from him again for well over 15 years.

One morning, Manuel Acosta arrived in a suit on the porch of the home where he grew up. Over an hour later my grandmother found him standing on the sidewalk, a middle aged man carrying a valise full of gifts for the family that would not let him in.

Living as an openly gay or lesbian Latino and exercising your unique power eliminates old obstacles while creating new ones. In certain respects, you may be breaking with your family, friends and community. By living as a queer among Latinos and a Latino among queers, there is the hope of establishing those relationships based on courage and honesty instead of fear and shame. We needn't feel like guests in our own homes, never entirely free to be ourselves. It is only in rejecting or suppressing any aspect of our identities as queers or Latinos that we guarantee our own personal isolation. The problem is not that we are alone as gay and lesbian Latinos. On the contrary, our political, social and personal *barrios* are richer by virtue of our diverse identities.

Coming out and living honestly as a gay or lesbian Latino may reveal what is good and powerful in your life. It may not be possible to resolve all of the conflicts and contradictions of belonging to more than one world but you do not have to resign yourself to a life dictated by prejudice and fear. Instead, you can choose to reconcile and integrate the worlds you span.

Several more years passed between the day my grandmother and Manuel Acosta saw one another again on that street in Van Nuys, and the phone call from a sister-in-law telling her he was dead. Although he had been beaten to death almost a year earlier the family had decided to spare the expense of a funeral and to keep the news from her. When the police had called, her brother Freddy denied knowing anyone by the name of Manuel Acosta.

Somewhere in the 1950s Vivian and Manuel Moreno, my grandparents, drove to the Potter's Field near La Puente where Manuel Acosta was buried in a communal grave with five John Doe's. They tried to claim his body but had no way of knowing where to find him in the grave. They returned home. And 35 years later they told the story of Manuel Acosta to their queer grandson and afterward we sat in silence, remembering or just imagining my great uncle whom I had never heard of before.

Our families may reject us but we belong to them nonetheless. The same is true of our friends, our churches, our neighborhoods and our country. We must not abandon them. They are ours. Even if it is impossible to stay, they remain ours for as long as we claim them; for as long as we attempt to reconcile our queer and Latino communities and identities; for as long as we educate ourselves about our rights and how to obtain them. As long as we do all that we have power, we have hope and we do honor to the memories of every queer Latino and Latina who lived or died alone, finally bringing them home to us where they belong.

Resources

National Directory of Latina/o Lesbian and Gay Organizations
(The following information is current as of 1992)

NATIONAL
LLEGO — The National Latina/o
  Lesbian & Gay Organization
P.O. Box 44483
Washington, DC 20026
202-544-0092

CALIFORNIA
GELAM — Gente Latina de Ambiente
48 San Jose Avenue, Suite 3
San Francisco, CA 94110
415-285-6921

GLLU — Gay & Lesbian Latina/os
  Unidos
P.O. Box 85459
Los Angeles, CA 90072
213-660-9681, 665-2196

Hogar Latino — Orange County
  Latina/o Lesbians & Gays
c/o Gay & Lesbian Community Center
  of Orange County
12832 Garden Grove Blvd., #A
Garden Grove, CA 92642
714-534-0250

LLEGO: California — Statewide
  Latina/o Lesbian & Gay
  Organization
P.O. Box 40816
San Francisco, CA 94140
415-647-7655

MUJERIO — Bay Area Latina Lesbians
c/o The Women's Building
3543 18th Street, Box 23
San Francisco, CA 94110
415-255-1316

Raices Latinas — Grupo de apoyo
c/o The Center
2017 East 4th St.
Long Beach, CA 90804
213-434-4445

Grupo Cultural Hispano
34 Putnam
San Francisco, CA 94110
415-641-1868 or 415-285-0719

VIVA — Lesbian & Gay arts
   organization
1022 North Virgil, Suite 444
Los Angeles, CA 90029
213-232-8482 (24 hour bilingual hotline)

COLORADO
GALA — Gay & Lesbian Latina/o
   Alliance
869 Santa Fe
Denver, CO 80204
303-623-9153

DISTRICT OF COLUMBIA
ENLACE — Coalition of Gay &
   Lesbian Latinos
P.O. Box 45211
Washington, DC 20026
202-332-0069

ILLINOIS
ALA — Grupo de Ambiente
   Latinoamericano
606 W. Barry, Box 202
Chicago, IL 60657
312-477-0735

LLENA — Latina Lesbianas En
   Nuestro Ambiente
606 W. Berry, Box 202
Chicago, IL 60657

NEW YORK
Boricua Gay & Lesbian Forum
P.O. Box 7108, Grand Central Station
New York City, NY 10163-6027
914-476-9732

HUGL — Hispanic United Gay &
   Lesbians
P.O. Box 226, Canal Street Station
New York City, NY 10019
212-691-4181

Las Buenas Amigas — New York City
   area Latina Lesbiana Group
P.O. Box 627, Stuyvesant Station
New York City, NY 10009

Latina/o Lesbian & Gay Coalition of
   New York
77 Poplar Drive
East Hills, NY 11576
516-621-0047

Lesbiana Latina History Project —
   Documentation Center
P.O. Box 627, Stuyvesant station
New York City, NY 10009
212-677-1289

OHIO
Gay & Lesbian Hispanics of Central
   Ohio
49 E. Moler St.
Columbus, OH 43207
614-444-5607

PENNSYLVANIA
FUEGO Latino
P.O. Box 40047
Philadelphia, PA 19106-5041
215-224-4934

PUERTO RICO
CCG — Colectivo de Concientizacion
   Gay
Apartado 1003, Estacion Viejo San Juan
San Juan, PR 00902
809-782-9600

TEXAS
AMIGA — All Mujeres Interested In
   Getting Active
P.O. Box 980134
713-520-5667

ALLGO — Austin Latina/o Lesbian &
   Gay Organization
P.O. Box 13501
Austin, TX 78711
512-472-2001

COMPANERAS: El Nuevo Canto —
   Political & Social Protest
1636 Kipling, Suite 4
Houston, TX 77006
713-529-4472

ELLAS — State-wide network of
   Lesbiana Latinas
P.O. Box 1175
San Antonio, TX 78294
512-228-0201

GLHD — Gay & Lesbian Hispanics of
   Dallas
P.O. Box 35023
Dallas, TX 75302
214-521-3458

GLHU — Gay & Lesbian Hispanics
   Unidos
P.O. Box 70153
Houston, TX 77270
713-880-GLHU or 270-4548

Paz Y Liberacion — Publication about
   Gay Latinoamerica
P.O. Box 66450
Houston, TX 77266

WASHINGTON
LLEGO — Seattle
1406 Western, Suite 802
Seattle, WA 98101
206-623-5782

Asian-Pacific Islander Issues: Identity Integration and Pride

Terry S. Gock

Introduction

Although the intended readers of this article are primarily those of Asian Pacific descent, I hope that non-Asian readers will gain a better understanding and deeper appreciation of Asians and Pacific Islanders through this exploration of the process of becoming positive and proud of who we are as Asian Pacific lesbians and gay men. This article will first briefly look at the relevant socio-historical context. Since I am a psychologist the process of identity integration is of particular interest to me. Therefore I will present a "model" of how such integration might occur and what kinds of experiences might contribute to positive identity integration for lesbians and gay men of Asian Pacific descent. As a gay Asian-American man myself, I know the struggle to integrate these identities from personal experience.

Some clarification of terminology may be helpful. In this article, the terms "Asians" and "Asians and Pacific Islanders" will be used interchangeably since Asians and Pacific Islanders share the same basic values, norms, and geographical proximity in their countries of origin despite discernible differences in physical appearance, cultural nuances, and ethnic background.

Socio-Historical Perspective

Although it was founded on the basic tenets of freedom and respect for differences, being different in the U.S. is not easy. The continuing struggle to deal with social and economic discrimination based on racial differences has been a prominent part of our collective history for the past 100 years. In more recent times, the quest for civil rights protection and social equality has extended to differences based on gender and sexual orientation. For Asians and Pacific Islanders, the struggle to attain equality and recognition despite being different in physical appearance and cultural roots lags somewhat behind the efforts of some of the other racial/ethnic minority groups, such as African-Americans.

Historically, while this country was rebuilding itself after the Civil War, with a new social structure in which black slavery was abolished, it was also busily passing laws (such as the Chinese Exclusion Act of 1882) which categorically excluded Asians from immigration, citizenship, and equal protection. In fact, it was not until the 60's that the remnants of such laws were completely repealed and many previously excluded Asians were finally allowed to become citizens of this country. Furthermore, the injustices and humiliation suffered by the over 110,000 persons of Japanese ancestry in concentration camps in this country from 1942 until the end of World War II bear witness to the intensity and the continuing power of deeply rooted racism against, and exploitation of, Asians in general. Following the Civil Rights movement in the '60s the Asian Pride movement began and then blossomed in the '70s.

For lesbians and gay men of Asian Pacific descent, developing a sense of pride and identity as a community has similarly lagged behind the mainstream lesbian and gay movement. With the mushrooming of many social, political, and other groups after the Stonewall Resistance in 1969, the modern era of the organized lesbian and gay movement in this country began. Asian Pacific lesbians and gay men, however, did not mobilize and establish any organized group until the mid to late '70s. While this delay may have affected the maturity of the Asian Pacific lesbian and gay movement when compared to that of other racial/ethnic minority lesbian and gay communities in this country, it has also offered some distinct advantages. We have been able to learn from the successes and failures of our predecessors in developing community and personal pride as lesbians and gay men of Asian and Pacific Islander descent.

Asian Pacific Lesbian and Gay Identity
Integration Process
It is not possible to be really proud of oneself without a fairly clear definition of who one is. One must also feel positive about this identity. For a lesbian or a gay man of Asian Pacific descent, this means having to deal with the process of integrating one's multiple identities derived from sexual orientation, gender, and race/ethnicity. My observation is that this multiple identity integration process is related to, but distinct from, the lesbian/gay identity development process described by the Australian psychologist Vivian Cass (1979) in her now classic model of how a positive gay or lesbian identity is formed. I believe also that it is distinct from the nongay ethnic minority identity integration process outlined by Atkinson, Morten, and Sue (1979). In other words, how affirmative one is about oneself as a lesbian or

gay person and how positive one is as an Asian-American certainly affects how proud one can be about one's lesbian/gay Asian identity. Nevertheless, the process of integrating one's multiple identities requires some additional and independent tasks not experienced by either those in the mainstream lesbian and gay community or those in the "straight" Asian Pacific Islander community.

How does one attain an integrated and positive gay and lesbian Asian Pacific Islander identity? The following model is adapted from Morales (1992) who has described a number of different "states" reflective of attitudinal and lifestyle changes as the awareness of multiple identities becomes more apparent and the process of change toward an integrated identity evolves.

State 1: Status Quo. During this state, there is the idealistic belief that one is being treated "as an individual like everyone else." Such statements as "I am not defined (and confined) by my lesbian/gay identity or by my Asian background" are common. Despite the subtle and not so subtle discrimination apparent in both the generally homophobic Asian and Pacific Islander community as well as the less than accepting mainstream lesbian and gay community, a utopian approach to life dominates both the perception of reality and the perception of the actions of others. At this state, an Asian lesbian or gay man tends to attract white lovers with the central focus of attraction being race or ethnicity.

State 2: Awareness of Identities. During this state, the realization of one's double minority status (and triple minority status for those Asian lesbians who are also identified with the women's community) often evokes significant emotional discomfort as one becomes keenly sensitive to the discrimination and prejudice which exist. For example, in a study by Dr. Connie Chan, over three quarters of the 35 Asian-American lesbians and gay men surveyed felt it was more difficult to come out to other Asians because of the grave concern about rejection and stigmatization (Chan, 1989). Similarly, discrimination persists in the mainstream gay and lesbian community as exemplified by the practice in some lesbian and gay establishments (e.g., bars and discos) of requiring more than the customary number of picture identity cards for admission by Asian clientele. The frustration of not being able to effectively integrate the different identity communities to which they belong often leads Asian Pacific lesbians and gay men to live different parts of their lives independently and to maintain separate groups of friends and associates who seldom intermingle.

State 3: Dilemma in Allegiance. During this state, the neat separation of different parts of one's life described in State 2 begins to break down. Concomitant with this predicament are the real and/or imaginary demands of the various communities or groups with which one associates. An example of this conflict can be seen in two concurrent California ballot measures in 1986. One was the so-called "La Rouche Initiative" which, for all intents and purposes at that time, aimed at legalizing discrimination against gay men under the guise of medical necessity because of AIDS. The other was the "English Only Initiative" which would legitimize prejudice against racial and ethnic diversity under the seemingly benign proposition to establish English as the "official language" of California. While there was no particular incongruity in opposing both initiatives, discomfort and distress arose because the agenda of the lesbian and gay community (which was working fiercely against the "La Rouche Initiative") and parts of the Asian Pacific Islander community (which was working equally hard against the "English Only Initiative") had little to do with each other. In fact, a number of Asian lesbians and gay men expressed feeling an insidious sense of betrayal to one community if they were to commit more of their resources to the other during this political process.

State 4: Selective Allegiance. During this state, a primary identification with one of the communities predominates. Perhaps due to the strong ties to their cultural roots, a significant number of Asian gay men tend to identify themselves with the nongay Asian and Pacific Islander community at this state although some do choose to align themselves with the mainstream gay community. In contrast, because of the oppressively hierarchical sex role expectations espoused by the traditional Asian and Pacific Islanders, many Asian lesbians seem to feel more comfortable identifying with the Asian women's community, the mainstream feminist movement, or lesbian groups. Despite the identification with a primary community during this state, feelings of resentment and frustration abound because of the lack of integration among the different communities. In fact, as noted by Dr. Chan (1989) in the survey mentioned above, Asian Pacific lesbians and gay men often express a desire to feel complete by being supported for who they are both as Asians and as lesbian or gay.

State 5: Integrating Identities. During this state, the primary identification with a community gives way to a more fluid and contingent identity. The question "do you identify yourself as a `lesbian or gay Asian' or as an `Asian who happens to be lesbian or gay'" often results in the response "it depends" followed by an explanation of how one determines primary identification based on different situations. In other words, the process of integrating multiple identities at this state involves moving back and forth between one's affiliation with the Asian Pacific community and with the lesbian and gay community (as well as with the women's community if an Asian lesbian is so identified). Such movements are a dynamic process which, I believe, continues throughout our lifetime.

As you who are Asian-American read through the five states described above, you may find descriptions from more than one state which fit you. As pointed out by Morales (1992): "It is possible that persons may experience several states or parts of states at the same time . . . (p.131)" It is not important to label yourself as being in a particular state. What is important is to use this model as a map or guide as you journey through the process of identity integration. As you struggle with the seemingly conflicting demands of commitment, and the fear of being alienated from either of your communities, you will find that mastery of your feelings, validation, and pride will be the rewards of the struggle.

Resources To Become Lesbian/Gay, Asian, and Proud
The model described above provides a road map or guide for understanding the multiple identity integration process experienced by lesbians and gay men of Asian Pacific descent. As such it should help you locate yourself in the integration process and see what might be ahead for you. For more concrete help there is one effective route to obtaining information and support for yourself and that is in the organizations which have been established specifically by and for Asian Pacific lesbians and gay men in the past ten to fifteen years. In fact, there is now at least one such organization in practically every major city in the U.S. and Canada with a sizable population of Asians and Pacific Islanders. It is thus not difficult for those living in these areas to contact the available groups. While there is currently no national network to centralize relevant referral information, those Asians and Pacific Islanders who live in areas without identifiable lesbian and gay Asian specific organizations can likely be referred to resources through mainstream gay agencies (such as lesbian and gay community services centers) and hotline programs, either locally or in nearby cities with a relatively high concentration of Asian Pacific residents.

The available Asian-Pacific lesbian and gay resources can generally be divided into two types. In order to provide the necessary safe space for their participants, there are organizations which offer programs (such as rap groups) open only to Asians and Pacific Islanders. Other organizations are more socially oriented and tend to include both Asians and non-Asians in their activities. Although some of these groups have names which denote a co-sexual membership make up, one needs to check with a specific group of interest to determine the gender balance of the membership.

A major advantage of participating in these Asian-specific gay groups and organizations is that they tend to provide a safe space to more fully explore and integrate one's multiple identities. Just the experience of being with other lesbian and gay Asians in a supportive and structured environment often helps reduce the feelings of isolation and alienation one develops from being in strictly gay non-Asian settings, or strictly nongay Asian surroundings. Moreover, in the mainstream lesbian and gay culture where role models who are Asians and Pacific Islanders are few and far between, such organizations provide an opportunity to know people who have successfully integrated their gay and Asian identities. This is especially important for those in the early stages of developing their identity as lesbians and gay men of Asian Pacific descent.

We have examined some aspects of the Asian lesbian and gay identity integration process. I hope this chapter will serve as a catalyst for further inquiry into the special experiences of Asian-American gays and lesbians. For those of you who are

Asian-American and gay, I hope you will continue your struggle to be that person who takes pride in your multiple identities. I encourage you to work toward integration not only of your own positive self-image, but toward integration of the diverse communities in which you live and love, to which you give the gift of your unique and graceful presence.

References

Atkinson, D.R., Morten, G., & Sue, D.W. (1979). *Counseling American minorities.* Dubuque, IA: Brown.

Cass, V.C. (1979). *Homosexuality identity formation: A theoretical model.* Journal of Homosexuality, 4, 219-235.

Chan, C.S. (1989). *Issues of identity development among Asian-American lesbians and gay men.* Journal of Counseling & Development, 68, 16-20.

Morales, E.S. (1992). *Counseling Latino gays and Latina lesbians.* In S.H. Dworkin & F.J. Gutierrez (Eds.). *Counseling Gay men and Lesbians: Journey to the End of the Rainbow.* Alexandria, VA: American Association for Counseling and Development.

Native[1] Gay and Lesbian Issues:
The Two-Spirited

Terry Tafoya

"Long ago, when the world was young, Coyote was going along . . ." (or perhaps it was Raven, or Wiskijiac, or Dukwebah, or Rabbit . . .) . . . with these words, a number of the Native stories of the Americas begin to tell of an unbroken connectiveness of past, present, and future. The stories provide a framework of understanding how the world works, how one identifies oneself as a member of a tribe, a clan, a community; what to value and what to avoid. These include issues of sexuality and gender.

Coyote, someone common to many tribes, plays with everything — sexual behavior, gender identity, boundaries and bodies. This Trickster always challenges an audience to think and to deal with concepts of transformation. Often in the stories, when "Evil" (and this term seems inappropriate, but it is a term forced by English usage and convention — "Disharmonic" might be a more accurate term), is encountered, it is not seen as something to be destroyed in some final Armageddon, but as a force or energy that is to be transformed.

For example, in a Pacific Northwest legend, Coyote confronts the Blood Monster Wawa-yai, a giant who kills people by draining them of blood. Offering him baskets full of blood soup, Coyote tempts him into excess, until Wawa-yai has ingested so much blood that he can barely move his enormous bloated body. Coyote then taunts the monster into chasing him, but Wawa-yai's belly is now so

---

[1]"Native" is the term deliberately chosen over "Native American", since many of the experiences discussed are relevant to the aboriginal people of Canada and Central and South America.

huge he can not fit through the Longhouse door, and he bursts as he runs against the thorn-lined doorframe. As Coyote watches, these exploding bits and pieces of the monster turn into mosquitoes. "Evil" is not eradicated, but turned into something that is more in balance with the universe, and indeed, the universe would not be in balance without the "Evil". Coyote's action is to stabilize the world by playing with the excess until harmony is restored. If this story is used to form a metaphor for AIDS, or substance abuse (contemporary monsters that steal and destroy loved ones in the manner of Wawa-yai), a European worldview of this story (e.g., Hansel and Gretel destroy the Witch) would focus on the eradication of the enemy — the dragon is slain, and everyone else lives happily ever after. But just as in substance abuse and real life, where "Evil" doesn't disappear when treatment begins, the "Evil" takes on a more manageable form that a person can live with on a daily basis. A mosquito may be a problem, but not of the significance of the Blood Monster. There is a place for everything in Creation — a fundamental belief of most Native communities.

Most Native communities tend not to classify the world into concrete binary categories of the Western world — Good/Bad; Right/Wrong; Male/Female; Gay/Straight, but rather into categories that range from appropriateness to inappropriateness depending on the context of a situation.

For example, a Navajo man asked a nonIndian man for food to feed his family including his wife, who was about to give birth. The nonIndian agreed, but asked why the man's family was going hungry when it was well-known what a good hunter he was. The Navajo replied, "Because it is not appropriate that I who am about to receive a life should be taking life at this time." In other words, hunting is not seen as right or wrong, but only understandable in the context of a relationship.

This worldview is critical in understanding Native concepts of sexuality and gender, which do not always fit comfortably and neatly into general American concepts of Gay/Straight, or Male/Female. Indeed, even the discrete categories that exist for social science research will not always make conceptual sense to Native people who may have a far more sophisticated taxonomy addressing spirituality and function, rather than appearance. For example, how does an Euro-American system of "Gay/Straight" classify a man who wants to be anally penetrated by a woman wearing a dildo?

When Native American people discovered Columbus five centuries ago, they presented a unique conundrum of identity. Not only did most tribes not organize themselves by kings and queens in European tradition, but the majority classified members as having more than two genders. This radical (for Europeans) way of seeing the world brought swift and tragic responses. The Spanish explorer Balboa, for example, declared such individuals who were not considered male or female to be "sodomites", and literally had them torn apart by his dogs in the 16th century. Thus, from the very beginning of European contact, Native people learned not to openly discuss matters of sexuality and gender with the newcomers, because they could be killed for being "different". Most American citizens are unaware of Native history and reality. For example, American Indians did not become citizens of the United States until 1924. When the reservations were created by the federal government, the superintendents of the reservations were all appointed Christian missionaries of various denominations, with the mandate to "civilize" American Indians by converting them to Christianity, often by withholding food and starving them into submission. Federal Boarding Schools were set up for Natives (American Indians and Alaskan). Natives were not permitted to attend public school until the mid-1930s. There are still a number of Indian Boarding Schools operating today. Children were forcibly removed from their parents, sometimes at gunpoint, to deliberately prevent them from growing up with the influence of their culture and language.

This forced segregation and isolation had a devastating impact on Native communities as a whole. Critical teachings and attitudes regarding sexuality and gender that would have been provided at the time of puberty for example, were never passed on in many families and tribes because the young person was away at Boarding School. Such things were not permitted to be discussed. In addition, there was an incredible loss of Native lives through exposure to European diseases to which Native people had no immunity (a situation that has a number of parallels to the AIDS epidemic... the newspaper editorials of the 1880s of the Pacific Northwest condemn Native Americans for having unacceptable sexual behaviors and multiple partners, and declared their deaths by infectious disease to be "God's punishment"). It is estimated that in the Pacific Northwest, 80% of the Native population died within two generations of European contact.

It is fascinating in working with the Native "Gay and Lesbian" community, to discover how often even those individuals who were denied access to their tribal histories of alternative gender roles and identities manifest the "duties and responsibilities of office" that were an integral part of being "different" before and after European contact. These traditional roles include teaching, keeping the knowledge of the elders, healing, child-care, spiritual leadership and participation, herbal wisdom, interpretation, mediation, and all forms of artistic expression.

Of the 250 or so Native languages still spoken in the United States, at least 168 of them have been identified as having terms for people who were not considered male or female. In the anthropological literature, the most common word used to describe such an individual is "Berdache". This is an unfortunate historic choice, reflecting as it does an old Persian term for a male sexual slave. The word was picked up in the Middle Ages by Europeans during the Crusades and its pronunciation and spelling evolved into its contemporary form.

When the French fur traders, explorers and missionaries encountered Native people in North America who did not fit European standards of gender roles, they used the term "Berdache" to describe them. In the 17th century, the word in French implied someone who engaged in receptive anal intercourse. It also has a connotation of someone with a biologically male identity, and so tends to exclude Native people who are biologically female. Some modern writers suggest the term "Amazon" to discuss the biological females who take on an alternative gender role. Berdache also indicates a sexual behavior that may or may not be relevant to a particular individual. Neither of these foreign terms are well known to traditional Native people.

In other words, asking a tribal member, "Do you have a Berdache or Amazon tradition in your community?" may bring about a confused stare. Asking a Navajo, "Do your people have Nadle?" or asking a Lakota, "Do your people have Winkte?" may get a very different response, as people recognize their own language's term for such people. Many contemporary Native people have difficulty in being comfortable with identifying themselves as Gay, Lesbian, or Bisexual, feeling as though they are "being herded" into such categories by the power of English. In response to this, the term "Two-Spirited" or "Two-Spirited People" seems to be gaining a greater acceptance for many of today's Native people, in lieu of "Berdache", "Amazon", or Gay/Lesbian/Bisexual. "Two-Spirited" indicates that someone possesses both a male and female spirit.

A number of non-Native Gay, Lesbian, and Bisexual researchers and writers have suggested the Two-Spirited tradition as an historic "Gay" role model since it often carries with it a sense of positive acceptance or even celebration within many Native communities. For example, a European-American gay male nurse reported being surprised and delighted to be visiting a Catholic priest on an Apache Indian reservation when a proud mother came in and told the priest, "My sixteen year old son is attracted to other men. We need to arrange for him to be initiated with the Medicine men". The nurse was amazed to discover that there was a respected and sanctioned role for such a young person among the Apache, and to note that the mother's response was somehow different than his own mother's had been when his own sexual orientation became known.

Unfortunately, the simplistic reductionism (Berdache-Gay) of many non-Native writers often fails to see that while the Two-Spirited People and Gay/Bisexual/Lesbian people experiences and worldviews overlap, they are not the same thing. The Two-Spirited position is not one determined primarily by sexual orientation. The role is one of a spiritual/social identity for Native people, as opposed to psycho-sexual identity. Paula Gunn Allen (Laguna/Sioux) suggests seeing the Berdache as a gender role, rather than a sexual identity. Tribal concepts do not stress individuality in the manner of Euro-American concepts, but instead focus on relationships, contexts, and interactions. In short, "Gay" can be seen as a noun, but "Two Spirit" is a verb. (This is meant as a metaphoric statement, where a noun is person, place or thing, where a verb deals with action and interactions).

The rigidity of the English language prevents even many self-identified Gay/Bisexual/Lesbian Natives from dealing with fluidity of gender and sexual roles, if the only categories that exist in a valued way are "homosexual/heterosexual". Native tradition emphasizes transformation and change, and the idea that an individual is expected to go through many changes in a lifetime. Indeed, many tribes anticipate that someone will change his or her name more than once, since a person at age 45 is not the same person he or she was at ten. Hence, a name change seems most appropriate.

While hardly identifying as "Asexual" (a lesser used category used by some researchers to indicate a Gay or Lesbian who is not active with males or females), some Two-Spirited people will not be involved on a sexual level with a biologically same-gendered partner, although an emotional/affectionate bonding can occur. This may be a matter of personal choice, an individual's medicine path (a traditional Native term that indicates one's spiritual behavior and connotates a combination of destiny and free choice), or a result of a specific spiritual vision/perception of their appropriate behavior. This should in no way distract from the fact that a number of Native people very strongly identify as members of the Gay/Lesbian/Bisexual community. But to see "Gay/Straight" as the only possible categories of sexual identity for Native people (and certain other ethnic groups in India, Burma, the Mid-East, etc.) is grossly misleading and out of touch with historic and contemporary reality. It is also seen as very reasonable that Two-Spirited people can be heterosexual, and one's partnering may change over a period of time. In many tribes, there was a history of polygamy, or polyandry — multiple spouses. This may still have an influence on how Native Two-Spirited people deal with relationships.

One of the impacts of the Gay/Lesbian/Bisexual movement has actually been to limit the options of younger Native people who are now (in English) informed that they are "gay" or "lesbian" when they begin showing behaviors that in earlier times would indicate they were "Lamana" or "Bote" or another traditional category. Native concepts of masculinity and femininity are so significantly different from European-American concepts of gender that they confuse the issue even more. For example, Jamake Highwater suggests: "...in hypermasculine societies, machismo is of the utmost importance in both heterosexual and homosexual males. In social systems that place less importance on distinction of sex, like those of many North American Indian tribes, there is a full spectrum of acceptable sexual behavior that makes the dualistic connotation of heterosexuality as opposed to homosexuality meaningless, and which therefore does not place a stigma on women who behave in a masculine manner or on men who behave in a feminine manner." (1991, p.82)

Interviews and research data obtained by the author with over 200 interracial same-sex couples indicates a higher rate of bisexuality (as defined by behavior rather than identity) among Native populations in America than in any other ethnic group studied, which may reflect the more fluid concept of gender relations and sexual expression (Tafoya & Rowell 1988, Allen 1989, Tafoya 1989). Indeed, in unpublished data based on interracial same-sex partners, there was a higher reported rate of heterosexual experience among the self-identified gay and lesbian Natives than among the other ethnics, even after the Native subjects had entered into a long-term (over a year's duration) same-sex relationship (Tafoya, 1992).

Native individuals may be quite comfortable with their presented identity shifting its emphasis on so-called "masculine/feminine" behavior, depending upon social context and the behavior/identity of a partner. In other words, a Two-Spirited person may become increasingly "masculine" within a specific environment, or when in a relationship with a "feminine" partner, regardless of biological gender. This appears increasingly complex, simply because the English language does not permit this discussion in a useful manner, with its emphasis on gendered pronouns and fundamental categories of Male/Female. Jay Miller (1992) offers a six gendered Native model, of 1) Hyper-Masculine (warriors and athletes, often reared away from women), 2) Ordinary Males, 3) Berdaches, 4) Amazons (or biological female Berdaches), 5) Ordinary Females, and 6) Hyper-Feminine. This model would also take into consideration a very strong femininely identified (e.g., Hyper-Feminine) individual who would partner an Amazon. At issue with high-risk reduction in HIV Prevention, this has significance, because in the two presented examples, the traditional communities would not consider such partnerships to be "homosexual", since they are classified as different genders. As a result, a commonly asked question "are you a man who has sex with other men", will honestly be answered "no" by someone who has sex with a Berdache or in some cases, with some Two-Spirited people. (With the risk of being tedious, it should be emphasized that in HIV transmission, "sex" with any gender is not at issue — rather certain forms of sexual expression carry risk factors and then only if one or more partners are HIV-positive.)

Yet another alternative would be to see European concepts of gender and sexuality as being polar opposites, or different ends of the same stick. One is either/ or male or female; gay or straight. Native American concepts usually prefer circles to lines. If one takes the line of male/female; gay/straight, and bends it into a circle, there are an infinite number of points. Just so, there are theoretically an infinite number of possible points of gender and sexual identity for an individual that can shift and differ over time and location.

Historically, the status of the Two-Spirited person was valued in many Native communities, since an ordinary male sees the world through male eyes, and an ordinary female sees the world through female eyes. However, a Two-Spirited person (who possesses both a male and female spirit, regardless of the flesh that is worn) will always see further. For this reason, many Two-Spirited people have become Medicine people, leaders and intermediaries between men and women, and between tribal communities and non-Native people. Their greater flexibility provides greater possibilities to discover alternative ways of seeing oneself and the world.

Because of the influence of the Federal Boarding School system and certain forms of Christianity, some tribal groups may be as homophobic as any other rural community, although Native attitudes tend towards a much greater tolerance and respect for personal choice than found in most Euro-American groups. For some individual Native people, their first contact with the formal category of "Berdache" or Two-Spirited, may be in a college course on anthropology, or a gay pride presentation. In those communities where the traditional role of the Two-Spirited has declined, many younger Native people report seeking partners and experiences off the reservation believing they are "the only one" in their community. As an adult, they discover the frequency of same-gender sexual and emotional involvement they had been happening on the reservation all the time.

Finally, the role of the Two-Spirited person is critical in its relationship to those who are not Two-Spirited. The alternative behaviors and creative option of the Gay and Lesbian community inform the entire society of what possibilities exist, and like the Coyote legends, offer guidelines and directions for exploring and living life to its fullest potential. A man or a woman is more clearly and accurately defined by the existence of a Two-Spirited person, just as a straight person may more fully understand him or herself in coming to know and understand Gay and Lesbians.

References

Highwater, Jamake. *Sex and Myth*, Harper and Row, NY, 1990.

Miller, Jay. "A Kinship of Spirit," in *America In 1492*, Alvin M. Josephy, Jr., ed., Alfred A., Knopf, NY, 1992: p.309.

Tafoya, Terry, and Rowell, Ron. "Counseling Native American Lesbians and Gays," in *The Sourcebook on Lesbian/Gay Health Care*, M. Shernoff and W.A. Scott, eds., National Lesbian and Gay Health Foundation, Inc., Washington, D.C., 1988: pp. 63 - 67.

Tafoya, Terry. "Pulling Coyote's Tale: Native American Sexuality and AIDS," in *Primary Prevention of AIDS*, V. Mays, G. Albee, and S. Schneider, eds., Saga Publications, Newsbury Park, CA, 1989: 280 - 289.

Suggested Reading

Unfortunately there are simply not that many materials available that specifically address Native Gay and Lesbian issues. Among those most relevant are:

Roscoe, Will. *Living the Spirit: A Gay Native American Anthology*, St. Martin's Press, 1989.

Roscoe, Will. *The Zuni Man-Woman*, St. Martin's Press, 1991.

Williams, Walter. *The Spirit and the Flesh: Sexual Diversity in American Indian Culture*, Harper and Row, 1987.

Resources

Gay American Indian Association
3004 16th St.
Suite 203
San Francisco, CA 94103
(415) 255-7210

WeWah and BarCheAmpe
111 E. 14th St.
Suite 141
New York, N.Y. 10003

American Indian Gays and Lesbians
P.O. Box 10229
Minneapolis, Minnosota 55458

National Native American AIDS Prevention Center
3515 Grand Ave.
#100
Oakland, CA 94610
1-800-283-AIDS

American Indian AIDS Institute
333 Valencia Street
Suite 200
San Francisco, CA 94103

Tahoma Two-Spirits
P.O. Box 4402
Seattle, Washington 98104

Vancouver Two-Spirits
P.O. Box 598, Station A
Vancouver, British Columbia, Canada V2S 1V4

Two-Spirited People of the 1st Nations
476 Parliament St.
#202
Toronto, Ontario, Canada M4X 1P2

Nichiwakan N.G.S.
616 Broadway Avenue
Winnipeg, Manitoba, Canada R3C 0W8

THE GAY AND LESBIAN CULTURAL SCENE

An Explosion of Creativity

Michael Lassell

Once upon a time, when I was a child — somewhere between the fall of Rome and Stonewall Riots — I went to my first play, *The Clown That Ran Away*, performed without sets by students in a local high school auditorium. I don't know what it was about that experience that was qualitatively different from singing, drawing, television and movies, all of which were a normal part of my life as heir to the American middle-class, or even from writing (my precocious first poem having been composed at age eight), but my life changed irrevocably that drizzly Saturday afternoon as some gangly but enthusiastic teenaged thespian ran up and down the linoleum-tiled aisles in a polka-dot jumpsuit enlisting audience support.

I had encountered Art, and I wanted to live in its arms forever.

Needless to say, I didn't then know that I was gay, although it was already clear that I was "different." I had managed by third grade to convince teachers that I was a far happier puppy left inside with my Crayolas to interpret scenes from *Mary Poppins* while the crew-cut boys went outside to whip themselves into an athletic frenzy that would have excluded me even if I had turned up ready and willing.

Three days into puberty, however, I realized that my life-long difference had something to do with sex, and that that difference — as well as all the others (race, class, religion, body odor) — were not only tolerated but encouraged by the arty kids of my high school drama club and their turtle-necked, guitar-strumming friends.

Now, a life in the world of art has long been an option for people of our tribe, from Aristophanes to Kit Marlowe, from Tchaikovsky and Walt Whitman to Gertrude Stein and Phranc, for the very reason that the art arena — unlike that of, say, politics or business — values eccentricity and individuality of expression above all else, beyond even the power of that expression to persuade or, for that matter, to communicate at all. Gangrenous conformity, which I choked down at home with every meal, was anathema to the long-haired, bohemian adolescents I hung around with, a crowd that spent its afternoons listening to Vivaldi and the Beatles, discussing *Naked Lunch* and *Last Exit to Brooklyn* as well as Great Books in French, and organizing folk music concerts to benefit the NAACP. Needless to say, more than a few of us "swung the other way." Of course, my own other-way-swinging, widely acknowledged, was entirely theoretical at the time, despite my passionate crush on the school's leading actor, the memory of whom still makes me sigh.

It wasn't until I was in college — some years after the assassination of JFK (during which I was rehearsing with some 200 other choristers for a country-wide choral concert) — that I had another art experience to rival in my psyche *The Clown That Ran Away*. It was another play, this one called *Fortune and Men's Eyes* by John Herbert. It premiered in 1967 at the Actors Playhouse in Greenwich Village, about a hundred yards from where I now lived. It was set in a prison cell, and it was, in no uncertain terms, about homosexuality.

It certainly wasn't the first play about homosexuals (that honor belongs, in modern times, to *The Green Bay Tree*, a Broadway melodrama of the 1920s that introduced America to a young Brit name Laurence Olivier as a deviant youth, art imitating life once again). *Fortune* was, however, the first contemporary work I'd ever seen (although I'd already read John Rechy, William Burroughs, Jean Genet, Oscar Wilde, and even Constantine Cavafy by then). For me, this was liberation of a higher order.

If that long-ago children's play had introduced the artist in me to art, the much more adult drama introduced the homosexual in me to gay art. It told me that I could not only make art, but I could make art about myself and the men I loved and/or lusted after (which was pretty much all of them in those days). Why it took a play to push my consciousness over an edge I resisted despite all my reading was, I suppose, the immediacy of the living experience right there in front of my eyes.

The following year, *The Boys in the Band* took New York by storm, and two undergraduate friends of mine and I created a tiny ripple in a small liberal-arts college by performing a one-act play by Sam Shepard. I played a role written for a woman; we played the relationship as one between two men. God did not strike me dead, although the performances were held in the basement of the pristine university chapel. The college was not consumed by avenging fire. Sam Shepard did not sue us. No one told my parents.

By the next year I was living in London and seeing the plays of Joe Orton in their earliest productions, hanging out with real-live gay actors from the Old Vic and the English company of *Hair*, and writing openly about being gay (although not well enough to be published). Homosexuality was no longer theoretical. Within months of my return home, the blessed drag queens of the Stonewall Inn changed history in a far more immediate way than the first moon walk, later that summer, and made my life a whole lot easier.

Gay art started to become a reality, even if it was often amateurishly ad hoc. Professionalism could come later. In the first wave of the Stonewall movement just *doing* it was paramount. And do it, we did. By the time the film version of *Boys in the Band* was released, it was no longer politically correct, and I picketed dutifully, handing out leaflets in a suburban shopping mall to bewildered passersby explaining why this self-hating segment of the homosexual population in no way represented the spectrum of gay and lesbian experience. Naive as I was, the link had been made between self-esteem and being out, and between them and the creation of art that told the truth, and between all of that and the oppression of silence.

By 1979 William M. Hoffman was able to collect enough already-produced plays to publish *Gay Plays: The First Collection*, including work by such colleagues as Robert Patrick, Lanford Wilson, and Jane Chambers. In 1983, Harvey Fierstein's *Torch Song Trilogy* won a Tony Award as Best Play of the year, and its Broadway producer, John Glines, thanked his lover on national network TV, not only using the word, but giving his name. America gasped, I shrieked out loud, jumped up across the room to dance and cavort with my own lover, and gay art skipped merrily forward even unto the heart of the mainstream — at least in theory.

Meanwhile, the dykes and fags were everywhere. Novelist Edmund White and poet Richard Howard, among others, were inducted as members of the ultra-prestigious American Academy of Arts and Letters. Andy Warhol, himself perhaps asexual, was not only America's most famous painter, he created an entire gay-inspired universe that became so much the aesthetic of New York that Tennessee Williams hired Candy Darling, a Warhol drag superstar, to play the leading woman in a late play called *Small Craft Warnings*. Later, the decidedly not asexual Keith Haring took up where Warhol left off. Robert Mapplethorpe began to make his famous series of "sado-masochistic" self-portraits. By the early 80s, we were everywhere, and letting the world know.

When the realities of the AIDS epidemic finally hit us, the mood of the community, of course, changed, as did the content of the art we were making. The quantity of that art and the passionate commitment of the artists gave gay- and AIDS-themed art a credibility it had not yet had. If anything, AIDS only spurred us on to more aggressive aesthetic postures. In *The Normal Heart*, Larry Kramer, an outspoken minor novelist, became a raging major playwright when he accused New York Mayor Koch and the *New York Times* of homophobic genocide in a conspiracy to keep the nature of the AIDS plague quiet until it was grotesquely too late. AIDS refocused the community's energy. Sex became less overtly important than the very right to life.

Despite the loss, the grief, the ongoing horror of AIDS, despite the dismissal of gay/lesbian art by many of our own leaders, our own artists, as "irrelevant" in the face of AIDS and corporate/government inaction, openly gay and lesbian art, literature, and media — much of it addressed AIDS, both directly and metaphorically — continue to flourish in every major city in the country, and in many less urban areas as well.

By 1992 estimate, three specifically gay/lesbian books ran off the presses *every day,* and no one ever pretended to be able to read them all. In *The Big Gay Book,* John Preston's encyclopedic compendium of our community's resources — an indispensable socio-cultural survival manual — some hundred pages are given over to "Gay Culture" from literary magazines and journals to lavender theater, opera, film, and video.

Writers, for example, meet annually to exchange ideas and give each other prizes. The increasingly significant Lambda Literary Awards (the "Lammys," as they are known) are bestowed by the community's own national gay/lesbian literary magazine, *Lambda Book Report,* an offshoot of one of America's dozens of independent lesbian/gay bookstores. Many of our gay/lesbian literary heroes/heroines continue to contribute to the world of words. They and their aesthetic offspring continue to win important recognition for their work. Openly lesbian Adrienne Rich has even won the prestigious National Book Award. Gay and lesbian writers who are successful in the mainstream, like Allen Gurganus, author of the best-selling *The Oldest Living Confederate Widow Tells All,* are coming out more and more publicly, and so-called "mainstream" publishing houses are printing our books with ever-greater frequency.

But the world of books and publishing is not our only venue by any means. An openly gay contemporary choreographer like Mark Morris, who frequently creates *serious* drag roles for himself, becomes so important to the dance world that no less a ballet giant than the decidedly heterosexual Mikhail Baryshnikov dances with him. But Morris is not alone in the gay dance vanguard. There are, for example, Britain's "bad boy" Michael Clark (who played Caliban in Peter Greenaway's film *Prospero's Books*) and brilliant African-American choreographer/dancer Bill T. Jones. John Kelly, who is a dancer by training, has segued over into the circle of "performance art" (that hardest to define medium), where he has many gay/lesbian colleagues, including, for example, Holly Hughes and Tim Miller (two names that became notorious when the National Endowment for the Arts in 1990 rescinded their grants because they are openly "queer").

Not all the arts, however, are equal: There are arts and then there are arts — the fine and the popular. And the expensive-to-make popular arts, like film, television, and records, have been less fertile ground for gay and lesbian artists. Because the media are profit-driven, broad public reaction of an unsophisticated kind — or, rather, executive anticipation of that reaction — determines electronic fare, and many people widely known to be gay or lesbian not only to insiders but to the public, still maintain a facade of heterosexual "respectability" in order to curry favor with the consumer public. Ultimately, of course this nonsense will end, even if it takes AIDS to help end it.

Even Hollywood has addressed our presence, if not our issues, although American studio films invariably portray us as evil or grotesque, even when they are trying to be sincere, as in *Prince of Tides,* for example, and *The Fisher King,* both of which feature "sympathetic" stereotypical gay men and heterosexual men of large-hearted tolerance. Some of the more vicious portraits of gay men and lesbians are too egregious even to mention the names of the film here, but they are in no short supply.

Thanks to insightful independent and foreign filmmakers, both conservative and decidedly revolutionary, we have had our moments on screen. Since *The Boys in the Band*, after all, we have been treated to some excellent more-or-less "mainstream" movies: *Maurice, Kiss of the Spider Woman, My Beautiful Laundrette, Another Country, Death in Venice*, even *La Cage aux Folles*. More experimental fare has been offered by *Carravagio* and *Edward II* (both by Derek Jarman); *Taxi zum Klo*; the late Arnie Breson's *Parting Glances*; and *Constant Companion*. There have also been incredibly powerful documentaries, including the Oscar-winning *The Life and Times of Harvey Milk, Before Stonewall*, and *Improper Conduct*, the late Nestor Almendros's look at homophobia in Castro's Cuba.

There are all manner of encouraging signs in the film industry. Lesbian filmmaker Debra Chasnoff in 1992 thanked her lover when she received an Academy Award for her documentary *Deadly Deception*. On the same telecast, a posthumous Best Song Oscar was awarded to Howard Ashman for his work on an animated Disney film, *Beauty and the Beast*. The award was movingly accepted by Ashman's surviving lover in a speech that was widely reported as the most affecting moment of the evening. The same evening, a semi-closeted lesbian actress gave a thinly coded acceptance speech that was well understood by her "tribe of outsiders."

Despite idiotic oppression, young gay and lesbian filmmakers of enormous talent, vision, and drive follow the lead of the trailblazers — Cocteau, Genet, and others — to create highly individualistic and often breathtakingly passionate short and feature-length films about the kind of gay men and lesbians we have never seen depicted in a Hollywood studio product, even those produced, written, directed, and starring gay men and lesbians.

Not only do these films win awards at international festivals more enlightened than the American marketplace, but we organize and flock to film/video festivals of our own. What is, perhaps, most encouraging is the expertise and finesse of this product. The feminist world was shocked when respected documentary filmmaker Yvonne Rainer came out at age 56. But other lesbians and gay men have never been in the closet. Jan Oxenberg, for example, has been making experimental lesbian films for over twenty years, and has been winning awards almost as long.

And there is a whole crop of energetic talents on the horizon: Marlon Riggs, an African-American who has dealt in *Looking for Langston* and *Tongues Untied* not only with matters of masculinity and homosexuality, but American racism; Gregg Araki, the Asian-American Angeleno who created *The Living End* and who deals directly with AIDS and the malaise of his generation; Todd Haynes, whose *Poison* incorporated metaphoric references to AIDS and specific, erotic references to Jean Genet; and Tom Kalin, whose *Swoon* takes a look at gay child murderers Leopold and Leob in a decidedly provocative way. Occasionally an openly gay director, Gus Van Sant for example, even "breaks through" to the heterosexual art-house crowd. Though his first film, *Mala Noche*, was clearly "avantgarde," he grabbed some "inside the fringe" attention with *Drugstore Cowboy* (Starring Matt Dillon) before enlisting River Phoenix and Keanu Reeves to star as male hustlers in *My Private Idaho*.

Music has also been a difficult area for gay artists, at least in the record industry sense of music. There are, of course, gay and gay-friendly solo acts and groups: Deee-Lite, the Pet Shop Boys, Morrissey , Jimmy Sommerville, Jane's Addiction, and the Red Hot Chili Peppers. And they prosper. But the closet hangs over many. Freddie Mercury of Queen, for example, did not come out until shortly before his death from AIDS. There are also major gay and lesbian names in the record business, but most are in the closet, especially the older label artists. Some of the biggest names in the music business are generally acknowledged to be gay thanks to statements made in interviews in the more permissive 1970's, but some of those have somewhat retrenched their positions. Liberace denied his homosexuality past the point of plausibility. Little Richard, on the other hand — bless his outrageous heart — is less equivocal.

The classical music world is more open to gay and lesbian singers and musicians, although conductors, I am assured by a singer who inhabits that world, must be married. And perhaps it is because our legacy is so palpable in the world of music, with gay forefathers to name like Aaron Copeland, Samuel Barber, Virgil Thompson, and Benjamin Britten. Ned Rorem, one of this country's most important living composers, is not only openly homosexual, but has written about it in a series of famous (some say "infamous") diaries. He has even become musically involved with the AIDS arts movement, as one of a dozen composers who set AIDS poetry to music for the *AIDS Quilt Songbook*. (Even the AIDS Quilt is art: It is credited as the largest quilt, in fact the largest piece of folk art, in history).

Opera and ballet, of course, have long appealed to gay people, and many singers, musicians, and dancers are, of course, lesbian and gay, even though they are rarely public about it. However, when the Metropolitian Opera decided to commission its first opera in decades, both the libretto and the score were written by gay men — Bill Hoffman (author of *As Is*, which went from Broadway to PBS) and John Corigliano, respectively — and the gala opening-night audience at the Met was far more noticeably gay than ever.

Broadway has long appealed to gay people, and our tribe has made extraordinary contributions to the world of the legit stage (as well as in the off-Broadway and off-off-Broadway avant-garde movements). Until recently we have not been often represented on commercial stages, even though, of the performing arts, theater has been most responsive and responsible to gay/lesbian issues. With such gay giants in our past as Tennessee Williams and William Inge, the legacy continues with some of the most produced playwrights in the country: Terrence McNally, Lanford Wilson, Christopher Durang. And there is a whole new crop of playwrights waiting in the wings: Jon Robin Baitz, Tony Kushner, and Cheri Morraga to name only a few. AIDS, of course, has taken its toll of talent in this community, robbing us of Michael Bennett, for example, playwright Robert Chesley, and genius of the contemporary absurd, Charles Ludlum, whose off-the-wall work is carried on by his surviving lover, Everett Quintin in New York City.

In 1983 we were shocked to hear that *Torch Song Trilogy* won a Tony for Best Play on Broadway. In 1992, the Tony telecast included a specifically gay segment from William Finn's Tony-nominated musical *Falsettos*, and Finn himself won Tonys for book and music. Each year, many Tony nominees and winners have been homosexual. Nonetheless, although Leonard Bernstein all but came out late in his life, some of the most talented and powerful men and women on Broadway are still in the closet.

What is most extraordinary about the explosion of creativity our community has experienced — and produced — is that gay art of great quality exists over so broad a base in this country, not just in the biggest cities but in all cities with any gay/lesbian population at all. Gay/lesbian theaters, bands, orchestras, chamber-music ensembles, poetry series, choirs and choruses (from classical to gospel), and even stand-up comedy troups now prosper, and draw audiences from all segments of society.

Interestingly enough, the increased visibility of gay men and lesbians in all creative fields has created as well as solved some problems. There is, for example, the issue of censorship, both by the government, by institutions supported directly or indirectly by the government, and by other arts institutions. This censorship has focused largely on expressions of sexuality by politically challenging artists of all persuasions, but primarily on gay men and lesbians. It is not the sexuality of the artists that has been persecuted by funding agencies, but the expression of homoeroticism (by which is meant anything remotely related to homosexuality) in the work. The censorship has been based, therefore, not on sexual identity or orientation, but on how far out the artist has come in her or his work.

The controversy surrounding the National Endowment for the Arts, which is being held hostage by forces of the far Right in Washington, focused on two areas, performance art, and the traditionally sacrosanct world of gallery and museum "fine art." Now, there have been gay and lesbian artists since the beginning of time, many of them among the first ranks of cultural history, and some of the most important living modernists are also homosexual — men like Robert Rauschenberg and Jasper Johns, Robert Indiana, even the wildly popular David Hockney.

The artists who are being censored are younger, and angrier. Their work often examines the relationship of homosexuality, AIDS, and government irresponsibility with respect to our own community and other communities: the poor, the homeless, people of color. Photographer Robert Mapplethorpe, who died of HIV-related disease, is one of the better known targets of censorship. The late David Wojnarowicz, a writer as well as an artist of the first rank, is another.

Nonetheless, shows that confront AIDS, homophobia, and sexuality continue to find homes in privately held spaces that owe no allegiance to the federal government, or any state or local agency funded by the federal government. Like other minority groups before us, we have learned the lesson that if we wish to show our work and be free of censorship, we must create our own institutions. And in New York City, for example, there are three galleries that exist for the exclusive showing of gay and lesbian art.

There is the issue, too, of the mainstream. Many gay and lesbian artists wrestle with the concept of cultural ghettoization. Are we making art for one another, or for everyone? And is making art for ourselves not enough? If art is a means of liberation, as it surely is, then it is the making that liberates. However, if art is a conduit of enlightenment, as it surely has been — the classical theorists have been clear that the purpose of art was both entertainment and education — then reaching beyond our community is also important.

Many of our community's best writers, for example, are published by so-called "mainstream" publishers — people like Allen Ginsberg and Judith Grahn, Kate Millet and Dennis Cooper, Paul Monette and Dorothy Allison, Sarah Schulman and the whole New York Violet Quill set: Felice Picano, Andrew Holleran, Edmund White. The list, in fact, is almost as long as a list of our authors. But the question remains, do any nongay people read these books? And the answer is assumed, by those mainstream presses, to be no. "If a gay title sells 50,000 copies in hardcover," a publisher recently told me "it's because 50,000 gay people bought it." There is obviously a great deal of work to be done.

Another interesting consideration is the very notion of "gay" or "queer" sensibility in art. This is the idea that gay men and women make "gay art" even when the theme is not specifically homosexuality. Spanish film director Pedro Almodóvar, who is openly gay, is one such talent. Although he appeals to a wide audience, his sexual politics are definitely all-inclusive, and he has found great support in the gay community. Sometimes, it is argued, more can be done subtly, even surreptitiously, to win support than can be done in a style of confrontation.

Representing, perhaps, another extreme, there are even those well-known artists in our community who believe that during the AIDS crisis, at least, art is virtually meaningless. All artists, they believe, ought to put their energies into direct political action to end the epidemic. This touchy issue continues to burn, as does the question of the "politically correct" in art and the gay/lesbian artist's various responsibilities: to him or herself, to his or her art form, to the tribe, to our allied minority communities, and to society as a whole. The issue of censorship, so seemingly simple, is rather complicated by the portrayal of women in traditional pornography. How far can and should we go as gay men and lesbians to assert our rights to say and make anything at all? And how do we evaluate the relative good of free expression vs. protecting exploited groups? All of these are questions in the air that must be addressed by every gay man and lesbian making art today.

Furthermore, it is not uncommon, as we produce more and more work to greater and greater acclaim, to hear the notion voiced that gay men and lesbians control art, that we have cornered the powered positions and are shoving our issues onto stages and into galleries, concert halls, and performance spaces. There is even some truth to this notion. Many artists who are out of the closet have succeeded in their art and have come to control venues like the Lincoln Center Theater and important regional theaters throughout the country.

It is understandable that an openly gay artistic director who has a modicum of self-esteem will undoubtedly be more predisposed to producing a gay-themed play, ballet, or performance piece. It is, of course, not true that gays and lesbians control the arts; just that we are more apparent in the arts than elsewhere, partly because of the visibility of what we do, partly because people care about those activities, and partly because we have always existed in the arts. We were once, however, quieter about it than we are now.

The bottom-line of the post-Stonewall explosion is that gay and lesbian artists have real choices now that we did not have even a decade ago. Yes, we may decide to work in small gay arenas for a gay audience, but many of us have found it possible to work in the broader cultural arena. Ironically, competition from main-stream venues has actually become a problem for gay/lesbian bookstores, as B. Dalton, Brentano's, Tower Books, and Rizzoli now offer gay and lesbian authors individual and group readings that would never have taken place a decade ago no matter how many gay employees a given outlet might have had.

Finally, it is important to remember that in the arts, as in all areas of life, we are often curtailed by internalized homophobia as well as by the homophobia of others. And that is why we must work to overcome it. Silence, the AIDS crisis has taught us, equals death. And the censoring of our work by agents of the federal govern-ment has taught us that censorship equals murder. We must never forget, however, that self-censorship is suicide. And suicide, our enemies in the Roman Catholic Church piously instruct us, is an unpardonable sin.

We have come far enough to know for certain that we are bound by no limits whatever except those we create for ourselves.

YOUNG PEOPLE: THE FUTURE OF OUR COMMUNITY

The Brave New World of Gay and Lesbian Youth

Teresa DeCrescenzo

A NEW LOOK

Young gays and lesbians today look very different from their youthful counterparts of ten, or even five years ago. It is a fresh, brash presentation. It's in your face. It's aggressive. Our young people today dress to impress. Or, is it to distress or to bother? Or, perhaps it is, in part, to demonstrate to their elders that they have acquired the sense of pride, self respect, and individuality for which early gay and lesbian activists worked so hard.

There is a stridency in much of the "new look" sported by gay and lesbian youth, mirroring the militant attitudes of ACT-UP and Queer Nation, direct action groups whose membership is largely made up of young people. At the same time, there is still the uncertainty of youth even as they chant, "I'm here, I'm queer!" The subtext seems to be, "I'm here, I'm Queer, *notice me.*"

ACT-UP, the AIDS Coalition to Unleash Power, has had a substantial impact on the national agenda like few other groups in the history of the gay movement. It has also been an especially attractive group to young people, because of its loose organizational style. While the "no hierarchy" strategy of ACT-UP has, from time to time, gotten in the way of its effectiveness, that same approach has offered its youthful membership the opportunity to express themselves fully, to be heard, and to have substantial impact on the direction the organization takes. It has also actually expedited important, impressive actions taking place, without large committees and boards of directors to impede activities.

There are ACT-UP chapters all over the country. Some, such as ACT-UP, Los Angeles, have specific working groups designed to deal with adolescents.[1] It would be too ponderous to attempt to list them all in this chapter. In larger cities, ACT-UP will be listed in your directory, or can be located through your local gay and lesbian community service center. If there is no community service center in your area, ask around. ACT-UP uses high visibility. Your local chapter won't be hard to find.

While there will always be the naturally effeminate boy in the gay world, there is no longer the automatic "sissification" of young gay males as an essential part of the discovery of being gay. Stereotypically effeminate behavior among young gays occurs for a number of reasons. Sometimes a transitory part of the coming out process, it may be adopted as behavior gays believe that straights expect of them. Or, it may serve as a protest against years of suppressing one's homosexuality. Other times, "campy" behavior functions as a means of self protection. If a "witty" gay male can keep everyone laughing, chances are he won't be the target of as much discriminatory behavior, including hate crimes, such as "gay-bashing."

Young lesbians are experiencing a similar transition. The formidably gray, drab, lesbian bar has become nearly as extinct as the dinosaur. Stylish clubs for young lesbians are proliferating. Fashion is in. Lipstick is in. Role playing is out. So is heavy drinking. Feeling good and looking good are in.

For many of those not inclined to lipstick and high fashion, athleticism is in. Being a young lesbian who is interested in sports no longer means being automatically labelled as a butch. Being physically fit and athletic are signs of pride and self respect. Drugs and alcohol don't fit into this young lesbian scene, either. The lesbian community will, of course, always happily accommodate our butches. We just will no longer be forcing our youngsters into one role or another, either because of an outdated set of stereotypes, or a lack of role models.

DEVELOPMENTAL ISSUES

With a much wider range and "variety" of role models, young gays and lesbians are freer to develop in the ways that are most natural for them as individuals. It is the clear responsibility of older gays and lesbians to optimize developmental opportunities for our young counterparts. There has recently been an encouraging surge of programs being developed throughout the country aimed at doing just that.

One of the best known programs for high school age youth is Project 10, Los Angeles Unified School District's pioneering counseling program for lesbian, gay

---

[1] In 1991, ACT-UP/LA formed a working group - Youth Action. Youth Action can be contacted at (213) 413-2838, or the ACT-UP/LA office at (213) 669-7301.

and bisexual students.[2] Founded in 1984, by Fairfax High School science teacher Virginia Uribe, the program has now expanded to more than fifty schools in the district. Many other school districts throughout the country have adopted similar programs, using Project 10 as the model. These programs provide opportunities for young gays and lesbians to meet each other in a safe environment. Just knowing that you are not alone is often enough to make the difference for a gay or lesbian high school student. In addition, finding supportive adult role models among the teachers and school counselors makes students aware that we gay and lesbian people come in both genders, and in all sizes, shapes and colors.

Programs such as Project 10, and others operated outside the school setting, either by social service agencies, or in some instances by the young people themselves, play an important role in providing young gays and lesbians with both socializing and socialization opportunities. Probably the oldest — and most activist — gay and lesbian youth group in the country is the Boston Alliance of Gay and Lesbian Youth (BAGLY).[3] This is one of the groups which holds firmly to the concept of youth having power within the organization. Adults are used as consultants, and for various kinds of support, but the young people basically run the organization. Begun in 1981, BAGLY offers a wide range of activities for gay and lesbian youth, including co-gender meetings, women's meetings, speakers services, and numerous planned "special events", such as dances, movies, and other outings.

There are two groups in San Francisco for gay and lesbian youth. The Lavender Youth Recreation and Information Center (LYRIC) provides non-alcoholic dances, trips to sporting events, and "rap groups" for young gays and lesbians.[4] The Bay Area Sexual Minority Youth Network specializes in providing pen pals as a means of young people being able to contact other young gays and lesbians. When writing to BASMYN, be sure to include your name and address, and tell enough about yourself so that you can be matched with a pen pal.[5]

In Washington, D.C., the Sexual Minority Youth Assistance League (SMYAL) provides services to youth, age twenty-one and under. There are support groups, training and education programs, and a help line. Most of the youth who participate in SMYAL live at home, and come from surrounding suburbs to Washington for the groups.[6]

---

[2]*Project 10 offers a handbook on addressing gay and lesbian issues, and consultation to administrators and staff personnel. Write, or call: Virginia Uribe, Ph.D., Fairfax High School, 7850 Melrose Avenue, Los Angeles, Ca., 90046, (213) 651-5200.*
[3]*BAGLY's address is Box 814, Boston, MA 02103. The phone number is (800) 422-2459.*
[4]*LYRIC can be reached through the Women's Building, 3543 18th Street, San Francisco, Ca., 94110, or phone (415) 703-6150.*
[5]*Write or call BASMYN, at P.O. Box 460268, San Francisco, Ca., 94146-0268, (415) 541-5012.*
[6]*For further information about SMYAL, phone (202) 546-5940. To reach the Helpline, call (202) 546-5911, Mon. – Thur. 7 – 10 p.m.*

Outside of small cities, there are numerous grass roots organizations being formed to meet the needs of gay and lesbian youth. Many of these groups are begun by youth themselves, and use adults for information, guidance and support. One such group, founded by an eighteen year-old in Kansas, is called Sexual Orientation Support (SOS). They meet in a local high school, and provide leaderless support groups.[7]

Until recently, the only places gay and lesbian youth, especially minors, could go in order to meet others like them were situations more suited to older people, such as bars and cruising areas. While these venues have a legitimate place in the adult gay community, they have a significant drawback, in that they usually offer a sexual encounter as a possibility, even a desirable outcome. There is nothing inherently wrong with social settings where there is a built in erotic element. The problem for young gays and lesbians in these environment is that the natural developmental process is hampered by presenting them with "sexual intercourse" opportunities *before* they have had sufficient "social intercourse" opportunities.

Erik Erikson, who has probably done the most important work on human development in this century, produced a model of the "stages of life" that we all go through, from birth to death. In the fifth stage of development, into which adolescence falls, Erikson notes that "so much of young love is conversation".[8]

That's why it is so essential that we provide our young people with opportunities to learn "social intercourse", to fall in love without sexual demands. These opportunities will enable them to acquire the skills necessary to move to the natural next step of development, that of "sexual intercourse". That's what makes "youth only" programs so important. They offer young gays and lesbians an environment free from sexual pressure, in which they will be able to develop non-erotic friendships with members of the same — and opposite — sex. That is certainly preferable to the way it has been historically, especially with young gay males too often having to begin courting behavior by skipping to the end result, sexual contact. Young people of both genders, of course, have sexual drives and urges. It's just that it's important that they be encouraged to explore those feelings as a natural outgrowth of peer interaction and socialization.

Erikson also talks about how important it is that an adolescent be affirmed by his peers, while at the same time learn from the larger society what are acceptable behaviors and lifestyles. The role of providing those learning opportunities so necessary to the well-being of our youngers must be assumed by the established older, adult gay and lesbian community. We must do it for ourselves and for our

---

[7] *SOS is a local group in Lawrence, Kansas. Their phone number is not listed here because they do not have the resources to field large numbers of phone calls. If you live in this part of the country, you should be able to find this group.*

[8] *This stage of development, the fifth in Erikson's model, is called "Identity vs. Confusion". From Erikson, E.H.,* Identity: Youth and Crisis, *Norton Books, New York, 1968.*

kids; and, in increasing numbers, we seem to be doing it. The proliferation of groups specifically for young gays and lesbians is also evidence that they, too, feel the strong need for their own venues.

CULTURAL CONCERNS

Before considering some specific ideas and suggestions about what kinds of things we might do to enhance the quality of life for young gays and lesbians, it might be a good idea to appraise some of the racial, ethnic and cultural differences among gay and lesbian youth.

Lesbian and gay youth of color can be thought of as being tri-cultural. They live within their own ethnic minority community, whether African-American, Asian-American, Latino or Latina, Native American, or Alaska Native. In addition, they live in the gay and lesbian community, where they may experience discrimination, or at least a lack of understanding, because of their race or ethnicity. Finally, of course, they live in the majority community, where racial prejudice and homophobic reactions occur all too often. These young people who live as a minority within a minority, often feel isolated, and afraid of losing their support systems. Attempting to integrate all three parts of their lives "requires a constant effort to maintain oneself in three different worlds, each of which fails to support significant aspects of a person's life."[9]

Racial and ethnic minority youth may experience particular difficulties in coming out to their families. For example, gender role behavior is very important among Latinos and Latinas. There is a sharp dichotomy between masculine and feminine, which begins very early in life, and is initially taught as early as age four or five. The culture is shaped and built that way, and departures from that which is familiar, such as homosexuality, are viewed stereotypically in the extreme. Gay men are thought of as effeminate, whether they are or not, and are called "jotos", or "fairies". Lesbians are thought of as masculine, whether they are or not, and are called "monflores", or "manflower". Thus the labels are used to stigmatize the person, making understanding a natural development very difficult, especially for the families. The labels are often sometimes used by more gender-typically "masculine" gay Latinos themselves as a way to avoid defining themselves as "gay". After all, they rationalize, if I'm not effeminate, I must not really be gay.

The anticipation of rejection by families has been a central problem for Latina lesbians and Latino gay males, since fear of bringing shame, of "scorching the family name" means coming out absent from the family support that is especially important in this culture. So, for young Latino/Latina gays, there is often an feeling of particular isolation in the coming out process.

---

[9] *For a more thorough discussion of this issue, please refer to* Homosexuality and Family Relations, *Harrington Park Press, New York, 1990, (pp. 217–239).*

If there have been precious few role models for Hispanic-American youth, there have been almost none for young black gay men and lesbians. In African-American families, youngsters who show homosexual tendencies are often deliberately isolated, to "control" this behavior. Such a child might be sent to live with an aunt or a grandparent or other relative, who lives in a setting deemed less likely to allow for the development of a homosexual orientation. There has historically been nearly complete disownership of homosexuality in the black community, labeling it, instead, a "disease caught from whites". The black gay or lesbian has often been seen as a sellout to his or her racial heritage. The sense of shame is less about "the family name", and more about disgracing "the race". The injunction, again, has been to be invisible in one's own community, since being a gay male has been seen as going against the masculine image of the African-American male. For many black, gay males, the choice has been to reject being gay, or to reject (and be rejected by) their own cultural community.

The good news is that all of this has been changing at a pretty rapid pace over the past decade. The emergence of a strong, proud African-American gay and lesbian community has established a potent national presence, and has enabled the creation of the Black Gay and Lesbian Leadership Forum, the National Coalition for Black Lesbians and Gays, and other organizations throughout the country.[10]

A number of grass roots organizations and special interest groups have also developed from within the gay and lesbian Latino and Latina communities. These groups celebrate their ethnicity and their cultural heritage alongside their gay pride, and do not view themselves as a "disgrace" to their families. Participants in these groups stage festivals, march in gay pride parades throughout the country, and are legitimate role models for their young parallels. They are also leaders in national minority AIDS prevention coalitions.

SOME YOUTH RESOURCES

Remarkably, there are currently more than *six hundred* organized gay and lesbian groups on college and university campuses throughout the country. Many of them host annual "gay and lesbian pride week" on campus, during which there are informational sessions, workshops, lectures, rallies, films, dances, even live stage performances. Others mount ambitious and impressive conferences annually, at which there are academic presentations of research on gay and lesbian life, panel

---

[10] *The National Coalition for Black Lesbians and Gays is located at Box 19248, Washington, D.C., while the Black Gay and Lesbian Leadership Forum can be reached at Box 29812, Los Angeles, Ca., 90027, (213) 667-2549. For a more comprehensive listing of African-American, Asian-American, and other racial and ethnic special interest groups, please refer to* The Big Gay Book, *by John Preston, Penguin Books, New York, 1991.*

discussions of different aspects of the gay experience, nationally known keynote speakers, and a wide range of socializing opportunities for conference participants.

Some gay and lesbian student groups host "kiss-ins", "coming out day", "blue jeans day", and other special events on campus, aimed at increasing gay and lesbian visibility among their peers. These special events also afford supportive non-gay students a chance to show their backing for equal rights for gay and lesbian students. While campus newspapers often give space to gay and lesbian issues, some universities actually have their own on-campus newspaper exclusively devoted to exploring issues of interest to the gay and lesbian student population. These publications also serve to educate the rest of the student body about gay and lesbian concerns.

Many colleges have lesbian sororities and gay fraternities, which are officially recognized by the administration, and enjoy full status alongside other, more traditional sororities and fraternities. The trailblazer among these groups was the UCLA sorority, Lambda Delta Lambda, which was featured along with Harvard University's Harvard-Radcliffe Gay and Lesbian Student Association, in Time Magazine. Such groups now exist in institutes of higher learning from California to Vermont. The National Gay and Lesbian Task Force, a Washington, D.C. based national gay and lesbian membership organization, maintains a comprehensive list of campus groups and other resources for students. For information about campus groups in your area, or for help with starting such a group, contact NGLTF.[11]

Possibly the best resource for students and campus professionals with regard to dealing with gay concerns on campus, in addition to NGLTF, is the newsletter, "Out on Campus", which is published by The Standing Committee for Lesbian, Gay, and Bisexual Awareness of the American College Personnel Association. The newsletter is free to members of the committee. Committee membership, which is open to anyone, is available at a modest cost, with a special rate for students.[12]

Most large cities have a gay and lesbian community service center of some sort, usually offering counseling and referral services, along with AIDS prevention education. The Los Angeles Gay and Lesbian Community Services Center is the nation's oldest and largest center, with a sizeable youth department, offering a wide range of services. Many other, smaller centers throughout the country also have programs for youth, ranging from single services such as a telephone hotline, to drop-in counseling, shelters, and in some instances, a full range of residential, psychosocial and case management services. Additional resources for gay and lesbian youth not mentioned elsewhere in this chapter include, in the Minneapolis-St. Paul area, the group known as "Lesbian and Gay Youth Together" meet every

---

[11]*National Gay and Lesbian Task Force, 1734 14th Street, N.W., Washington, D.C., 20009, (202) 332-6483.*
[12]*For information on "Out on Campus", contact Joan Campbell, Campus Housing, M/C 579, University of Illinois at Chicago, 818 Wolcott Avenue, Room 317SRH, Chicago, Il., 60612.*

Sunday, in an informal, safe environment. Meetings are open to youth ages 15 to 21.[13]

In Portland, Oregon, there are several youth resources, including a Youthline that operates from 3–5 p.m., Mondays through Fridays,[14] a social and support group for those under 21 who are gay, lesbian, or unsure,[15] and a student group.[16]

Salt Lake City, Utah, has a youth group,[17] as do Cleveland, Ohio; Las Vegas, Nevada; St. Louis, Missouri; San Anselmo, California; Eugene, Oregon; and Berkeley, California.[18]

For a list of other available youth programs, or to start one in your community, contact either NGLTF, or the Oregon-based newsletter, "Getting Ready".[19]

SPECIALIZED RESOURCES

In spite of the many challenges facing gay and lesbian youth as a stigmatized minority, most appear to make the transition into adult life remarkably undamaged. The majority of our resilient young people emerge as healthy adults from the struggles associated with adjusting to the role of being gay or lesbian in a society that has not done enough to ease the passage for them. Still, there are some for whom the challenges are simply too daunting, and they find that they need specialized services, sometimes including out of home placement, or a special school setting.

---

[13]*Meetings are at 2025 Nicollet Ave. South, from 4:30 to 6:30. Adult advisors can be reached at (612) 822-8870, or contact the Minnesota Task Force for Gay and Lesbian Youth, at (612) 224-3371.*
[14]*Youthline can be reached at (503) 233-1113.*
[15]*Windfire meets on Thursdays, from 7 - 9 p.m., in the meeting room of the Multonomah County Central Library, 801 SW 10th Avenue, (503) 223-8299.*
[16]*Oregon Lesbian, Gay and Bisexual Campus Union, P.O. Box 4925, Portland, Oregon, 97208, (503) 236-2597.*
[17]*The Youth Group, Box 3832, Salt Lake City, Utah, 84110, (801) 328-3737.*
[18]*In Cleveland, call (216) 522-1999, or write to PRYSM, Lesbian/Gay Community Service Center, 1418 West 29th St., Cleveland, Ohio.*
In Las Vegas, call (702) 383-8386, or write Gay Youth Alliance, 1117 South Main Street, Las Vegas, Nevada.
In St. Louis, call (314) 533-5322, or write Growing American Youth, 11 South Vanderventer, St. Louis, Missouri.
In San Anselmo, California, call (415) 475-1115, or write Rainbow's End, 100 Sir Francis Drake Blvd., San Anselmo, California, 94960.
In Eugene, Oregon, call (503) 346-3360.
In Berkeley, California, call (510) 841-6224, or write Romper Room, Pacific Center for Human Growth, 2712 Telegraph Avenue, Berkeley, Ca. 94704.
[19]*"Getting Ready", while published mainly for teens in group home and foster care, also serves as a resource for information about gay and lesbian youth programs throughout the country. Subscriptions are also available. Contact Northwest Media. P.O. Box 56-S, Eugene, Oregon, 97440, (503) 343-6636.*

There are at least two specialized school programs for gay and lesbian youth who find the mainstream school setting too difficult at some time or another during their high school years. Each has the goal of mainstreaming youth back into regular school, whenever possible. Each is actually a part of the school district in which they are located. The oldest such program is the Harvey Milk School, begun in 1985, in New York. A more recent arrival is the EAGLES Center, in Los Angeles, which opened its doors to twelve students in 1992. Both programs emphasize counseling and support as a part of the educational process.[20]

The main task of adolescence is the development of a sense of "self", leading to the emergence in young adulthood of an autonomous and independent person. This is a time for the maturation of psychological, biological and social processes. Completion of this vital developmental task can be greatly affected by the inner discovery that you are gay or lesbian. The ability to successfully integrate into society, and to achieve this maturation, can be impaired if the experience of disclosure, both to self and others is stigmatizing. Negative coming out experiences at any age, but particularly during adolescence, can trigger a chain reaction of problems, including feelings of isolation and depression, drug and alcohol abuse, school and employment difficulties, or running away from home. When these problems occur, it sometimes becomes necessary for youngsters to be placed out of their homes, either in temporary foster care or group home care.[21] During this time, social workers and case managers work with the youth and their families, to effect reunification as soon as possible.

CHALLENGES FOR GAY AND LESBIAN ADULTS

Whether a gay or lesbian youth lives at home, or is temporarily living away from home, it is important for there to be intervention, in some manner, by healthy, well-adjusted gay and lesbian adults who can not only give guidance, but also model the positive aspects of being part of the gay community. If you are a gay or lesbian adult, here are a few ideas about how to do that. For example, if you are an attorney, offer your consultation to your local legal society or professional association about the needs of gay and lesbian youth, particularly those who are in the juvenile justice system. If you are a social worker, do the same for your local child protective

[20]*Consultation and training are available from both school programs. For Harvey Milk, contact the Hettrick-Martin Institute, 401 West Street, New York, N.Y., 10014, (212) 633-8920, Frances Kunreuther, Executive Director. For the Eagles Center, contact GLASS - Gay and Lesbian Adolescent Social Services, 8901 Melrose Avenue, #202, West Hollywood, Ca., 90069-5605, (310) 288-1757, Teresa DeCrescenzo, Executive Director; Jerry Batty, EAGLES Director.*
[21]*Gay and Lesbian Adolescent Social Service, Inc., (GLASS), is a Los Angeles based, youth serving agency, providing foster and group homes for gay and lesbian minor youth around the country. GLASS also provides training to other agencies, both private and public.*

services agency, and ask them to set up a seminar on issues involving gay and lesbian youth in placement.

Get in touch with the school district in your city or town. Ask them if they have a special program for gay and lesbian youth. If they do, congratulate them. If they don't, help them to contact Project 10, and to get their manual.[22] Offer to help them to set up the program.

Volunteer at your local gay and lesbian community service center, in the youth department. If they don't have one, offer to help them begin a service delivery program for gay and lesbian youth.

Consider becoming a foster parent yourself. It can be a very rewarding experience. If your local department of children's services, or department of social services, child protective services (or whatever it is called in your state) isn't aware of the opportunities for gay or lesbian foster parenting, ask them to contact GLASS[23] for assistance in creating and utilizing this valuable resource.

Reading Suggestions

Getting accurate, unbiased information into the hands of gay and lesbian youth is critically important to their development. There are a number of books about gay and lesbian life available for both young people and their families. A classic in the genre, written by teens for teens, is *One Teenager in Ten*,[24] originally published in 1983, and still in print.

Another definitive book written by teens for their peers is *Young, Gay and Proud*.[25] This book offers young gays and lesbians practical advice on self-discovery, disclosure, handling hassles at school, and has a particularly good section on how to change things, offering such practical tips as, "find out who the okay people are at school", "see what you and your friends can do about someone getting picked on for being gay". This section might seem a bit "soft" by current standards of militancy, but all of the advice is sound. The new edition is updated, to include AIDS education and safer sex guidelines. The new incarnation also features new art work as well.

Another "oldie", but well worth finding a copy of, is *A Way of Love, A Way of Life: A Young Person's Guide to What it Means to Be Gay*.[26] This book is a primer for young gays and lesbians, and those who love them. Ignore the reference section in the back, since it is now understandably outdated, given that the book was originally published in 1979.

---

[22]*Project 10: 7850 Melrose Avenue, Los Angeles, Ca., 90046.*
[23]*GLASS provides foster parent training and supervision, and operates a mentoring program, matching young gays and lesbians with "older siblings".*
[24]One Teenager in Ten: Writings by Gay and Lesbian Youth, *edited by Ann Heron, Alyson Publications, Boston, 1983.*
[25]Young, Gay and Proud, *Alyson Publications, Boston, 1991.*
[26]A Way of Love, A Way of Life: A Young Person's Guide to What it Means to Be Gay, *by Frances Hanckel and John Cunningham, Lothrop, Lee & Shepard Books, New York, 1979.*

More recently published books worth reading include: *Understanding Sexual Identity: A Book for Gay Teens and Their Friends*,[27] a slim book, which appears aimed at upper middle class kids, and is careful not to take a very strong stand on anything, does offer some helpful suggestions to the younger teen, who may not be at all sure about being gay; *Bridges of Respect*,[28] which effectively analyzes the impact of homophobia on young people; this book would be excellent for use in a discussion group, and it also has a helpful directory of organizations; *Life Drawing*,[29] a novel about a gay male adolescent's first love, which also addresses racism, as a "story within the story;" *Gloria Goes to Gay Pride*,[30] a cleverly illustrated children's book about a lesbian couple and their child, as they prepare to enjoy this special day.

There has been a virtual explosion of books for and about the families of gays and lesbians. The first, and one of the best, is *Now That You Know: What Every Parent Should Know About Homosexuality*,[31]. Others include: *My Son Eric*,[32] in which a mother tells of how she came to accept her gay son; *Coming Out to Parents*,[33] which offers guidance to gays, lesbians and their parents in dealing with the coming out process within a family; *Beyond Acceptance*,[34] which presents a series of first person accounts of how parents have managed to move beyond the initial stages of accepting their gay or lesbian children. These are just a few of the many excellent books available to young lesbians and gays, as well as to their families.

There are a number of books written for professionals working with gay and lesbian people. One especially scholarly work is *Gay and Lesbian Youth*,[35] which includes many studies and theoretical papers on gay and lesbian youth. Most large and medium size cities have a gay, lesbian, or feminist book store, where most of the books mentioned here should be available.[36]

[27]*Understanding Sexual Identity, Janice E. Rench, Lerner Publications, Minneapolis, 1990.*
[28]*Bridges of Respect, Kay Whitlock, American Friends Service Committee, Philadelphia, 1989 (2nd ed.).*
[29]*Life* Drawing, *Michael Grumley, Grove Weidenfeld, 1991.*
[30]*Gloria Goes to Gay Pride, Leslea Newman, Alyson Wonderland, Boston, 1991.*
[31]*Now That You Know: What Every Parent Should Know About Homosexuality, Betty Fairchild and Nancy Hayward, A Harvest/HBJ Book, New York, San Diego, revised edition, 1989.*
[32]*My Son Eric, Mary Bohrek, Pilgrim Press, New York, 1979.*
[33]*Coming Out to Parents: A Two-Way Survival Guide for Lesbians and Gay Men and Their Parents, Marey Borhek, Pilgrim Press, New York, 1983.*
[34]*Beyond Acceptance: Parents of Lesbians and Gays talk about their experiences, Carolyn Welch Griffin, and Marian J. and Arthur G. Wirth, Prentice-Hall, New Jersey, 1986.*
[35]*Gay and Lesbian Youth, Gilbert Herdt, Editor, Harrington Park Press, New York, 1988.*
[36]*Support your local gay, lesbian, and feminist bookstores. If you are unable to acquire these books locally, there are two gay owned bookstores with multiple locations, a toll-free number, and the ability to ship orders. They are: Lambda Rising, at (800) 621-6969, and A Different Light, at (800) 343-4002.*

Many larger cities also have gay libraries, or at least substantial lesbian and gay sections in their main library branch. Among the cities that do have a library or an archive are Philadelphia and New York on the east coast; San Diego, San Francisco, and Los Angeles on the west coast; Chicago and St. Paul in the midwest; Fort Lauderdale in the southwest; and Seattle in the northwest. If you want a complete listing of all known lesbian and gay libraries and archives in America, or if you are interested in starting a library in your own community, contact the Gay and Lesbian Library Service.[37]

Anyone wanting to be helpful to gay and lesbian youth should find their nearest Parents and Friends of Lesbians and Gays chapter (P-FLAG), and attend a meeting.[38] Gay and lesbian youth should also attend meetings. These groups can provide information, guidance and support for youngsters who are struggling with coming out to their families.

Each year since 1988, on October 11, there is a national "coming out day", regionally coordinated all over the country. This is a very positive "upbeat" event, designed to enhance self-esteem, openness, and unity among gays and lesbians. The goal is to increase the visibility of lesbians and gay men. It would be an excellent activity for gay and lesbian youth.[39]

The more information people have, the more barriers of ignorance and prejudice come tumbling down. Recently, my own eighteen year-old cousin, Jennifer, who was at the time in her last semester in a private, Catholic high school in Rhode Island, heard a lecture on "sexual behavior" in her Sociology class. She noticed that there was nothing much said about the subject of homosexuality. The lecture wasn't particularly negative, except for the reiteration of the church's position on homosexuality, that it is essentially okay to be gay or lesbian, you are just not allowed to "act on it". Jen volunteered that she has a cousin who is a lesbian, in a successful, long-term relationship, and offered to bring in a book that I had sent her about gay and lesbian relationships.[40] In addition, she volunteered to bring in a video tape that I had sent her of the black tie dinner-dance my partner and I gave to celebrate our fifteenth anniversary.

The discussion among the students that followed the viewing of the video was remarkable. Her classmates were not only impressed that Jen "didn't feel funny around us", but they were also impressed by the quality of our lives, by how much

---

[37]*Gay and Lesbian Library Service, McFarland & Company, Box 611, Jefferson, N.C., 28640.*
[38]*For information on the chapter of Parents and Friends of Lesbians and Gays— Parents-FLAG — nearest you, contact the Federation of Parents and friends of Lesbians and Gays, Inc., at (800) 432-6459.*
[39]*National Coming Out Day headquarters is at P.O. Box 8270, Santa Fe, New Mexico, 87504, (800) 445-NCOD.*
[40]*The book was* Permanent Partners: Building Gay and Lesbian Relationships That Last, *by Betty Berzon, available in paperback at most gay, lesbian, and feminist bookstores.*

more like them we were, rather than *different from them*. They were also "pretty blown away" by the sight of more than one hundred gay men and lesbians dancing together, in various combinations of partners, men dancing with men, men dancing with women, women dancing with other women.

This experience has to have had a rippling effect for those young people in that class. They, no doubt, went home and told their parents about it, and undoubtedly discussions ensued around the dinner table. They also probably told other students at school, and more dialogue was spurred. And, somewhere among all of the people who shared this experience with Jennifer, either directly or indirectly, you may be sure that a young gay boy or lesbian was touched, validated, encouraged to feel better about what may be only a suspicion, or a full-fledged conviction that he or she is gay. The unlikely appearance of that book, and that video tape in that Catholic school in Rhode Island might very well have been the starting point in the development of a positive gay or lesbian identity for some boy or girl struggling with that possibility. The teacher took notes from the book, and informed the class that he would use those notes in teaching this class in future years.

That is the gift we gay and lesbian adults have to offer our youngers, to open our lives to them in any way we can, to tell them our stories, to share our successes, to impart hope for a life that is viable and productive, free of injunctions to hide and pretend about something that is natural and understandable.

The Positively Gay Discussion Guide

FOR USE IN EDUCATIONAL, TRAINING AND PERSONAL GROWTH PROGRAMS

Changing attitudes toward one's self or others when those attitudes have been held a long time and are deeply ingrained in one's thinking is a very difficult thing to accomplish. Social psychologists tell us that one of the best approaches to attitude change is through social facilitation — learning in the context of an experience *shared* with others. Based on that knowledge we suggest use of group discussion of the contents of this book to enhance the probability that real attitude change, with regard to the objectives below, will occur.

OBJECTIVES OF THIS DISCUSSION PROGRAM

For Gays
To better understand the options and opportunities for growth open to gay people, and to explore ways of making use of these possibilities in their lives.

For Nongays
To become better informed about issues of concern to lesbians and gay men in their everyday lives, and to increase understanding of how these issues influence the thoughts, feelings and actions of gay people.

WHO MIGHT USE THIS DISCUSSION PROGRAM

Gay

It might be used by:

(1) any two people who've read the book and want to go more deeply into the significance of its contents for themselves;

(2) a gay person with her/his family to help them understand better what the lives of gay people are about;

(3) a gay organization, such as a community service center, a student union, a social or political club or a religious group, to structure personal growth groups.

Nongay

It might be used by:

(1) a group of parents or other relatives of gays who want to inform themselves about gay life;

(2) a church or other community service group to conduct gay/straight dialogue;

(3) a college or university, for human sexuality courses or graduate curricula in the helping professions;

(4) a mental health or social service agency for in-service training;

(5) a law enforcement agency for human relations training;

(6) an organization conducting continuing education courses for physicians, lawyers or other professionals in allied fields.

SCHEDULING THE SESSIONS

It is suggested that the program be divided into twelve sessions, each dealing with one area of special interest:

Session 1 — Developing a positive gay identity (Berzon, Thompson, Preston chapters)

Session 2 — The new gay and lesbian world (Podolsky, Bronski, DeCrescenzo chapters)

Session 3 — Growth for gay and lesbian couples (Berzon, Toder chapters)

Session 4 — Improving family relationships (Berzon, Fairchild chapters)

Session 5 — Resolving religious issues (Eger, Johnson, Nugent chapters)

Session 6 — Concerns of gay and lesbian parents (Abbitt/Bennett, Carron chapters)

Session 7 — Adjustments to aging (Martin/Lyon, Berger/Kelly chapters)

Session 8 — Job security and voting power (Link/Coleman, Debaugh chapters)

Session 9 — Financial planning (Jacobson/Wright chapter)

Session 10 — AIDS: its impact on our lives (Shernoff, Wolverton chapters)

Session 11 — Special issues of gay and lesbian people of color (Folayan, Gutierrez, Gock, Tafoya chapters)
Session 12 — The gay and lesbian cultural scene (Lassell chapter)

A variety of formats is possible.

SIZE OF THE DISCUSSION GROUP

The best size for a discussion group of this kind is probably 8 to 12 members, though the program can also be used with smaller or larger groups.

Suggestions for Structuring the Sessions

If there is an instructor, trainer or leader, he or she should ask that chapter material related to each session be read by the members before the group meets. If there is no designated leader, a volunteer from the group could act as coordinator, or that role might be rotated among the members.

The following questions (or similar ones) might be used to give form to the discussion:

1. What did you learn from the material you read that you didn't know before?
2. What was it most helpful to read, whether you knew it before or not?
3. What surprised you most in what you read?
4. If you were trying to educate someone about gay life, what in the material you read would you particularly want them to know?
5. What in your own personal life can you relate to the material you've read?

To encourage participation by everyone in the group you might:
1. Go around the group for each question, having the members answer each one for themselves.
2. Or, go around the group having each person choose one of the questions to answer.

If you use the above suggestions, the initial, structured interaction should be followed by open discussion in which opportunity should be provided for participants to talk about any of the material covered in the session and how they feel about it.

It is likely that whatever needs motivated group members to participate in the first place will determine the directions the discussion takes at this point. Those needs should be cooperated with but care should be taken to provide opportunity for *all* persons involved to be heard from.

It is hoped that this book, and others like it, will encourage and facilitate discussion of these issues in as many forums as possible, public and private. The conspiracy of silence attending the concerns of gay people has been broken. It is crucially important that we talk, and keep talking. There must never be such a conspiracy again.

Contributors

DIANE ABBITT is an attorney in private practice. A long time gay and lesbian community activist she presently serves on the Board of the Human Rights Campaign Fund. The mother of two grown sons, she lives in Los Angeles with her law partner and lover of eighteen years, Roberta Bennett.

ROBERTA BENNETT is an attorney in private practice, specializing in family law. She is currently a Board member of the Victory Fund, a fundraising organization that contributes to the campaigns of gay and lesbian political candidates. The mother of two grown daughters, she lives in Los Angeles with her law partner and lover of eighteen years, Diane Abbitt.

RAYMOND M. BERGER, Ph.D. is the author of *Gay and Gray: The Older Homosexual Man* (Alyson, 1984) and co-author of two popular research textbooks. He has been published widely in the areas of homosexuality, and scholarly publishing practices. Dr. Berger provides consultation to authors seeking to publish: The Getting Published Program, 350 Wild Apple Road, Goldendale, WA 98620.

BETTY BERZON, Ph.D. is a psychotherapist, in private practice, specializing in work with lesbians and gay men, and their families, since 1972. She is the author of PERMANENT PARTNERS: BUILDING GAY AND LESBIAN RELATIONSHIPS THAT LAST (Dutton, 1988, also available in paperback). She lives in Los Angeles with Teresa DeCrescenzo, her partner of nineteen years.

MICHAEL BRONSKI is the author of CULTURE CLASH: THE MAKING OF GAY SENSIBILITY (South End Press, 1984). He is a columnist for Z Magazine, and The Guide. His articles on books, film, politics and sexuality have appeared in *Gay Community News, the Boston Globe, Radical America*, and *The Advocate*. He has been involved with gay liberation for over twenty-three years. He lives in Boston.

JEFF CARRON is a professional band leader and singer. He served on the Board of the Municipal Elections Committee of Los Angeles (MECLA) for three years and was a member of the Los Angeles Gay and Lesbian Police Advisory Task Force for three years. He lives in Los Angeles with his daughter Jenny and his lover, Spencer Howard.

THOMAS F. COLEMAN is an attorney and president of EEO Seminars, a Los Angeles-based firm providing consulting services to corporations on marital status and sexual orientation discrimination in the workplace and the consumer marketplace.

R. ADAM DEBAUGH has served the Universal Fellowship of Metropolitican Community Churches as a committed lay person for over seventeen years. In 1975 he started the UFMCC Washington Field Office, becoming the first person to lobby the Congress full-time for gay and lesbian civil rights legislation. In 1992 he retired as UFMCC Mid-Atlantic District Coordinator to devote his energies to Chi Rho Press, a gay and lesbian publishing house.

TERESA DECRESCENZO, a Licensed Clinical Social Worker, has worked with adolescents since 1970. She is founding Executive Director of Gay and Lesbian Adolescent Social Services (GLASS), an agency providing long-term residential and foster care to sexual minority youth, and AIDS-affected infants and children. She is also a psychotherapist in private practice. She lives in Los Angeles with her partner of nineteen years, Betty Berzon.

DENISE L. EGER is presently the rabbi of Congregation Kol Ami (Voice of My People) in Los Angeles. Previously she served as rabbi of Beth Chayim Chadashim for four years. She has worked extensively with people with AIDS. Denise was raised in Memphis, TN and was ordained at Hebrew Union College - Jewish Institute of Religion. She writes and teaches in addition to her rabbinical duties.

BETTY FAIRCHILD lives in San Francisco. In 1970 she learned that one of her children is gay. For many years she worked actively with P-FLAG groups and has counseled and corresponded with hundreds of lesbians and gay men and their parents. She is co-author of NOW THAT YOU KNOW, a highly thought of guide-book for parents (updated and revised edition, Harcort, Brace, Jovanovich, 1989).

AYOFEMI FOLAYAN is a cultural worker and political activist committed to creating healthy dialogue between all the communities she represents as an African-American lesbian-feminist with disabilities. She is currently an artist-in-residence at the Gay and Lesbian Community Services Center in Los Angeles.

TERRY S. GOCK, Ph.D., a clinical psychologist in private practice, is also the Associate Director of the Asian Pacific Family Center of Pacific Clinics in Los Angeles County. A member of the founding steering committee of "Asian Pacific Lesbians and Gays, Inc." in 1981, he is currently chair-elect of the Committee on Lesbian and Gay concerns of the American Psychological Association.

ERIC-STEVEN GUTIERREZ is a writer and performance artist. A 1984 graduate of Harvard, his fiction has been published in the anthologies "Blood Whispers: LA Writers on AIDS," and "Indivisible: New Short Fiction by Gay and Lesbian West Coast Writers." He is Executive Editor of *High Performance Magazine.*

RONALD J. JACOBSON is a graduate of the U.C.L.A. School of Law, and is a member of the California Bar. He is currently the Vice President for Business Affairs, Network Television Division, Paramount Pictures.

REV. BILL JOHNSON, Ed. D., is a United Church of Christ minister and certified sex educator. The first openly gay person ordained in modern times (1972), he founded the United Church Coalition for Lesbian/Gay Concerns. He serves as Secretary for AIDS Programs and Ministries Coordination for the United Church Board for Homeland Ministries and lives in Lakewood, Ohio.

JAMES J. KELLY, Ph.D., has been a social work educator and researcher for twenty years. He served as consultant to the United Nations World Assembly on Aging. Currently professor and Director, Department of Social Work, California State University (Long Beach, CA 90840-0902) Dr. Kelly has published in the areas of gerontology, AIDS, and homosexuality.

MICHAEL LASSELL is the author of two volumes of poetry, *Poems for Lost and Un-Lost Boys* (Amilia, 1985), and *Decade Dance* (Alyson, 1990), the winner of a Lambda Literary Award. A career journalist, his writing has appeared in such anthologies as *Gay and Lesbian Poetry in Our Time, Poets for Life: 76 Poets Respond to AIDS, Men on Men 3, High Risk, Indivisible, Hometowns, Queer City, and Flesh and the Word* among others. He lives in New York City.

DAVID LINK is an attorney who practices public interest law and criminal appeals in Los Angeles. He is the author of a Loyola University Law Review article on the rights of same-sex couples. A playwrite and essayist, he has completed his first novel.

DEL MARTIN and PHYLLIS LYON, inseparably, are co-founders (1955) of the Daughters of Bilitis, the first national Lesbian organization. They have been a couple for 39 years, 37 of those years active in the Lesbian, Gay, Bisexual and Women's movements. Their book *Lesbian/Woman*, in its 20th anniversary (updated) edition, chronicles the changes they have seen from the 50's to the 90's.

BRIAN McNAUGHT is an educational consultant and trainer on the issues facing gay people. His primary work is with corporations and universities. He is the author of *On Being Gay* (St. Martin's Press, 1988) and is featured in the video *On Being Gay* (TRB Productions). He lives in Atlanta, GA.

ROBERT NUGENT is a Catholic priest. He is the co-founder of New Ways Ministry in Washington, D.C. He is editor of *A Challenge to Love: Gay and Lesbian Catholics in the Church* (1983); author of *Prayer Journey for Persons with AIDS* (1990); and co-editor of *Building Bridges: Gay and Lesbian Reality and the Catholic Church*. He is a graduate of Yale Divinity School and presently resides in Baltimore.

ROBIN PODOLSKY is a writer and performance artist. Her work has been anthologized in *In a Different Light: An Anthology of Lesbian Writers, Blood Whispers: L.A. Writers on AIDS*, and *Indivisible*. She contributes to *L.A. Weekly, High Performance Magazine, ArtPaper*, and *The Advocate*. In 1991 she received a Special Citation from PEN Center, New York City, and a Media Award from the Gay and Lesbian Alliance Against Defamation.

JOHN PRESTON is the former editor of *The Advocate*. He's written and edited more than thirty books, among them the novel *Franny the Queen of Provincetown*, the Alex Kane adventure series, and such anthologies as *Hometowns: Gay Men Write About Where They Belong* and *Personal Dispatches: Writers Respond to AIDS*. He lives in Portland, Maine.

MICHAEL SHERNOFF, MSW, is a psychotherapist and is founder and co-director of Chelsea Psychotherapy Associates in New York City. He is a past Board member of the National Lesbian/Gay Health Foundation. He co-authored the original programs on "Eroticizing Safer Sex" that have been used around the world to help gay men learn how to have satisfying sex lives without spreading HIV.

DR. TERRY TAFOYA, of Taos Pueblo and Warm Springs Native Heritage, a professor of psychology at Evergreen State College and the University of Washington, Seattle, is an internationally-acclaimed storyteller and presenter on such topics as cross-cultural communication, substance abuse, AIDS prevention, multicultural education and psycholinguistics.

MARK THOMPSON is Senior Editor (for the arts) of *The Advocate*, the national gay and lesbian newsmagazine. He edited the anthologies: *Gay Spirit: Myth and Meaning* (St. Martin's 1987) and *Leatherfolk: Radical Sex, People, Politics, and Practice* (Alyson 1991) which was nominated for a Lambda Literary Award. He lives in Los Angeles with his life partner, Malcolm Boyd.

NANCY TODER, Ph.D., a clinical psychologist and psychoanalyst in private practice in Los Angeles, specializes in working with lesbians. Active in the feminist and lesbian movements since 1971, she has a chapter on lesbian sexuality in *Our Right To Love*. She is the author of *Choices*, a novel about lesbian love and the development of lesbian identity.

TERRY WOLVERTON is a writer of fiction, poetry, essays, and dramatic scripts, whose work has been widely published and anthologized. She co-edited *Indivisible: New Short Fiction by Gay and Lesbian West Coast Writers*, (Plume Fiction), and *Blood Whispers: L.A. Writers on AIDS*. She is currently working on her first novel, *The Labrys Reunion*.

JOHNATHAN A. WRIGHT is a graduate of the U.C.L.A. School of Law and is a member of the California Bar. He has specialized in trust, probate, estate planning and employee benefit law for over eighteen years.

Our books are available at all bookstores, or can be special ordered. You are welcome to order directly from us. Please send your order with your check, money order, or credit card information to the address on page 302.

AIDS TREATMENT NEWS
Volume 2 (Issues 76 through 125)
John S. James
Here is the second volume of collected newsletters, presenting the most complete information on experimental AIDS treatments and research, dated from March 1989 through March 1991. Edited only for updating and safety, the newsletters are presented complete and intact, comprehensively indexed for subjects, symptoms, medications, research topics, and so on.
ISBN 0-89087-614-2
$16.95 quality paperback, 300 pages

AIDS TREATMENT NEWS
Volume 1 (Issues 1 through 75)
John S. James
Collected in one volume with a complete index are the first 75 issues of the widely respected newsletter of the same name. Covering standard and experimental therapies for AIDS and its associated illnesses, this is the only easy-to-use reference available to the layperson but with first-only information for the professional as well.
ISBN 0-89087-553-7
$12.95 quality paperback, 560 pages

THE Q JOURNAL: A Treatment Diary
Paul Reed
The remarkable journal of a writer who, while mourning the death of his lover, embarked on an experimental HIV treatment program with the Chinese drug, Compound Q. This intimate diary probes many issues at the heart of AIDS today—loss, hope, research, treatment, anger, coping, and the courage to go on living.
ISBN 0-89087-628-2
$8.95 quality paperback, 176 pages

LONGING
Paul Reed
Hailed by *The New York Times* for its style, this haunting novel of San Francisco in the early 1980s also made the *Christopher Street* bestseller list. A tale of evocative moods and driving passions, this novel remains a popular gay classic.
ISBN 0-89087-597-7
$7.95 quality paperback, 192 pages
ISBN 0-89087-540-5
$14.95 hardcover, 192 pages

SERENITY: Support and Guidance for People with HIV, Their Families, Friends and Caregivers
Second Edition
Paul Reed
In discussing frankly the emotional turmoil of facing AIDS, *Serenity* is an empowering book that leads the reader honestly from despair to action to hope. Counseling for full awareness of one's own medical condition and for early intervention, this book has been thoroughly updated for the 1990s.
ISBN 0-89087-604-5
$6.95 quality paperback, 128 pages

LOVING SOMEONE GAY
Revised and Updated
Don Clark, Ph.D.
For some a diagnosis of AIDS, ARC, or HIV seropositivity can be an unexpected disclosure about their sexuality, and families and friends must confront dual feelings about gay people at the same time as grappling with the diagnosis of their loved one. In this updated edition, the challenges of AIDS are frankly discussed along with guidelines to understanding, accepting, and supporting gay people.
ISBN 0-89087-505-7
$8.95 quality paperback, 290 pages

PSYCHOIMMUNITY & THE HEALING PROCESS
Third Revised Edition
Jason Serinus, C.H.T.
Many individuals with HIV disease seek alternative therapies either as a complement to their medical care or as an independent path towards healing. *Psychoimmunity & the Healing Process* offers a different way of understanding AIDS and immune dysfunction, and includes a thorough alternative approach to potential therapies.
ISBN 0-89087-461-1
$12.95 quality paperback, 400 pages

EXTENDED HEALTH CARE AT HOME
Evelyn M. Baulch
With advances in AIDS therapies, many patients find themselves able to receive some treatments at home. *Extended Health Care at Home* is a guide to coping with problems involved in any kind of home health care: finding a home nurse; getting the home ready; supplies and equipment; handling pain. Includes a section on the special needs of people with AIDS.
ISBN 0-89087-539-1
$9.95 quality paperback, 272 pages

LIVING IN HOPE: A 12-Step Approach for Persons at Risk or Infected with HIV
Cindy Mikluscak-Cooper, R.N. and
Emmett E. Miller, M.D.
The first and only 12-step program for people with AIDS, ARC or HIV infection, this ground-breaking book uses the familiar 12-step approach to help cope with the AIDS epidemic. Especially strong in the use of daily affirmations and guided imagery, this book weaves together the powerful tools of change and self-healing in a proven method.
ISBN 0-89087-629-0
$12.95 quality paperback, 300 pages

FACE TO FACE: A Guide to AIDS Counseling
James W. Dilley, Cheri Pies, Michael Helquist
This easy-to-read guide to the emotional problems encountered in AIDS is geared for both the patient and the professional. It covers such topics as the emotional responses to HIV seropositivity, the psychological ramifications of neurological problems in HIV disease, and the special needs of the variety of affected populations—minority communities, IV-drug-using groups, women, and gay men.
ISBN 0-89087-583-9
$14.95 quality paperback, 350 pages

AIDS LAW FOR MENTAL HEALTH PROFESSIONALS
Gary James Wood J.D., et al.
This text explores the legal and ethical issues confronting therapists when they treat people with concerns about HIV infection. Focusing on California law, *AIDS Law for Mental Health Professionals* discusses issues relevant to practitioners everywhere—the duty to treat, the duty to warn, confidentiality, and suicide.
ISBN 0-89087-601-0
$19.95 quality paperback, 272 pages

KVETCH
T.R. Witomski
From the master of searing wit and scalding humor comes this collection of wry essays that stirred controversy when published. Included are "101 Things to Do with a Straight Man," "How to Cruise the Met," and the highly debated "Zeitgeist or Poltergeist: Why Gay Books Are So Bad."
ISBN 0-89087-578-2
$7.95 quality paperback, 132 pages

. . . SO LITTLE TIME
Mike Hippler
Over 50 essays on gay life collected into one volume from Hippler's award-winning columns, on topics ranging from politics, family, sports, and travel to religion, sex, AIDS, and gay role models. Included are some of Hippler's most popular pieces, such as "Dear Abby, Am I Too Gay?", "How to Meet Lesbians," and the wrenching "Visit to an AIDS Ward."
ISBN 0-89087-609-6
$11.95 quality paperback, 288 pages

For Groups, Organizations, Health Care Institutions:
These books are available in bulk at special discounts. Please write or call our Special
Sales Department.

CELESTIAL ARTS Publishing
P.O. Box 7123
Berkeley, CA 94707

(510) 845-8414